standard grade study-mate

GW00745976

W A C Sharp

- **a handbook of concise revision notes, practice questions and practical advice**

chemistry

second edition

Hamilton Publishing

standard grade study-mate

chemistry second edition

First published 1991
Second edition 1995
© W.A.C. Sharp 1991, 1995

ISBN 0 946164 28 2   2nd edition
(ISBN 0 946164 16 9   1st edition)

A catalogue record for this book is available from the British Library.

Orders can be made *direct* over the phone
Contact Thomson Litho, Hamilton Publishing (Sales)
on (013352) 33081

Access and Visa Cards accepted

Letter accepted with school or personal cheque

Published by
Hamilton Publishing
A division of M & A Thomson Litho Limited
10–16 Colvilles Place, Kelvin Industrial Estate,
East Kilbride G75 0SN

Printed and bound in Great Britain by
M & A Thomson Litho Ltd., East Kilbride, Scotland

INTRODUCTION

Standard Grade Chemistry will be one of a number of subjects which you need to master at the end of your fourth year in school. Chemistry, like many of the other subjects, involves 'jargon', words that are not used in everyday life.

Chemicals are all around us and are used by people who have no knowledge of chemistry. Maybe you say 'Please pass the en ay see el, Dad!', but more likely you will say 'Pass the salt'. If someone who had not studied chemistry overheard you reading aloud some of the equations in Chapter Seven of this book, they would perhaps think that you were talking a foreign language. One of the aims of this book is to help you master the 'language' of chemistry. The first twelve chapters contain concise revision notes of all the *knowledge and understanding* that you will require for Standard Grade Chemistry.

Being able to apply this knowledge is called *problem solving*. Only one chapter, Chapter Thirteen, is devoted to this, but you will find plenty of questions on problem solving throughout the book. The secret of mastering problem solving is to get plenty of practice in it. Questions about knowledge and understanding and problem solving are found together in the exams which you sit. You will find them similarly presented in the practice questions in this book. Problem solving questions are identified by

Advice is given on tackling different types of questions which are now asked in Standard Grade Chemistry exams. Included in the *practice questions* are many of the 'grid' type.

Reference is often made to the *Data Booklet*, published by the Scottish Examinations Board. As this is so commonly used in schools, it has not been reproduced here. It is assumed that you have been given a copy of this by your school.

This *Standard Grade Study-Mate* has all you need to know to help you make the grade in Chemistry. *Good Luck!*

◀ S C O T V E C

Some questions may be of help to students following the Stage 1 SCOT-VEC units (modules). These questions are not intended as assessment material. Lecturers and teachers should refer to the current unit descriptors for details of the test specifications and performance criteria.

WACS

Grid Questions: Note to Teachers

The grid questions in this book are intended for revision purposes only. The grid questions used in tests and prelims should conform to the current SEB arrangements. At present there should be between four and six boxes as answer choices, and no more than two correct answers.

WACS

ACKNOWLEDGMENTS

The Author and Publisher would like to thank the following for permission to reproduce copyright material in this book:

The Scottish Examination Board for the extracts on pages 1, 3 and 4 from the 1990 Standard Grade Chemistry examination paper, and the table of solubilities on page 48 from the *Data Booklet*;

ICI for the photograph on page 46;

The Building Research Establishment, Fire Research Station, for the photograph at the top of page 84 (BRE Crown Copyright 1991).

CONTENTS

PREPARING FOR THE EXAM

This book provides a summary of all the *knowledge and understanding* in the fifteen topics of Standard Grade Chemistry. It will also provide you with help to develop your skills in *problem solving*.

Practical abilities are not covered, although they are referred to. Practical abilities will be taught and assessed by your class teacher.

▶ HOW YOU WILL BE ASSESSED

Standard Grade Chemistry is assessed both during the course in your school and in an external exam which you will take at the end of your fourth year.

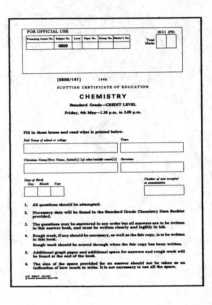

Element	Assessment
Knowledge and understanding	School exams and external exam
Problem solving	School exams and external exam
Practical abilities	School assessment only

A lot of your success in Standard Grade Chemistry may depend on your school assessments. However, a good performance in the external exam is important.

In the external exam there are two papers: *General* and *Credit*. In each of the papers there will be questions on *knowledge and understanding* and on *problem solving*. Many of the problem solving questions will be applications of your knowledge.

▶ GETTING ORGANISED

In your school you will probably have made your own chemistry notes.

Organise your school work by putting your notebooks in order and numbering them. Write on the cover of each notebook the names of the topics they contain. If you have loose-leaf notes, then see that they are in the sequence in which you worked through the topics, and make sure that each topic has a title at the start.

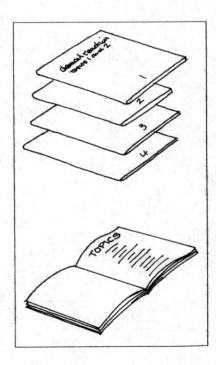

You may find a few things here which are *not* in your own notes. You may have been absent for a time or you may have gone at a slower pace in some of the topics. If you know *everything* in your school notes and *everything* in this book, then you should achieve a Grade 1. If you miss out parts of some topics, then you will have to settle for less.

There may be a few differences between your school notes and some of the notes in this book. If you are concerned about differences, then ask your chemistry teacher to advise you.

▶ GENERAL AND CREDIT

The work has not been separated into *General* and *Credit* as you will sit *both* of these papers. Quite simply Credit work is more difficult than General work. In problem solving you will have to handle more information in Credit questions than in General questions. You should aim to do well in *both* papers. However, if by chance you do well in the Credit paper and badly in the General paper, this will not count against you.

▶ STUDYING CHEMISTRY

Organise your notes.
This will make revising an easier task for you.

Do not learn by reading.
A pencil and paper are essential for studying chemistry. You can never learn to draw cyclobutane by looking at it. Draw and redraw formulae, diagrams, tables and flowcharts. Your best writing is not needed for revision and you should put the paper you have used into the bin when your revision session is over.

Take your own time.
There are 15 topics of unequal lengths. Aim to revise each topic several times. Don't waste time on the easy work — yes, there is easy work! Spend more time on the work involving chemical calculations, formation of ions, cells, electrolysis, redox and the structure of polymers. A chart of your work plan will be a help — remember to include rest days and breaks.

Decide for yourself how long a period of revision is best for you. Fifteen minutes is probably too short. More than an hour is almost certainly too long.

Avoid distractions.
It may be tempting to watch your favourite TV progamme whilst trying to learn about isomers, or to study and sunbathe at the same time. However, the fewer distractions that you have the better.

Your notes are your own.
Write as many extra comments and references into your notes as you wish. You may have written about catalysts in Topic 2. Beside this you may want to write 'See Haber process, Topic 14, or catalytic converters, Topic 5'. Such additions of your own are called 'cross-references'.

▶ THE EXAM

In each paper the same number of marks, usually 30, will be given for knowledge and understanding and for problem solving.

Two kinds of questions are asked. *Part 1* contains questions in which you must select a letter (or letters) in a grid. The questions in *Part 2* require you to write your own answers.

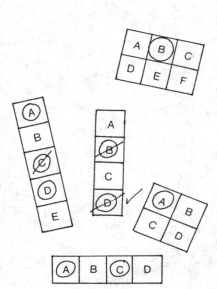

Part 1

At the Start of Part 1 you will find advice on how to answer the questions. As well as reading this advice, you should also be careful in reading the questions themselves.

You may be told how many correct answers to select.

'Identify the **two** substances which . . .'
Or you may be asked to identify for yourself how many answers to choose.

'Identify the statement(s) which can be applied to . . .'
In all these questions it is important that you select the correct number of letters. You will lose marks if your circle too many or too few.

If you make a mistake and want to change it, then make it clear which answer(s) you have finally selected.

Look for words in **bold type**. You may not always be asked to identify a correct statement. However, the examiner is not trying to trick you. Important words such as **two**, **incorrect** or **both** will be emphasised.

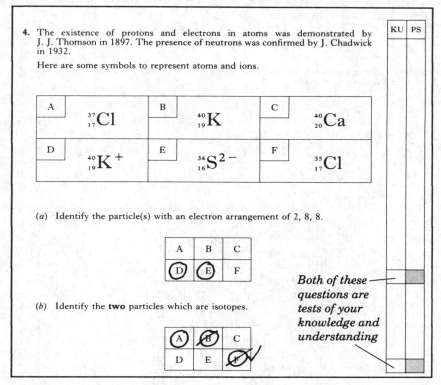

4. The existence of protons and electrons in atoms was demonstrated by J. J. Thomson in 1897. The presence of neutrons was confirmed by J. Chadwick in 1932.

Here are some symbols to represent atoms and ions.

A $^{37}_{17}Cl$	B $^{40}_{19}K$	C $^{40}_{20}Ca$
D $^{40}_{19}K^{+}$	E $^{34}_{16}S^{2-}$	F $^{35}_{17}Cl$

(a) Identify the particle(s) with an electron arrangement of 2, 8, 8.

A	B	C
Ⓓ	Ⓔ	F

(b) Identify the **two** particles which are isotopes.

Ⓐ	B̶	C
D	E	F̶✓

Both of these questions are tests of your knowledge and understanding

(a) You must decide for yourself how many letters to circle.

*(b) You are told that there are **two** correct answers. They are A and F. As you can see, several changes have been made but it is clear that A and F are the answers that have finally been decided on.*

Part 2

In Part 2 the number of marks will be indicated. The number of marks and the space provided for the answers are a guide as to how much you should write.

Answer exactly what you are asked. If you are asked to '**Name** the element which is a liquid metal', then give the name, mercury, and not the symbol, Hg. If you are asked for a '**word equation**', then do not write a chemical equation. Never write equations or formulae with charges unless you are asked to.

Always '**show your working clearly**' in calculations. If you have made a mistake somewhere, you will still get marks for the parts which are correct. A wrong answer on its own will always get no marks.

There is a lot of reading in some questions. There are a lot of clues contained in the words. Drawings often contain help. They may remind you that copper(II) oxide is a solid or that hexane burns. Look for hints.

Your diagrams are not meant to be works of art. They should, however, be realistic and whatever you draw must work. A stencil will help you, and a ruler should be used for straight lines. There are no sausage-shaped test tubes or pear-shaped beakers in your chemistry lab. Labels should be accurate, with names of substances rather than formulae, with lines touching the correct part of the diagram.

When presenting information, use the methods asked for in the question. Make sure that you draw a **line graph** if that is what is asked for, and not a bar graph. You may lose marks if you get it wrong.

Remember that you may get different grades for knowledge and understanding and problem solving. If you have a bad memory and do badly in knowledge and understanding, you may still do well in problem solving. Make sure that you can look up information in the *Data Booklet*, construct tables and both draw and use graphs.

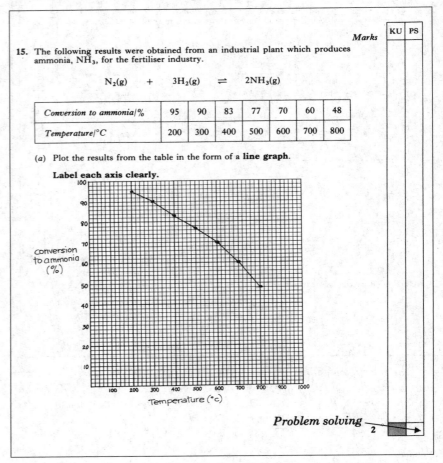

15. The following results were obtained from an industrial plant which produces ammonia, NH_3, for the fertiliser industry.

$$N_2(g) \quad + \quad 3H_2(g) \quad \rightleftharpoons \quad 2NH_3(g)$$

Conversion to ammonia/%	95	90	83	77	70	60	48
Temperature/°C	200	300	400	500	600	700	800

(a) Plot the results from the table in the form of a **line graph**.
Label each axis clearly.

Problem solving — 2

(a) *Marks are given for correct figures on each axis, labels and units.* **Line graph** *has been emphasised. You will lose marks for points which have not been accurately plotted. You will usually find another piece of graph paper at the end of the exam book. Use this if you make a mess of the first one.*

15. **(Continued)**

(b) Making use of the graph, calculate the amount of ammonia produced at 450 °C, when 280 kg of nitrogen reacts with excess hydrogen.

(b) *From the graph, at 450°C the conversion to ammonia is 80%.*

$N_2 + 3H_2 \rightleftharpoons 2NH_3$
1 mole of N_2 gives 2 moles of NH_3
28g of N_2 gives 2×17g of NH_3
280 kg of N_2 gives 340 kg of NH_3
mass of ammonia = 80% of 340 kg

$$= 340 \times \frac{80}{100} = 272 \text{ kg}$$

NH_3
$N\ 1 \times 14 = 14$
$H\ 3 \times 1 = \underline{3}$
$fm = \underline{17}$

All working has been shown. This means that marks can be earned even if the final answer is wrong. Take care that the correct units (kg in this question) are used.

CHEMICAL REACTIONS

In chemistry there are two common kinds of changes: **physical changes** and **chemical reactions**.

► PHYSICAL CHANGES

There are three **states** of matter: solid, liquid and gas. A physical change is a change of state. Physical changes can usually be reversed easily. A melted ice lolly can be refrozen in the freezer. Steam from a boiling kettle will condense on a cold window.

The following are physical changes:

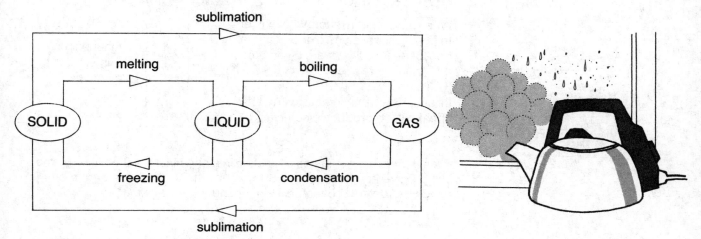

In a physical change there is no new substance forming, only a change of state. Physical changes always occur at a fixed temperature.

Substance	Melting point (°C)	Boiling point (°C)	State at room temp. (25°C)
water	0	100	liquid
oxygen	−218	−183	gas
iron	1537	2747	solid

► CHEMICAL REACTIONS

In a chemical reaction a new substance is formed. It may be very difficult or even impossible to reverse a chemical reaction. Imagine trying to 'unburn' petrol or to 'unrust' iron.

SIGNS OF CHANGE

New substances which form in chemical reactions may be in a different state. Adding some chalk to acid will cause bubbles of gas to form. This is called **effervescence**.

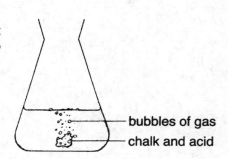

— bubbles of gas
— chalk and acid

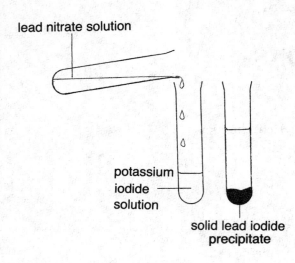

lead nitrate solution

potassium iodide solution

solid lead iodide precipitate

Sometimes when two solutions are mixed a solid forms. This solid is called a **precipitate**. In one of your practical techniques you may have added colourless lead nitrate solution to colourless potassium iodide solution and formed a yellow precipitate of lead iodide.

These changes in appearance or colour are signs of new substances forming. Chemical reactions are taking place.

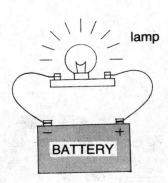

lamp

BATTERY

OTHER SIGNS OF CHANGE

When magnesium reacts with oxygen to form magnesium oxide, a great deal of *heat* and *light* are given out.

In a battery, zinc reacts with other chemicals to produce *electricity*.

magnesium burning in oxygen

Even if there are no flames or flashes in a chemical reaction, energy may still be given out. When an acid reacts with an alkali a thermometer is needed to detect the temperature change.

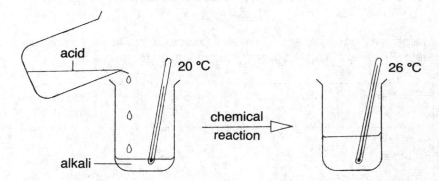

acid

20 °C

alkali

chemical reaction

26 °C

Energy has been given out in all of the chemical reactions described. Many reactions may require energy to be put in before they can take place. For example, many substances need to be heated before they will decompose (break up). In the kitchen both baking and cooking involve heating and chemical reactions.

Every chemical reaction is accompanied by an energy change.

▶ ELEMENTS — THE BUILDING BLOCKS

Elements are the simplest substances in chemistry. Each element has a **symbol** (e.g. C for carbon, He for helium). The names of the elements and their symbols are to be found in the periodic table (see page 131).

Most elements are metals and are very similar in appearance. Many of the metals have similar properties.

If a substance is an element, then its name will appear in the periodic table. Hydrogen and oxygen are elements. Water and salt are not elements; their names do not appear in the periodic table.

COMPOUNDS

Although there are only about one hundred elements there are many millions of **compounds**. A compound contains two or more elements joined together. The chemical name for a compound gives a clue to the elements in it.

The ending *-ide* indicates that the compound contains only two elements.

Compound	Elements present
zinc ox*ide*	zinc and oxygen
calcium sulph*ide*	calcium and sulphur
magnesium nit*ride*	magnesium and nitrogen

There are exceptions to this rule: hydroxides contain hydrogen and oxygen and another element (calcium hydroxide contains calcium, hydrogen and oxygen); and cyanides contain carbon and nitrogen and another element (potassium cyanide contains potassium, carbon and nitrogen).

When a name ends in *-ate* or *-ite* this indicates the presence of oxygen in addition to the other elements.

Compound	Elements present
copper carbon*ate*	copper, carbon and oxygen
potassium phosph*ate*	potassium, phosphorus and oxygen
sodium sulph*ite*	sodium, sulphur and oxygen

MIXTURES

The substances in a **mixture** have not reacted together.

Water is a *compound* of hydrogen and oxygen, not a mixture of hydrogen and oxygen. A *mixture* of the gases hydrogen and oxygen is also a gas but with quite different properties from those of water. Oxygen can be breathed, but water cannot. Hydrogen burns, but water certainly does not!

hydrogen

oxygen

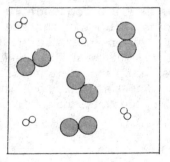

mixture   compound

A mixture of two substances has properties rather like those of the individual substances. A mixture can be separated again if the right method can be found.

Separating Mixtures

Filtration separates an insoluble solid from a liquid.

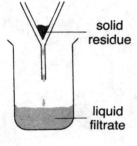

solid residue

liquid filtrate

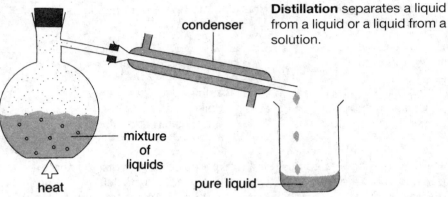

condenser

Distillation separates a liquid from a liquid or a liquid from a solution.

mixture of liquids

heat

pure liquid

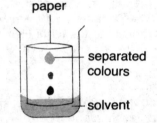

paper

Chromatography separates mixtures of colours into individual colours.

separated colours

solvent

SOLUTIONS

A liquid with a substance dissolved in it is called a **solution**. The liquid is called the **solvent**. The substance added to the liquid is called the **solute**. The solute can be solid, liquid or gas.

Lemonade is a solution of carbon dioxide (gas), sugar (solid) and flavouring (liquid) in water.

Solutions in water are called **aqueous** solutions. A solution in which no more solute can be dissolved is called a **saturated** solution.

Concentration

You will often meet the idea of **concentration**. The concentration of a solution tells you how much solute is dissolved in it. A lot of solute in a solution means that the solution will be **concentrated**. Little solute means the solution is **dilute**.

Later it will be shown that concentration is given by figures such as 1 mol/*l* and 0.1 mol/*l*. The bigger the number, the more concentrated the solution.

water

dilute

concentrated

► SPEED OF REACTIONS

Here are some examples showing how the rates of chemical reactions can be increased, and how this can be seen.

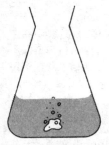

lump of chalk and acid

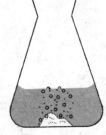

powdered chalk and acid

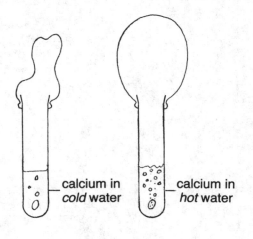

calcium in *cold* water

calcium in *hot* water

dilute acid and magnesium

concentrated acid and magnesium

The speed (or rate) of a chemical reaction can be increased by:
- using *powders* instead of lumps of solids;
- increasing the *temperature* of the reactants;
- increasing the *concentration* of the reactants.

CATALYSTS

Another way in which the speed of a reaction can be altered is by using a **catalyst**. A catalyst speeds up the rate of a reaction but is not used up itself.

For example, when a liquid called hydrogen peroxide is heated, it slowly decomposes to give oxygen. However, adding powdered manganese dioxide, a catalyst, produces oxygen much more quickly without heating. When oxygen has stopped coming off there is still as much catalyst left as there was at the start. If the powder is filtered and dried, its mass will be the same as it was at the beginning of the experiment.

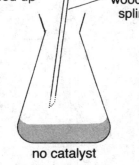

glowing wooden splint

no catalyst   catalyst

heat

Uses of Catalysts

Many catalysts are metals such as nickel, platinum and iron. They are used for making margarine, polythene, ammonia, sulphuric acid and many other substances.

Cars are now being fitted with catalytic converters. These convert harmful chemicals in the exhaust into other substances which are harmless.

In Chapter Twelve you will learn about biological catalysts called enzymes.

THE IDEA OF FAIRNESS

When powdered chalk was added to acid it reacted much faster than lumps of chalk did. But how can we be sure that this is a **fair comparison**?

The conditions that can be changed in a reaction are called **variables**. In this experiment the variables are:

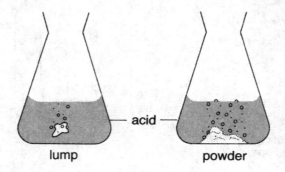

- the *temperature* of the acid;
- the *concentration* of the acid;
- the *size* of the chalk lumps;
- the *volume* of acid;
- the *mass* of chalk.

If only *one* of the variables is changed, e.g. the size of the chalk lumps, then the test is a fair one. If the results of two experiments are to be compared, then only *one* variable must be changed at a time.

PRACTICE QUESTIONS

1. In chemistry there are two common changes, physical and chemical.

A	B	C
burning a match	dissolving sugar	melting ice
D	**E**	**F**
milk going sour	meths and water mixing	water forming from hydrogen and oxygen
G	**H**	**I**
steam condensing	iron rusting	sand and salt mixing

(*a*) Which **four** boxes refer to chemical changes? ◄SCOTVEC

(*b*) Which **two** boxes refer to solutions forming?

(*c*) Which box refers to a **compound** forming from its elements? ◄SCOTVEC

(*d*) Which box refers to a change which is the **opposite** of boiling?

2. State the symbols of the following elements. ◀SCOTVEC

(a) carbon   (b) neon   (c) iron
(d) chlorine   (e) sodium   (f) chromium
(g) copper   (h) tungsten   (i) helium

3. Name the following elements. ◀SCOTVEC

(a) P   (b) N   (c) Ar
(d) K   (e) Pt   (f) Br
(g) Ca   (h) Au   (i) B

4. Name the elements in the following compounds. ◀SCOTVEC

(a) magnesium oxide   (b) zinc chloride
(c) potassium hydroxide   (d) copper carbonate
(e) barium iodide   (f) potassium sulphite
(g) calcium hydroxide   (h) sodium sulphide

5. Name the compounds formed between the following elements. ◀SCOTVEC

(a) zinc and chlorine   (b) iron and oxygen
(c) sodium and fluorine   (d) copper, sulphur and oxygen
(e) hydrogen and oxygen   (f) magnesium and nitrogen

6. A mixture of iron and sulphur is different from the compound iron sulphide.

Explain to someone who has not studied chemistry the difference between a mixture and a compound.

 7. You are given a mixture of sand and salt.

Describe how you could separate them. You must finish with dry samples of each.

8. A technician has to make up a chemical for a chemistry class to use. To make this he must dissolve solid copper sulphate in water.

(a) What are the names of the solute and solvent that he uses?
(b) What should he write on the label of the bottle?

9. Mixtures of substances can be separated in different ways.

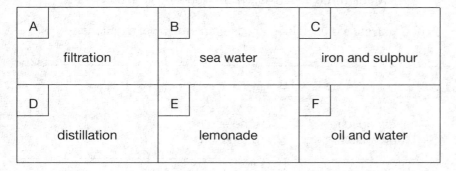

A filtration	B sea water	C iron and sulphur
D distillation	E lemonade	F oil and water

(a) Which box shows a method of separating mud and water **without** heating?
(b) Which **two** boxes show solutions?
(c) Which box shows a mixture of two solids?

PS **10.** Draw a **labelled** diagram of the apparatus you would use to filter muddy water. Your labels should include 'residue' and 'filtrate'.

11. The rate of a chemical reaction can be changed in a number of ways.

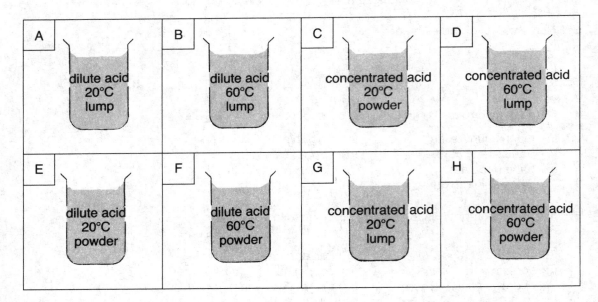

A	B	C	D
dilute acid 20°C lump	dilute acid 60°C lump	concentrated acid 20°C powder	concentrated acid 60°C lump
E	F	G	H
dilute acid 20°C powder	dilute acid 60°C powder	concentrated acid 20°C lump	concentrated acid 60°C powder

(a) In which experiment will the speed of the reaction be **greatest**? ◀ S C O T V E C

(b) In which experiment will the speed of the reaction be **slowest**? ◀ S C O T V E C

PS (c) Which **two** experiments could be chosen to show that changing the concentration of the acid altered the speed of the reaction? (There are several possible pairs of experiments.)

PS **12.** Lumps of ice were added to the acid in experiment **A** in question 11 above. This slowed down the rate of the reaction. Give **two** reasons why this should be. ◀ S C O T V E C

13. A group in a chemistry class carried out a practical investigation. This was intended to show that sugar lumps really do take longer to dissolve than the more usual powdered sugar.

PS (a) Decribe the experiment you could carry out to prove this.

PS (b) Name **three** variables which should be kept constant.

14. Catalysts are used in many different chemical reactions.

A	B	C
remains unchanged in a reaction	weighs less at the end of a reaction	cooling reactants
D	E	F
increasing the concentration of reactants	burning magnesium	manufacture of margarine

(a) Which box describes what happens to a catalyst in a chemical reaction?

(b) Which box gives a use of a catalyst?

(c) A catalyst can speed up a reaction.
Which box gives **another** way of speeding up a reaction?

15. In an experiment, a group of pupils added exactly 2.00g of powdered manganese dioxide catalyst to 20cm³ of hydrogen peroxide solution. Here is their report.

There was effervescence and a gas, which relit a glowing splinter of wood, formed. The formation of the gas slowed down and after 10 minutes it stopped.

The group carefully filtered the remaining solid, left it to dry and then reweighed it.

(a) What evidence is there in their report that a chemical reaction has taken place?

(b) Suggest the reason why the formation of the gas slowed down.

(c) What was the name of the 'remaining solid'?

(d) Manganese dioxide is a catalyst. What mass of dry solid would you expect the group to find?
Explain your answer.

ATOMS AND MOLECULES

▶ THE PERIODIC TABLE

Elements are classified by their arrangement in the **periodic table** (see also page 131). The vertical columns of elements are called **groups**.

Groups																		0
I	II											III	IV	V	VI	VII		He
Li	Be				H							B	C	N	O	F		Ne
Na	Mg				Transition metals							Al	Si	P	S	Cl		Ar
K	Ca	Sc	Ti	V	Cr	Mn	Fe	Co	Ni	Cu	Zn	Ga	Ge	As	Se	Br		Kr
Rb	Sr	Y	Zr	Nb	Mo	Tc	Ru	Rh	Pd	Ag	Cd	In	Sn	Sb	Te	I		Xe
Cs	Ba	La	Hf	Ta	W	Re	Os	Ir	Pt	Au	Hg	Tl	Pb	Bi	Po	At		Rn
Fr	Ra	Ac																

Ce	Pr	Nd	Pm	Sm	Eu	Gd	Tb	Dy	Ho	Er	Tm	Yb	Lu
Th	Pa	U	Np	Pu	Am	Cm	Bk	Cf	Es	Fm	Md	No	Lr

Radioactive and man-made elements

The elements in each group show similarities to the others in the group in their properties.

- All of the metals in Group I react violently with water and have to be stored under oil. They are called **alkali metals**.
- The elements in Group II all burn brightly.
- Group VII elements are called **halogens**.
- The Group 0 elements are called **noble gases**.

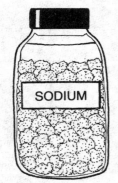

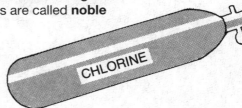

Group 0 elements do not feature much in chemistry as they are all very unreactive gases. This can, however, be an advantage. Helium is less dense than air and is safer for filling weather balloons than explosive hydrogen. Light bulbs are filled with argon rather than air so that the filament will last longer.

Most of the elements are metals. In the middle of the table is a large group called the **transition metals**. This group contains many useful metals such as iron and copper. The transition metals also include precious metals like gold and silver, and the only liquid metal, mercury. Here, too, are found the catalysts such as platinum nickel and iridium.

The last elements in the table are 'man-made' and are radioactive. Many of these man-made elements take the names of countries or scientists, e.g. Americium, Curium and Einsteinium.

► ATOMIC STRUCTURE

Elements are made up of very small particles called **atoms**. Atoms themselves are made up of even smaller particles: **protons, neutrons** and **electrons**.

The diagram shows where these particles are arranged in an atom of lithium. Protons and neutrons are found in the **nucleus**, the centre of the atom. Electrons are found moving in paths outside of the nucleus and at a distance from it.

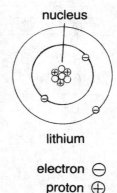

lithium

electron ⊖
proton ⊕
neutron ◯

Atomic particle	Mass	Electrical charge	Where particle is found in atom
proton	1	+	nucleus
neutron	1	0	nucleus
electron	almost 0	—	outside nucleus

There are equal numbers of protons and electrons in an atom. Because of this, individual atoms have no overall charge. Atoms are neutral.

Atoms are described by their atomic number and mass number. The **atomic number** is the number of protons in the atom. The **mass number** is the number of protons *and* neutrons in the atom. For example, an atom of sodium would be described as follows:

> mass number (11 protons, 12 neutrons) → 23
> atomic number (11 protons)   → 11 **Na** ← symbol

The elements are arranged in the periodic table in order of their atomic numbers.

Atoms of different elements have different atomic structures and may have very different chemical properties.

ELECTRON ARRANGEMENT

The chemical properties of elements are determined by their **electron arrangement**. Electrons are arranged in layers around the nucleus. The layers, or shells, are different **energy levels**. *For example,*

- boron has five electrons arranged 2, 3;
- sulphur has 16 electrons arranged 2, 8, 6.

You will *not* be asked to work out the electron arrangement of elements with more than eight electrons in their outer levels. In any case, the electron arrangements of *all* the elements can be found in the *Data Booklet for Standard Grade Chemistry* (SEB).

Level	Number of electrons
1	2
2	8
3	8 (this level *can* take up to 18)
4	8 (this level *can* take up to 32)

Outer Electrons

The **group number** of an element is given by the *number of electrons in the outer level*. All the elements in Group I have one electron in their outer level. All those in Group II have two electrons in their outer level, etc.

It is the number of electrons in the outer level which determines the chemical properties of an element.

IONS AND ATOMS

An **ion** is a charged atom. An atom can become charged by *gaining* or *losing* electrons. The number of electrons in an ion will be greater or less than in a neutral atom:

- *more* electrons than protons in a *negative* ion;
- *fewer* electrons than protons in a *positive* ion.

The table shows the numbers of atomic particles in some atoms and ions.

	Protons	Neutrons	Electrons	
Na	11	12	11 (2, 8, 1)	same number of protons and electrons
F⁻	9	10	10 (2, 8)	one electron more than the number of protons
Mg²⁺	12	12	10 (2, 8)	two electrons less than the number of protons

There is more information about ions in Chapter Five.

ISOTOPES

The number of neutrons in atoms of the same element can vary. Atoms of an element with different numbers of neutrons, and thus with different mass numbers, are called **isotopes**. For example, there are two isotopes of carbon: $^{12}_{6}C$ and $^{14}_{6}C$.

Isotope	Protons	Neutrons	Electrons
$^{12}_{6}C$	6	6	6 (2, 4)
$^{14}_{6}C$	6	8	6 (2, 4)

The two carbon isotopes have the same chemical properties, and the two isotopes exist together in nature. All elements are made up of mixtures of isotopes.

Relative Atomic Mass

The **relative atomic mass** of an element is the *average mass number* of all its isotopes. The units are atomic mass units or 'amu'.

The relative atomic mass, because it is an average, is never a whole number.

In the *Data Booklet*, with the exception of chlorine, the relative atomic masses are given as being the mass numbers of the commonest isotope.

Atoms of different elements vary both in size and mass.

► BONDS

Molecules are groups of atoms held together by **bonds**. The bonds in molecules are called **covalent bonds**. Covalent bonds are formed by two atoms sharing a pair of electrons. Molecules are formed between elements which are both non-metals.

The chemical **formula** of a compound or element represents the number of atoms of the elements in the molecule. Here are some examples.

Molecule	Formula	Atoms present
H | H – C – H | H	CH_4	1 carbon, 4 hydrogen
F – F	F_2	2 fluorine
H – O – H	H_2O	1 oxygen, 2 hydrogen

From the molecules in the table above, it can be seen that:

- carbon atoms form four bonds;
- fluorine atoms form one bond;
- oxygen atoms form two bonds;
- hydrogen atoms form one bond.

The number of bonds which an atom forms is called its **valency** or combining power. For a *metal* element its valency is the *number of electrons in the outer shell*. For a *non-metal* element its valency is the *number of electrons by which it is short of a full outer shell*.

Group number	I	II	III	IV	V	VI	VII	0
Number of electrons in outer shell	1	2	3	4	5	6	7	8
Valency	1	2	3	4	3 (8–5)	2 (8–6)	1 (8–7)	0

As a full outer shell usually contains eight electrons, the valency of a non-metal element is 8 minus the group number.

COVALENT BONDS

The electrons in the outer level of an atom can be represented as follows.

hydrogen
1 electron

carbon
4 electrons

oxygen
6 electrons

chlorine
7 electrons

The electrons in the inner energy levels need not be shown when representing bonds. Only the outer electrons of an atom are involved in bonding.

The simplest molecule is that of hydrogen which forms when two hydrogen atoms share their electrons, as follows:

(H) and (H) join to give (H | H) with a molecular fomula H_2.

The molecule of hydrogen can be represented with electrons as: H ÷ H

Or without electrons as: H – H

Here are other examples of molecules.

Substance	Atoms	Molecule	Molecular formula
hydrogen oxide			H_2O
nitrogen hydride			NH_3
oxygen chloride			OCl_2

STRUCTURAL FORMULA

The **structural formula** of a compound represents the bonds in the compound as lines. The electrons in the bond are not shown.

Here is an example of how to draw the structural formula of the compound formed between nitrogen and hydrogen:

$$H - N - H$$
$$|$$
$$H$$

If electrons are to be shown, then they can be represented thus:

$$H \div N \div H$$
$$\cdot|\cdot$$
$$H$$

Molecules which contain only two atoms are called **diatomic molecules**. Seven elements, when uncombined, are made up of diatomic molecules. When uncombined with other elements, they are written:

$$H_2 \qquad N_2 \qquad O_2 \qquad F_2 \qquad Cl_2 \qquad Br_2 \qquad I_2$$

Compounds such as hydrogen chloride (HCl) and carbon monoxide (CO) also form diatomic molecules.

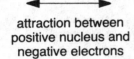

attraction between positive nucleus and negative electrons

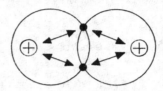

Atoms are held together in molecules by their shared electrons being attracted by the nuclei of *both* atoms.

Three-dimensional molecules

Molecules often have three-dimensional shapes. However, their structural formulae are always drawn as if they were flat.

The shape of a molecule like methane, CH_4, is called **tetrahedral**.

PRACTICE QUESTIONS

1. Elements are arranged in groups in the periodic table.

◀ S C O T V E C

A	B	C	D
sodium	iron	argon	chlorine
E	F	G	H
fluorine	lithium	nitrogen	zinc

(*a*) Which element is a noble gas?
(*b*) Which **two** elements are alkali metals?
(*c*) Which **two** elements are transition metals?
(*d*) Which **two** elements are halogens?
(*e*) Which **four** elements are gases?

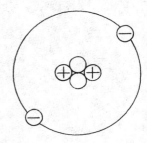

2. (*a*) Copy **and label** the diagram of an atom. ◄ S C O T V E C
        Use the labels 'electrons' and 'nucleus'.
    (*b*) Explain why the atom is neutral. ◄ S C O T V E C
    (*c*) Which element is represented by the diagram? ◄ S C O T V E C

3. Lithium and sodium are in the same group in the periodic table. Explain what it is about their atomic structures that makes them belong to the same group.

4. Copy and complete the following table. ◄ S C O T V E C

Particle	Charge	Mass	Where particle found in atom
proton		1	in nucleus
	0		
		almost 0	

5. Copy and complete the following table.

Atom	Number of protons	Number of neutrons	Number of electrons
$^{4}_{2}He$			
$^{19}_{9}F$			
$^{27}_{13}Al$			
	15	16	

6. Copy and complete the following table.

Ion	Number of protons	Number of neutrons	Number of electrons
$^{23}_{11}Na^+$			
$^{19}_{9}F^-$			
$^{24}_{12}Mg^{2+}$			
$^{32}_{16}S^{2-}$			

7. (a) Give the electron arrangement of the following atom and ions.
    (i) O^{2-} (ii) Ne   (iii) Na^+ (iv) Mg^{2+}

   PS

   (b) From your answers to (a), what do you notice about the number of electrons in the outer shell of positive and negative ions?

8. The two main isotopes of chlorine are $^{35}_{17}Cl$ and $^{37}_{17}Cl$.

   (a) Using the words 'mass number' and 'neutrons', explain why the above atoms are said to be isotopes.
   (b) The relative atomic mass of chlorine is 35.5. Explain why the relative atomic mass is not a whole number.

   PS 9. The structural formulae of molecules of some elements and compounds are given below.

   State the chemical formula of each of the following molecules.

   (a) 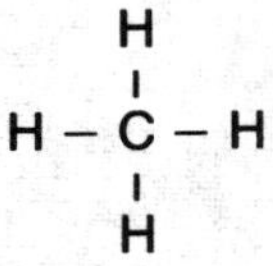
   ```
       H
       |
   H − C − H
       |
       H
   ```
   (b)
   ```
        Cl
        |
   Cl − C − Cl
        |
        Cl
   ```

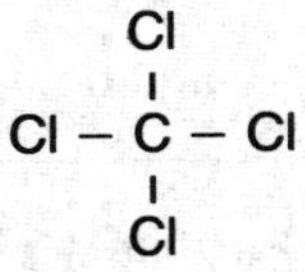

   (c)   H − F

   (d)   H − H

   (e) 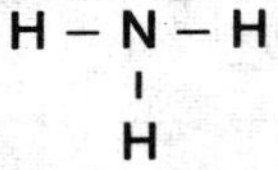
   ```
   H − N − H
       |
       H
   ```
   (f)   H − S − H

   (g) 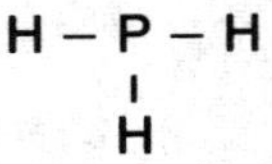
   ```
   H − P − H
       |
       H
   ```
   (h)
   ```
        Cl
        |
   Cl − C − F
        |
        F
   ```

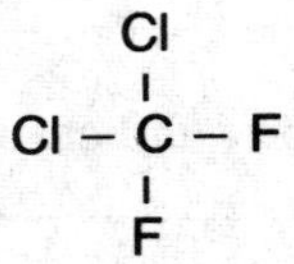

10. The structural formula of hydrogen oxide can be represented as:

    H – O – H

    Draw the structural formulae of the compounds formed between the following elements.

    (a) hydrogen and fluorine   (b) fluorine and oxygen
    (c) nitrogen and hydrogen   (d) carbon and hydrogen

11. Redraw the structural formulae of the compounds in question 10 showing the **outer** electrons of the atoms.

CHAPTER THREE
SYMBOLS, FORMULAE AND EQUATIONS

▶ SYMBOLS

Each element is given a symbol using the letters of the alphabet. As there are more elements than letters of the alphabet, some symbols are given more than one letter.

If there is only one letter in the symbol, a capital letter is used, for example hydrogen H, oxygen O.

Where two letters form the symbol, then the first is a capital letter and the second a small letter, for example bromine Br, zinc Zn.

Not all the symbols take the first letter of the English name of the element. Many elements were first named in languages other than English, for example tungsten W (wolfram), iron Fe (ferrum), mercury Hg (hydrargyrum).

It is important to write symbols correctly. Co is the symbol for the element of cobalt whereas CO is a poisonous compound called carbon monoxide.

▶ WRITING FORMULAE

The formulae of covalent compounds can be obtained from their structural formulae. The formulae of many compounds can also be written using the instructions which follow. All the compounds in the examples below contain only two elements.

1. The chemical formula of a compound is written by swapping over the valencies of the two atoms.

    The number '1' is always left out of formulae.

sodium oxide		
valency	1	2
formula	Na_2O	

nitrogen fluoride		
valency	3	1
formula	NF_3	

2. When both elements have the same valency no numbers are added.

magnesium oxide		
valency	2	2
formula	MgO	

aluminium nitride		
valency	3	3
formula	AlN	

3. The name of the compound may include 'mono' (meaning 1), 'di' (2), 'tri' (3), 'tetra' (4) or 'penta' (5). If it does, then the above rules are not followed. The formula must be written from the 'clues' in the name, for example:

carbon *mono*xide	CO
carbon *di*oxide	CO_2
*di*nitrogen *tetr*oxide	N_2O_4
sulphur *di*oxide	SO_2

4. The transition metals can each have many different valencies. Manganese, for example, can have valencies of 2, 3, 4, 6 and 7. A Roman numeral (I, II, III, IV, etc.) is used to indicate which valency should be used in writing the formula. Here are some examples.

iron(II) chloride	$FeCl_2$	(iron valency 2)
iron(III) oxide	Fe_2O_3	(iron valency 3)
vanadium(V) oxide	V_2O_5	(vanadium valency 5)

▶ WORD EQUATIONS

A chemical reaction can be described by a **word equation**. The chemicals at the start of a reaction are called **reactants** and those at the finish are called **products**. Here is an example.

Copper(II) chloride solution reacts with *zinc* to form *zinc chloride* solution and *copper* metal.

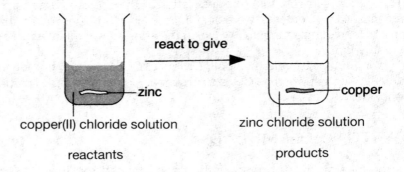

copper(II) chloride solution   zinc chloride solution

reactants   products

The word equation is:

copper(II) chloride + zinc → zinc chloride + copper

This is not the same as an equation which you might meet in your maths class. In an equation in chemistry:

'+' means 'and' or 'reacts with';
'→' means 'gives' or 'changes into'.

Here are other examples of word equations:

magnesium + oxygen → magnesium oxide
zinc + hydrochloric acid → zinc chloride + hydrogen
hydrogen peroxide → oxygen + water

There is a lot of information missing from a word equation. In the first example above, it is not stated that the magnesium must be heated.

A word equation is simply a list of the names of all the reactants and products in the reaction. Some detective work may be needed to find which elements are present in compounds. In the examples above, it can be seen that 'water' is 'hydrogen oxide' and that 'hydrochloric acid' is 'hydrogen chloride'.

▶ CHEMICAL EQUATIONS

A **chemical equation** gives the chemical formulae of the reactants and products instead of their names.

iron + sulphur   →   iron(II) sulphide
Fe + S   →   FeS

$$\text{hydrogen} + \text{chlorine} \rightarrow \text{hydrogen chloride}$$
$$H_2 + Cl_2 \rightarrow HCl$$

$$\text{magnesium} + \text{hydrochloric acid} \rightarrow \text{magnesium chloride} + \text{hydrogen}$$
$$Mg + HCl \rightarrow MgCl_2 + H_2$$

In the two equations above in which the element hydrogen appears, it is written as 'H_2'. Hydrogen is one of seven elements which occur as diatomic molecules. Always write the symbol for the element hydrogen as H_2 in a chemical equation. The other six elements, N_2, O_2, F_2, Cl_2, Br_2 and I_2, are also written in this way. All the other elements have their symbols written as if they were monatomic.

▶ STATE EQUATIONS

More information can be given by adding **state symbols** to a chemical equation:

(s) solid
(l) liquid
(g) gas
(aq) solution (in water or 'aqueous').

Here is an example of a chemical equation with state symbols.

$$\text{calcium carbonate} + \text{hydrochloric acid} \rightarrow \text{calcium chloride} + \text{water} + \text{carbon dioxide}$$
$$CaCO_3(s) + HCl(aq) \rightarrow CaCl_2(aq) + H_2O(l) + CO_2(g)$$

This chemical equation says:

'When *solid* calcium carbonate is added to hydrochloric acid (a *solution* of hydrogen chloride in water) a *solution* of calcium chloride, water (a *liquid*) and carbon dioxide *gas* are formed'.

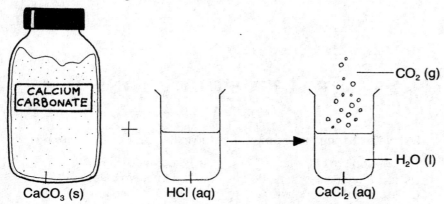

CaCO$_3$ (s)   HCl (aq)   CaCl$_2$ (aq)

▶ BALANCING CHEMICAL EQUATIONS

Here is the chemical equation for the reaction of hydrogen and chlorine.

$$H_2 + Cl_2 \rightarrow HCl$$

Here is the same equation written with the structural formulae of the compounds.

$$H—H + Cl—Cl \rightarrow H—Cl$$

It can be seen from the structural formulae that there are enough hydrogen atoms and chlorine atoms in the molecules of hydrogen and chlorine to form *two* molecules of hydrogen chloride, so it could be rewritten like this:

$$H—H + Cl—Cl \rightarrow H—Cl + H—Cl$$

or in a shorter form:

$$H_2 + Cl_2 \rightarrow 2HCl$$

This **balanced equation** states that:
'*1 molecule of hydrogen reacts* with *1 molecule of chlorine* to form *2 molecules of hydrogen chloride*'.

Here is an example for sodium reacting with sulphur to form sodium sulphide.

Word equation: sodium + sulphur → sodium sulphide
Unbalanced equation: $Na + S$ → Na_2S
Balanced equation: $2Na + S$ → Na_2S

In balancing a chemical equation, numbers are always put in front of formulae. Formulae themselves must *never* be altered in order to balance an equation.

Here are other examples of balanced equations. In each case the unbalanced equation has been written first.

methane + oxygen → carbon dioxide + water   hydrogen + oxygen → water
  $CH_4 + O_2$ → $CO_2 + H_2O$ $H_2 + O_2$ → H_2O
  $CH_4 + 2O_2$ → $CO_2 + 2H_2O$ $2H_2 + O_2$ → $2H_2O$

You will be expected to write word equations from descriptions of experiments in both the General and Credit exams. Unbalanced chemical equations with symbols and formulae will also be required in the General exam, and for the Credit exam you should, in addition, be able to write balanced chemical equations.

Symbols, formulae and equations are the 'language' of chemistry. Although they may account for only a few marks in your exams, it is essential that you master the 'language' if you are going to study chemistry further.

PRACTICE QUESTIONS

1. Write the chemical formulae of the following: ◀ SCOTVEC

   (a) sodium chloride   (b) fluorine oxide
   (c) magnesium sulphide   (d) aluminium oxide
   (e) carbon monoxide   (f) carbon disulphide
   (g) dinitrogen tetroxide   (h) copper(II) chloride
   (i) iron(III) oxide   (j) mercury(II) bromide

2. Name the reactants and products for each of the following chemical reactions. Give your answers in the form of a **table** with the headings 'reactants' and 'products'.

   (a) Sodium reacts with chlorine to form sodium chloride.
   (b) Magnesium reacts with copper(II) bromide to give copper and magnesium bromide.
   (c) Magnesium oxide is formed when magnesium is burned.
   (d) Chlorine reacts with sodium iodide to give iodine and sodium chloride.
   (e) Calcium carbonate decomposes when heated to give calcium oxide and carbon dioxide.

3. Write the **word equations** for the reactions in (a) to (e) in **2** above.

PS **4.** Copy the equations below and complete them by putting the names of the missing chemicals in the boxes.

(a) aluminium + chlorine → [ ]

(b) zinc + hydrochloric acid → zinc chloride + [ ]

(c) lead(II) nitrate + potassium iodide → potassium nitrate + [ ]

(d) sodium + [ ] → sodium oxide

(e) [ ] + copper(II) chloride → iron(II) chloride + copper

5. Write **balanced** chemical equations for the following. ◀ S C O T V E C
(Not all the equations will require to be balanced.)

(a) zinc + sulphur → zinc sulphide

(b) iron + copper(II) chloride → iron(II) chloride + copper

(c) calcium + chlorine → calcium chloride

(d) carbon + oxygen → carbon dioxide

(e) sodium + sulphur → sodium sulphide

(f) aluminium + sulphur → aluminium sulphide

(g) magnesium + oxygen → magnesium oxide

(h) hydrogen + oxygen → water

(i) hydrogen + chlorine → hydrogen chloride

(j) magnesium + hydrochloric acid → magnesium chloride + hydrogen

6. Copy and balance the following equations. ◀ S C O T V E C

(a) $CH_4 + O_2 \rightarrow CO_2 + H_2O$

(b) $H_2 + F_2 \rightarrow HF$

(c) $Mg + CO_2 \rightarrow MgO + C$

(d) $Al + Fe_2O_3 \rightarrow Fe + Al_2O_3$

(e) $Fe + HCl \rightarrow FeCl_2 + H_2$

7. Write **balanced state** equations for the following reactions.

(a) Magnesium metal reacting with steam to form solid magnesium oxide and hydrogen gas.

(b) Powdered iron and sulphur reacting to form solid iron(II) sulphide.

(c) A solution of copper(II) chloride reacting with magnesium to give a solution of magnesium chloride and copper metal.

(d) Calcium oxide powder reacting with hydrochloric acid (hydrogen chloride solution) to form calcium chloride solution and water.

HYDROCARBONS

▶ FUELS

A **fuel** is a chemical which gives out energy when it burns. Burning is also called combustion. In combustion a substance combines with oxygen and gives out energy. A chemical reaction in which energy is given out is called an **exothermic** reaction.

FOSSIL FUELS

Most fuels are derived from coal, oil or natural gas. These are called the **fossil fuels**.

Coal was formed over a period of millions of years. Decayed plant material was changed into coal by high pressures and temperatures.

Oil and natural gas were derived from the decayed remains of the bodies of sea organisms. Oil and natural gas were formed over a long period of time in a similar way to coal.

Coal is mainly composed of carbon whereas oil and natural gas are mixtures of **hydrocarbons**. Hydrocarbons are compounds made up of the elements carbon and hydrogen only.

Because one day our reserves of fossil fuels will be used up, these resources are said to be **finite**. Methods of using alternative sources such as solar, wind, wave and tidal power are being developed.

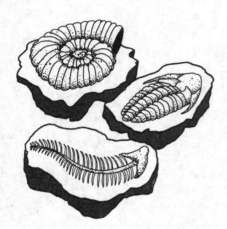

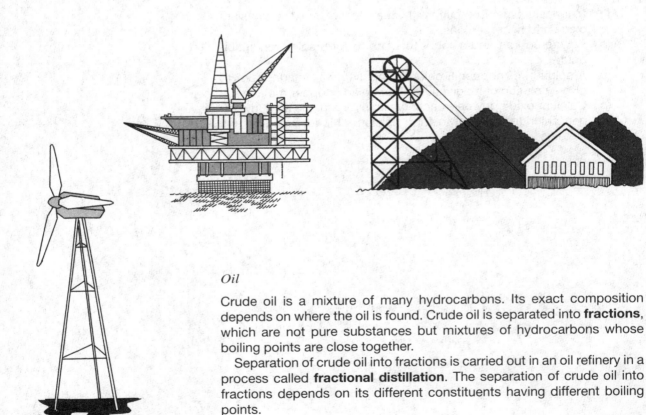

Oil

Crude oil is a mixture of many hydrocarbons. Its exact composition depends on where the oil is found. Crude oil is separated into **fractions**, which are not pure substances but mixtures of hydrocarbons whose boiling points are close together.

Separation of crude oil into fractions is carried out in an oil refinery in a process called **fractional distillation**. The separation of crude oil into fractions depends on its different constituents having different boiling points.

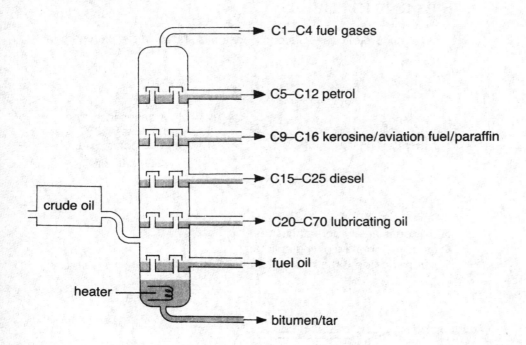

C1–C4 fuel gases

C5–C12 petrol

C9–C16 kerosine/aviation fuel/paraffin

C15–C25 diesel

C20–C70 lubricating oil

fuel oil

bitumen/tar

crude oil

heater

When crude oil is heated the fractions begin to boil. As the temperature at the bottom of the column is much greater than at the top, the fractions can be removed from the column where they reach the point at which it is cool enough for them to condense.

The fractions of oil have many similarities: they are all hydrocarbons and they all burn. The fractions differ both in the size and in the mass of their molecules. Their properties also vary in ways which are summarised in the following table.

Fraction	Properties
'light'–small molecules with short chains of atoms	gases or liquids which are easy to boil evaporate easily catch fire easily (flammable) low boiling points light in colour
'heavy'–larger molecules with longer chains of atoms	liquids which are more difficult to boil, or waxes or solids do not evaporate easily difficult to set on fire higher boiling points darker in colour viscous

A thick oily liquid is said to be **viscous**. The **viscosity** of a liquid is a measure of how 'runny' it is. Syrup is viscous, water is not viscous.

The ease with which a liquid catches fire is called its **flammability**. Liquids which catch fire easily are **flammable**. Fuels with low boiling points are highly flammable, their vapours are easily set on fire.

▶ BURNING FUELS

Air is a mixture of gases. Its composition is shown in the pie chart.

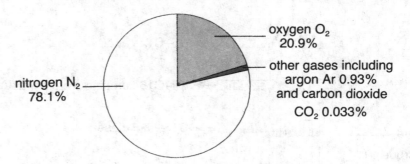

oxygen O_2
20.9%

other gases including
argon Ar 0.93%
and carbon dioxide
CO_2 0.033%

nitrogen N_2
78.1%

Nitrogen is a very unreactive gas.
Oxygen relights a glowing splinter.
Carbon dioxide turns lime water chalky (or milky).

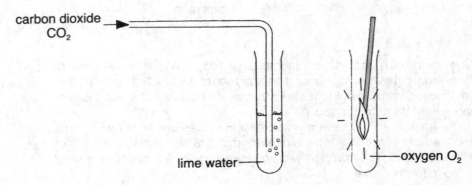

carbon dioxide
CO_2

lime water

oxygen O_2

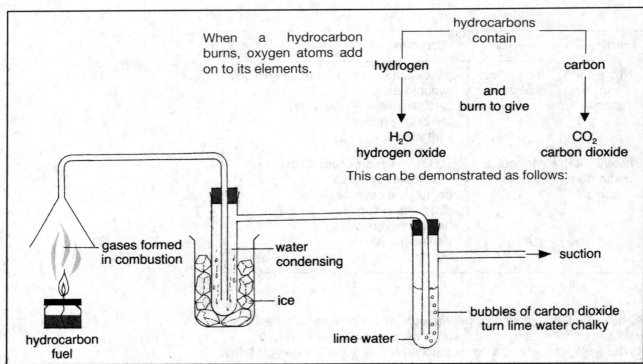

When a hydrocarbon burns, oxygen atoms add on to its elements.

hydrocarbons
contain

hydrogen

carbon

**and
burn to give**

H_2O
hydrogen oxide

CO_2
carbon dioxide

This can be demonstrated as follows:

gases formed
in combustion

water
condensing

suction

ice

bubbles of carbon dioxide
turn lime water chalky

hydrocarbon
fuel

lime water

If insufficient oxygen is present when a hydrocarbon fuel burns, then either carbon monoxide (a poisonous gas) or carbon (soot) may form.

POLLUTION

Gases present in air but which do not naturally occur are called pollutants and cause **air pollution**. Almost all of these pollutants are harmful.

Carbon monoxide (CO) is one gas which can pollute air. Sulphur dioxide (SO_2) and nitrogen dioxide (NO_2) are others.

Sulphur dioxide forms when the small amounts of sulphur in fossil fuels burn. Removing sulphur and sulphur compounds from fuels or from the chimney gases is now considered a priority, as oxides of sulphur combine with water to form acids which cause widespread damage.

The motor car is another cause of air pollution. Petrol is ignited in a car engine by a spark from the sparking plug. The enormous energy of the spark is enough to cause normally inactive nitrogen in the air to combine with oxygen and form oxides of nitrogen. Another pollutant is lead which is found in small amounts in the exhaust of cars which use petrol containing lead compounds. These lead compounds have been added to petrol to improve the performance of the car engine.

Car manufacturers have introduced a number of changes which will help to reduce air pollution from car exhausts. These are: *more efficient engines* with improved fuel-to-air ratios, reducing the amount of *carbon monoxide* produced; *lead-free petrol*, so removing *lead* from the exhaust gases; *catalytic converters* in exhausts which reduce the *oxides of nitrogen* and *carbon monoxide*. *Platinum* and *rhodium* are examples of metals used as catalysts.

Water and land pollution is another problem. Oil spillages at sea can cause serious damage to the environment and wildlife.

► HYDROCARBONS

There are many thousands of hydrocarbon compounds. This large number of compounds is possible because carbon atoms have the ability to form chains. Hydrocarbons are arranged into families or series according to their structural formulae. Three of these familes are **alkanes**, **cyclo-alkanes** and **alkenes.**

ALKANES

The fractions of crude oil are mostly made up of compounds belonging to a family of hydrocarbons called the alkanes.

Name	Structural formula	Shortened structural formula	Molecular formula
methane	H | H – C – H | H	CH_4	CH_4
ethane	H H | | H – C – C – H | | H H	CH_3CH_3	C_2H_6
propane	H H H | | | H – C – C – C – H | | | H H H	$CH_3CH_2CH_3$	C_3H_8
butane	H H H H | | | | H – C – C – C – C – H | | | | H H H H	$CH_3CH_2CH_2CH_3$ or $CH_3(CH_2)_2CH_3$	C_4H_{10}

The molecular formulae of the next four compounds are:
C_5H_{12} pentane; C_6H_{14} hexane; C_7H_{16} heptane; C_8H_{18} octane.

The first part of the name of each compound states the number of carbon atoms in the molecule:

    meth-   1 carbon atom;

    eth-   2 carbon atoms.

The second part of the name, the ending *-ane*, indicates that the compound belongs to the alkane series.

All of the members of the alkane series have similar chemical properties. A series of compounds such as the alkanes, in which all the members have the same name ending and similar chemical properties, is called a **homologous series**.

The **general formula** of the alkanes is C_nH_{2n+2}. If n = 1 the formula is CH_4. If n = 2 the formula is C_2H_6.

The first four alkanes are gases. The other alkanes listed above are liquids. From pentane to octane the boiling points of the liquids increase as the number of carbon atoms in the molecules increases.

The table illustrates how the properties of some alkanes change as the number of carbon atoms in their molecules increases.

Name	Formula	Melting point (°C)	Boiling point (°C)	Properties or uses
methane	CH_4	−183	−164	'North Sea' gas or 'natural' gas
butane	C_4H_{10}	−138	0	cigarette lighter fuel
pentane	C_5H_{12}	−130	36	liquid which boils easily
heptane	C_7H_{16}	−91	98	component of petrol
octadecane	$C_{18}H_{38}$	28	306	solid which melts easily
tricontane	$C_{30}H_{62}$	66	445	waxy solid

CYCLOALKANES

A second homologous series is the cycloalkanes.

Name	Structural formula	Molecular formula
cyclopropane		C_3H_6
cyclobutane		C_4H_8
cyclopentane		C_5H_{10}

A cycloalkane molecule contains a ring of carbon atoms. The general formula for the cycloalkanes is C_nH_{2n}. This is different from that of the alkanes. If n = 6 then the molecular formula is C_6H_{12}. This compound is called cyclohexane.

ALKENES

A third homologous series of hydrocarbons is called the alkenes. Alkene molecules, like alkane molecules, contain chains of carbon atoms. The general formula of the alkenes is C_nH_{2n}, the same general formula as the cycloalkanes.

In alkene molecules *two* of the carbon atoms in the molecule are joined by a 'double bond' as shown in the models.

Name	Structural formula	Shortened structural formula	Molecular formula
ethene	H H | | C = C | | H H	$CH_2{=}CH_2$	C_2H_4
propene	H H H | | | C = C – C – H |　　　| H　　　H	$CH_2{=}CH\ CH_3$	C_3H_6
butene	H H H H | | | | C = C – C – C – H |　　| | H　　H H	$CH_2{=}CH\ CH_2CH_3$	C_4H_8

The molecular formula of pentene is C_5H_{10}, hexene is C_6H_{12}.

Molecules are always drawn on paper as if they were two-dimensional, even though this is unrealistic. As the models show, molecules are three-dimensional.

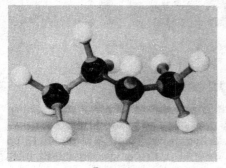

Butane

Cyclopentane

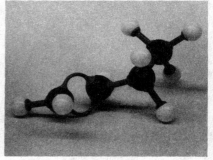

Butene

ISOMERS

As molecules are drawn in two dimensions, care must be taken to notice whether two structural formulae represent the same compound or different compounds. Here is an example.

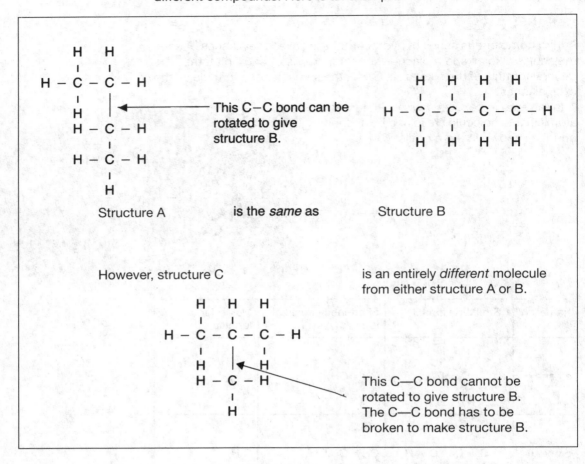

Structure A   **is the *same* as**   Structure B

However, structure C   is an entirely *different* molecule from either structure A or B.

Compounds which have the *same* molecular formulae but *different* structural formulae are called **isomers**.

Here are models of the molecules of the two isomers above.

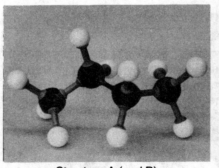

Structure A (and B)

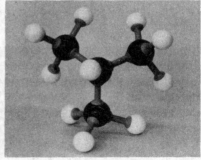

Structure C

SATURATED AND UNSATURATED HYDROCARBONS

Alkenes contain a double bond and are called **unsaturated** hydrocarbons. Alkanes and cycloalkanes are called **saturated** hydrocarbons.

A chemical test will distinguish between saturated and unsaturated hydrocarbons. Alkanes and cycloalkanes can be distinguished from alkenes by adding brown bromine solution.

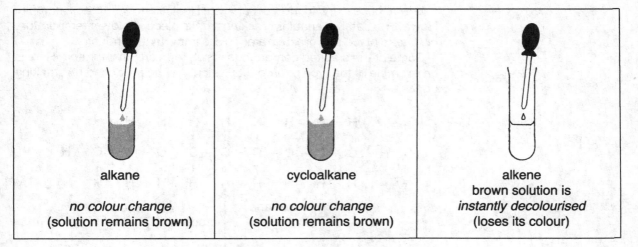

alkane	cycloalkane	alkene
no colour change (solution remains brown)	*no colour change* (solution remains brown)	brown solution is *instantly decolourised* (loses its colour)

When ethene reacts with bromine the following reaction occurs:

$$\begin{array}{ccccc} \text{H} & \text{H} & & & \text{H} \quad \text{H} \\ | & | & & & | \quad\quad | \\ \text{C} = \text{C} & + & \text{Br}_2 & \rightarrow & \text{Br} - \text{C} - \text{C} - \text{Br} \\ | & | & & & | \quad\quad | \\ \text{H} & \text{H} & & & \text{H} \quad \text{H} \end{array}$$

brown   colourless

The reaction of bromine with an unsaturated hydrocarbon is called an **addition** reaction. When hydrogen adds on to an alkene molecule the corresponding alkane molecule is formed. This is also an addition reaction.

$$\begin{array}{ccccc} \text{H} & \text{H} & & & \text{H} \quad \text{H} \\ | & | & & & | \quad\quad | \\ \text{C} = \text{C} & + & \text{H}_2 & \rightarrow & \text{H} - \text{C} - \text{C} - \text{H} \\ | & | & & & | \quad\quad | \\ \text{H} & \text{H} & & & \text{H} \quad \text{H} \end{array}$$

hydrogen   ethane

Alkenes can be used for the manufacture of plastics.

CRACKING

There are far more of the compounds with long chain molecules in the fractions of oil than are required. These long chain molecules can be made into shorter chains and more useful compounds by a process called **cracking**. Paraffin contains long chain alkane molecules and can be cracked as follows:

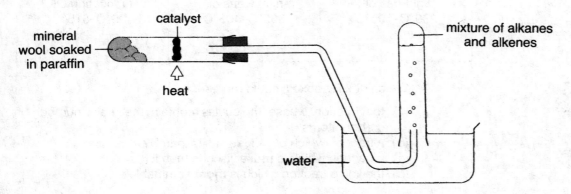

It is not necessary to use a catalyst. Heat alone will crack paraffin. However, a catalyst enables cracking to take place at a lower temperature or to take place at a greater rate. This is important in industry.

Some of the cracked compounds which form are unsaturated. Here is an example of the type of products which may be produced by cracking nonane.

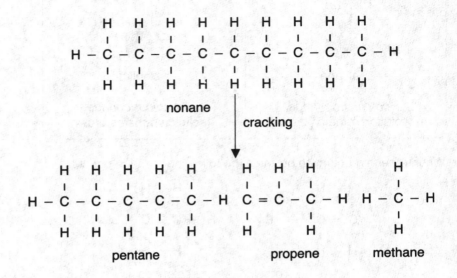

nonane

cracking

pentane   propene   methane

PRACTICE QUESTIONS

---

1. When crude oil is distilled, fractions are obtained which vary greatly in their properties and uses.

   Here are the names of some fractions and the temperature ranges over which they boil.

A	B	C
natural gas < 0°C	gasoline 40°C–180°C	kerosine 180°C–230°C
D	E	F
light gas oil 230°C–305°C	heavy gas oil 305°C–405°C	lubricating oil 405°C–515°C

Which box (or boxes) could represent:

(a) the fraction whose molecules contain the **least** number of carbon atoms?

(b) a fraction which boils **less** easily than D?

(c) a fraction which is **more** viscous than E?

(d) the liquid fraction which is **most** flammable?

2. Air is a mixture of gases including 79% nitrogen, 20% oxygen, less than 1% argon and traces of carbon dioxide.
Nitrogen is a largely unreactive gas; it gives no result with common chemical tests. Oxygen relights a glowing splinter and carbon dioxide can be identified by lime water which it turns chalky. Argon is a totally unreactive gas.

Present the above information in the form of a table with **three** headings.

3. Give the names of the products of complete combustion of the substances in the table.

Fuel	Combustion products
hydrogen carbon carbon monoxide methane ethene	

4. Hydrocarbons can be represented by molecular and structural formulae.

A	B	C
CH₄	$\begin{array}{cc} H & H \\ \| & \| \\ C & = C \\ \| & \| \\ H & H \end{array}$	C₅H₁₂
D	**E**	**F**
(cyclopropane structure) H H \\/ C / \ H–C———C–H | | H H	H H H | | | H – C – C = C | | H H	C₅H₈
G	**H**	**I**
H H | | H – C – C – H | | H – C – C – H | | H H	H H | | H – C – C – H | | H H	H | H – C – H | H .

Which box (or boxes) could represent:

(a) the structural formula of an alkene? ◀ SCOTVEC
(b) the structural formula of a cycloalkane? ◀ SCOTVEC
(c) isomers? ◀ SCOTVEC
(d) a substance which is **neither** an alkane nor an alkene nor a cycloalkane?
(e) pentane? ◀ SCOTVEC

5. Hydrocarbons are obtained from the fractional distillation of crude oil. Two common groups of hydrocarbons are alkanes and alkenes.

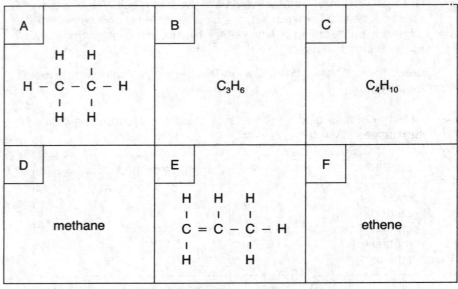

(a) Which **three** boxes show alkanes? ◀ S C O T V E C
(b) Which box gives the structural formula of a compound with the general formula C_nH_{2n}?
(c) Which box gives the molecular formula of an **alkane**?
(d) Which box represents an alkene with **two** carbon atoms? ◀ S C O T V E C
(e) Which **three** boxes could show **unsaturated** hydrocarbons?

6. (a) Draw the structural formula of the alkene with **four** carbon atoms and state its name. ◀ S C O T V E C
   (b)

$$H - \underset{\underset{H}{|}}{\overset{\overset{H}{|}}{C}} - \underset{\underset{H}{|}}{\overset{\overset{H}{|}}{C}} - \underset{\underset{H}{|}}{\overset{\overset{H}{|}}{C}} - \underset{}{\overset{\overset{H}{|}}{C}} = \underset{\underset{H}{|}}{\overset{\overset{H}{|}}{C}}$$

   (i) Give the molecular formula of the above alkene and state its name. ◀ S C O T V E C
    (ii) Draw the structural formula of the cycloalkane which has the **same** molecular formula.

7. The following two compounds are both gases and both have the same molecular formula.

$$H - \underset{\underset{H}{|}}{\overset{\overset{H}{|}}{C}} - \underset{\underset{H}{|}}{\overset{\overset{H}{|}}{C}} - \underset{}{\overset{\overset{H}{|}}{C}} = \underset{\underset{H}{|}}{\overset{\overset{H}{|}}{C}} \qquad\qquad H - \underset{\underset{|}{}}{\overset{\overset{H}{|}}{C}} - \underset{\underset{|}{}}{\overset{\overset{H}{|}}{C}} - H$$

compound A   compound B

(a) State the names of compounds A and B. ◀ S C O T V E C
 (b) Describe a chemical test which you could carry out to distinguish them.
(c) What name is given to such compounds with the same molecular formula and different structural formulae? ◀ S C O T V E C

8. Draw a **labelled** diagram of the apparatus which you would use to crack a liquid hydrocarbon such as paraffin and collect the product which is a mixture of gases.

9. When butane gas is passed over a heated catalyst it cracks as follows:

$$C_4H_{10} \rightarrow C_2H_6 + \text{compound X}$$

(a) Give the molecular formula and the name for compound X.

(b) Draw the structural formula of the compounds which form when compound X reacts with (i) hydrogen, (ii) bromine.

(c) What name is given to the type of reactions occurring in (b)?

CHAPTER FIVE

IONS

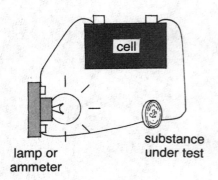

lamp or ammeter

substance under test

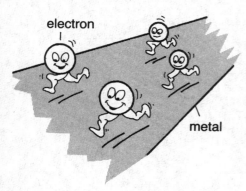

electron

metal

► ELECTRICAL CONDUCTIVITY

The diagram shows how the electrical conductivity of a substance can be tested. If the substance under test is a conductor of electricity, the lamp will light or there will be a reading on the ammeter.

Both **conductors** and **insulators** are important. Conductors carry electrical current in wires. Insulators do not conduct electricity and are used as sleeves on wires and casings for appliances.

Here is a summary of the electrical conductivity of substances.

Conductors	Non-conductors
metals carbon (graphite) solutions of metal compunds molten metal compounds	non-metals solid metal compounds non-metal (covalent) compounds in any state

Electricity travels along metals and carbon as an electric current. An electric current in a wire is a flow of electrons and is measured in amperes (A).

► IONS

The conductivity of molten metal compounds and solutions of metal compounds shows that metal compounds are not covalent. Metal compounds are not made up of molecules but are made up of charged atoms or **ions**. The conductivity of ionic compounds comes from a movement of ions, not electrons.

A battery or cell supplies a direct current (DC) in which electrons always move in the same direction.

The conductivity of an ionic solution is shown.

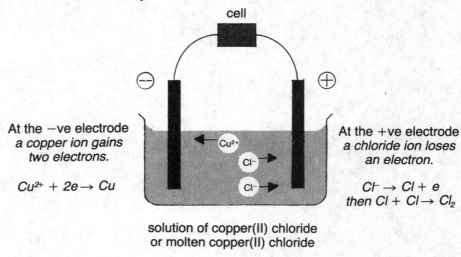

cell

At the −ve electrode
*a copper ion gains
two electrons.*

$Cu^{2+} + 2e \rightarrow Cu$

At the +ve electrode
*a chloride ion loses
an electron.*

$Cl^- \rightarrow Cl + e$
then $Cl + Cl \rightarrow Cl_2$

solution of copper(II) chloride
or molten copper(II) chloride

This experiment shows that metal ions have a positive charge and non-metal ions have a negative charge.

FORMATION OF IONS FROM ATOMS

A *positive ion* forms when a *metal atom loses its outer electrons*.

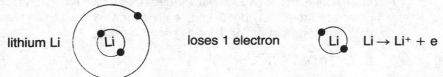

lithium Li   loses 1 electron $Li \rightarrow Li^+ + e$

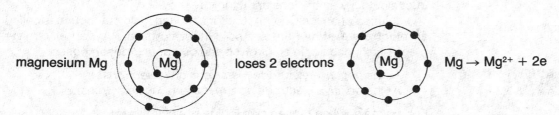

magnesium Mg   loses 2 electrons $Mg \rightarrow Mg^{2+} + 2e$

The opposite happens when non-metal atoms form ions.

A *negative ion* forms when a *non-metal atom gains enough electrons to have a full outer shell*.

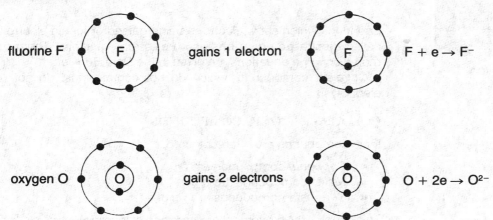

fluorine F   gains 1 electron $F + e \rightarrow F^-$

oxygen O   gains 2 electrons $O + 2e \rightarrow O^{2-}$

In each case the atoms reach the same electron arrangement as the nearest noble gas. Usually this means having eight electrons in the outer level.

IONIC FORMULAE

The formula of ionic compounds can be written to include charges, for example:

sodium chloride	Na^+Cl^-
magnesium oxide	$Mg^{2+}O^{2-}$
calcium fluoride	$Ca^{2+}(F^-)_2$

In each of the examples the total number of positive and negative charges in the formula are equal.

► NETWORK SOLIDS

Ionic compounds do not form molecules. Instead they form **networks** or **lattices**. These grow naturally as **crystals**.

In ionic networks each ion is tightly held by its oppositely charged neighbours, and the network is difficult to break down. Ionic compounds have high melting and boiling points and are solids at room temperature.

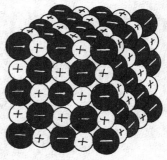

ionic crystal

There are no such strong forces of attraction between neighbouring covalent molecules. Covalent compounds may be solids but they are often liquids or gases. Covalent substances which have very high melting points contain a network of covalently bonded atoms. Examples of these are diamond (carbon) and sand (silicon dioxide).

ELECTROLYSIS

Ions which are tightly held in the network of the solid are set free to move when dissolved in water or melted. Solid ionic compounds do not conduct electricity as the ions are unable to move.

A solution of an ionic compound or a molten ionic compound is called an **electrolyte**. When an electric current flows through an electrolyte **electrolysis** occurs. In electrolysis the compound decomposes.

At the *negative* electrode *metal ions gain electrons*.
At the *positive* electrode *non-metal ions lose electrons*.

For example, when molten zinc iodide is electrolysed:

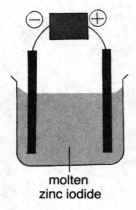

molten
zinc iodide

negative electrode	$Zn^{2+} + 2e \rightarrow Zn$
positive electrode	$I^- \rightarrow I + e$
	then $I + I \rightarrow I_2$

Equations which show electrons being gained or lost in electrolysis are called **discharge equations** or ion electron equations. The most common discharge equations are given in the *Data Booklet*.

Covalent compounds, which do not contain ions, do not undergo electrolysis.

COLOURS OF IONIC COMPOUNDS

Ionic compounds are often coloured.

- *Copper(II)* compounds are *blue*.
- *Nickel* compounds are *green*.
- *Chromate* compounds are *yellow*.

This enables the movement or **migration** of ions in electrolysis to be seen.

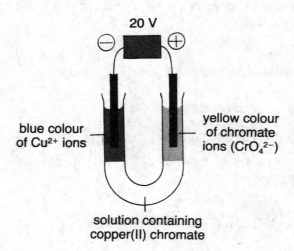

20 V

blue colour
of Cu^{2+} ions

yellow colour
of chromate
ions (CrO_4^{2-})

solution containing
copper(II) chromate

Blue copper(II) ions are seen to move towards the negative electrode showing that *copper(II) ions have a positive charge*.

Yellow chromate ions are seen to move towards the positive electrode showing that *chromate ions have a negative charge*.

SOLVENTS

Although water is a covalent liquid, it is unusual in being a slight conductor of electricity. Water contains a very small number of ions.

Many ionic compounds dissolve in water. Covalent compounds do not dissolve in water but can dissolve in covalent solvents such as hexane or propanone.

MORE ABOUT IONS

Not all ionic compounds contain only two elements. Those which have the name ending 'ate' or 'ite' also contain oxygen.

Here are examples of ions containing more than one kind of atom.

Ion	Formula	Valency
ammonium	NH_4^+	1
hydroxide	OH^-	1
nitrate	NO_3^-	1
carbonate	CO_3^{2-}	2
sulphate	SO_4^{2-}	2

The formulae of these and other ions are listed in the *Data Booklet*.

MORE ABOUT FORMULAE

To write the formula of a compound containing ions with more than one atom, each part of the name of the compound should be treated as one unit. The formulae are written by using the rule of 'swapping' over valencies. In the first example, the carbonate ion has been put in brackets to make the two units clear. It is really only necessary to use a bracket if a number subscript has to be added.

Charges may be added to formulae. It may be helpful to put a bracket round *each* of the ions although it is again only necessary when a number subscript has to be added.

ammonium carbonate 1　　2 $(NH_4)_2(CO_3)$	aluminium carbonate 3　　2 $Al_2(CO_3)_3$
aluminium sulphate 3　　2 $(Al^{3+})_2(SO_4^{2-})_3$	ammonium chloride 1　　1 $(NH_4^+)Cl^-$

PRACTICE QUESTIONS

1. Elements and compounds can be divided into two sets, conductors of electricity and insulators.

A carbon (graphite)	**B** copper	**C** mercury
D sodium chloride crystals	**E** petrol	**F** sulphur
G molten lead(II) bromide	**H** copper(II) sulphate solution	**I** sodium

(a) Which **three** boxes represent **solids** which are conductors of electricity?

(b) Which **two** boxes represent conductors of electricity through which **ions** flow?

(c) Which box represents a liquid which conducts electricity by a **flow of electrons**?

(d) Which box represents an ionic **solid**?

2. Carbon dioxide is a **gas** made up of molecules of CO_2. Magnesium oxide is a **network soild** made up of Mg^{2+} ions and O^{2-} ions.

Explain why carbon dioxide is a gas whereas magnesium oxide is a solid.

3. A student wrote the following in her notebook.

> Ionic solids such as sodium chloride do not conduct electricity. They do conduct when they are melted or dissolved in water. They conduct only when their ions are free to move.

Draw a diagam showing the arrangement of the ions in an ionic crystal, and use it to explain the note which the girl wrote.

4. When a copper(II) chloride solution was electrolysed, it decomposed to form copper (metal) and chlorine (gas).

   (a) Write the formula for copper(II) chloride showing charges.
   (b) Write the discharge equations for this electrolysis showing the formation of (i) copper, (ii) chlorine.

5.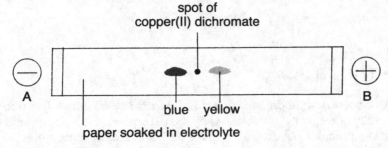

   spot of
   copper(II) dichromate

   A   blue   yellow   B

   paper soaked in electrolyte

   The experiment shown above is about ion migration. Copper(II) dichromate solution was spotted on to a piece of wet paper. The terminals A and B were connected to a source of 20 V direct current and the experiment was left for ten minutes.

   A blue colour was seen moving towards A and a yellow colour was seen moving towards B.

   (a) What does this experiment indicate about the charges on the two ions in copper(II) dichromate?
   (b) Why did the blue colour move towards A?
   (c) Why was a 'direct' current used?
   (d) Suggest why the paper was soaked in an 'electrolyte' and not simply water.

6. Write the formulae for the following compounds.   ◀ SCOTVEC
   (a) sodium nitrate   (b) potassium hydroxide
   (c) ammonium chloride   (d) ammonium hydroxide
   (e) copper(II) sulphate   (f) sodium carbonate
   (g) lithium carbonate   (h) ammonium sulphate
   (i) iron(III) nitrate   (j) aluminium sulphate

7. Rewrite the formulae in 6 above showing the charges on the ions.

ACIDS, ALKALIS AND CHEMICAL CALCULATIONS

► THE pH SCALE

An aqueous solution can be **acidic**, **neutral** or **alkaline**. The degree of acidity or alkalinity is measured by the pH scale and can be measured by using indicator paper, liquid 'Universal' indicator or a pH meter.

- In an *acid solution* there are *more* H^+ *ions than* OH^- *ions*.
- A *neutral solution* contains the *same number of* H^+ *ions and* OH^- *ions*.
- In an *alkaline solution* there are *more* OH^- *ions than* H^+ *ions*.

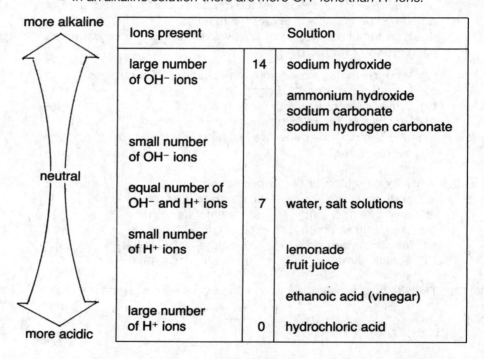

Ions present		Solution
large number of OH^- ions	14	sodium hydroxide
		ammonium hydroxide sodium carbonate sodium hydrogen carbonate
small number of OH^- ions		
equal number of OH^- and H^+ ions	7	water, salt solutions
small number of H^+ ions		lemonade fruit juice
		ethanoic acid (vinegar)
large number of H^+ ions	0	hydrochloric acid

more alkaline ↑   neutral   ↓ *more acidic*

Acid solutions contain a much greater concentration of H^+ ions than water. Alkaline solutions contain a greater concentration of OH^- ions than water. When an acidic or an alkaline solution is diluted with water the pH of the solution moves towards 7.

The table lists some common acids and alkalis.

Acids	hydrochloric acid	HCl
	nitric acid	HNO_3
	sulphuric acid	H_2SO_4
	phosphoric acid	H_3PO_4
	ethanoic acid	CH_3COOH
Alkalis	sodium hydroxide	$NaOH$
	potassium hydroxide	KOH
	calcium hydroxide	$Ca(OH)_2$
	ammonium hydroxide	NH_4OH

ELECTROLYSIS OF ACID SOLUTIONS

When acid solutions are electrolysed, **hydrogen** gas forms at the negative electrode.

$$H^+ + e \rightarrow H$$
then $H + H \rightarrow H_2$

A mixture of hydrogen and air explodes with a pop when ignited. This is a test for the hydrogen formed.

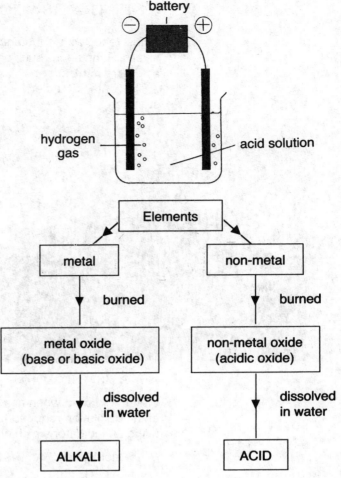

► MAKING ACIDS AND ALKALIS

Many acids and alkalis are formed from the oxides of elements.

Not all metal oxides dissolve in water to form alkalis. The table of solubilities in the *Data Booklet* indicates which metal oxides dissolve.

Here are examples of alkalis and acids forming.

Sodium forms sodium oxide which then forms the alkali sodium hydroxide.

sodium + oxygen → sodium oxide
sodium oxide + water → *sodium hydroxide*

Carbon forms carbon dioxide which then forms the acid carbonic acid.

carbon + oxygen → carbon dioxide
carbon dioxide + water → *carbonic acid*

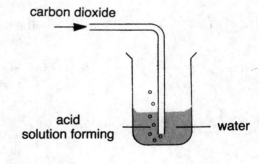

ACID RAIN

Many fuels contain traces of sulphur. When sulphur burns it pollutes the atmosphere with sulphur dioxide which dissolves in rain water to form **acid rain**.

Acid rain damages structures made from many materials. Buildings made from limestone or marble (calcium carbonate) slowly react with acid rain and become eroded. In many buildings a lot of fine detail has been lost over the years.

Acid rain also has a damaging effect on many metals, plant and animal life. Iron is one of the metals which is affected by acids and rusting is accelerated by contact with acid rain.

▶ NEUTRALISATION

Acids react with substances such as metals, bases, carbonates and alkalis. Substances such as these are called **antacids**. In such reactions acids are **neutralised**.

The antacid tablets which chemists sell neutralise acidity in the stomach.

Lime is an antacid which farmers dig into the soil to reduce its acidity. Lime can also be added to lakes and rivers which have become acidic. This encourages the return of living things which cannot tolerate acidity.

ALKALIS AND ACIDS

Water is formed when an acid is neutralised by an alkali. The volume of antacid solution required to neutralise an acid solution can be found by using an indicator which changes colour when the pH reaches 7.

$$\text{acid (pH} < 7) \qquad \text{alkali (pH} > 7) \qquad \text{neutral (pH} = 7)$$
$$H^+(aq) \quad + \quad OH^-(aq) \quad \rightarrow \quad H_2O(l)$$

As well as water another compound, called a **salt**, is formed. The pH of salt solutions is 7.

Naming Salts

The first part of the name of a salt is taken from the metal in the antacid. Salts take the second part of their names from the acid used.

Acid	Salt
hydrochloric acid	–chloride
sulphuric acid	–sulphate
nitric acid	–nitrate
phosphoric acid	–phosphate
ethanoic acid	–ethanoate

For example:

$$\textit{sodium} \text{ hydroxide} \quad + \quad \textit{nitric} \text{ acid} \quad \rightarrow \quad \text{water} \quad + \quad \textit{sodium nitrate}$$
$$NaOH \quad + \quad HNO_3 \quad \rightarrow \quad H_2O \quad + \quad NaNO_3$$

A salt is formed when the hydrogen ion, H^+, in an acid is replaced by a metal ion or an ammonium ion, NH_4^+.

Here are examples of salts:

sodium chloride (common 'salt')	$NaCl$
calcium nitrate	$Ca(NO_3)_2$
ammonium sulphate	$(NH_4)_2SO_4$

CARBONATES AND ACIDS

Carbon dioxide gas is formed, along with water and a salt, when an acid is neutralised by a carbonate.

sulphuric acid + copper(II) carbonate → water + copper(II) sulphate + carbon dioxide
$$H_2SO_4 + CuCO_3 → H_2O + CuSO_4 + CO_2$$

This equation can be written in a simpler way:

$$2H^+(aq) + CO_3^{2-}(s) → H_2O(l) + CO_2(g)$$

The ions which have been missed out are called **spectator ions**.

Many carbonates are insoluble in water and react with acids to form soluble salts. Here is how a salt solution can be made from an acid and an insoluble carbonate.

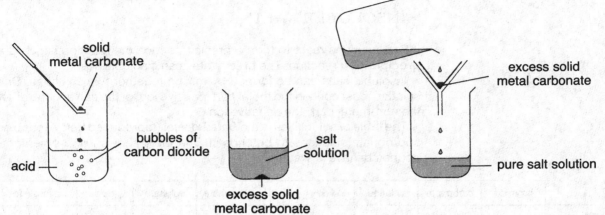

solid metal carbonate

acid

bubbles of carbon dioxide

salt solution

excess solid metal carbonate

excess solid metal carbonate

pure salt solution

As long as the reaction is taking place, bubbles of carbon dioxide will be seen forming. When the acid has been neutralised the bubbling will stop. Excess carbonate, which is insoluble, can then be removed by filtering, leaving a solution of the salt.

METAL OXIDES AND ACIDS

Metal oxides, many of which are insoluble solids, neutralise acids to form salts. It is usually necessary to heat the acid.

sulphuric acid + magnesium oxide → water + magnesium sulphate
$$H_2SO_4 + MgO → H_2O + MgSO_4$$

Omitting the spectator ions, this can be written:

$$2H^+(aq) + O^{2-}(s) → H_2O(l)$$

A salt solution can be made by adding a base to an acid by the same method described for a carbonate. When the acid has been neutralised the excess insoluble base will lie at the bottom of the beaker. Excess oxide can then be removed by filtering, leaving a solution of the salt.

METALS AND ACIDS

Some metals react with acids to form hydrogen and a salt.

magnesium + sulphuric acid → hydrogen + magnesium sulphate
$$Mg + H_2SO_4 → H_2 + MgSO_4$$

Water does *not* form when a metal reacts with an acid. Salts formed when metals react with acids are named in the same way as those formed in the other neutralisation reactions.

Metals such as sodium and potassium react violently with acids.

The metals chosen to make hydrogen are those known as the '**mazit**' metals: magnesium, aluminium, zinc, iron and tin.

SUMMARY OF NEUTRALISATION REACTIONS

acid	+	alkali	→	salt	+	water
acid	+	carbonate	→	salt	+	water + carbon dioxide
acid	+	metal oxide	→	salt	+	water
acid	+	metal	→	salt	+	hydrogen

Neutralisation by an alkali is the method which should always be chosen to make sodium, potassium and ammonium salts. Reacting an acid and a carbonate is the most convenient way of making other soluble salts. The end of the reaction can easily be seen and no heating is required. Metal carbonates are also much cheaper than metals and the reaction forms carbon dioxide rather than hydrogen which is a flammable gas.

▶ INSOLUBLE SALTS

If two solutions react to form a precipitate then the reaction is called a **precipitation** reaction. The precipitate is an insoluble solid.

Insoluble salts can be formed by mixing together two solutions. One solution must contain the metal part, positive ion, of the salt and the other the non-metal part, the negative ion.

The table of solubilities in the *Data Booklet* (reproduced below) enables appropriate solutions to be chosen. The table shows how some compounds behave in water.

	bromide	carbonate	chloride	iodide	nitrate	phosphate	sulphate	oxide	hydroxide
aluminium	—	i	—	—	vs	i	vs	i	i
ammonium	vs	vs	vs	vs	vs	vs	vs	—	—
barium	vs	i	vs	vs	vs	i	i	reacts	vs
calcium	vs	i	vs	vs	vs	i	s	reacts	s
copper(II)	vs	i	vs	—	vs	i	vs	i	i
iron(II)	vs	i	vs	—	vs	i	vs	i	i
lead(II)	s	i	s	i	vs	i	i	i	i
lithium	vs	vs	vs	vs	vs	i	vs	reacts	vs
magnesium	vs	i	vs	vs	vs	i	vs	i	i
nickel	vs	i	vs	vs	vs	i	vs	i	i
potassium	vs	vs	vs	vs	vs	vs	vs	reacts	vs
silver	i	i	i	i	vs	i	s	i	i
sodium	vs	vs	vs	vs	vs	vs	vs	reacts	vs
tin(II)	vs	i	vs	s	—	i	vs	i	i
zinc	vs	i	vs	vs	vs	i	vs	i	i

vs   means very soluble   (a solubility greater than 10 g/l)
s   means soluble   (a solubility of between 1 and 10 g/l)
i   means insoluble   (a solubility of less than 1g/l)
—   indicates that data is unavailable

Oxides which react with water form alkalis.

MAKING COPPER(II) CARBONATE

The table of solubilities shows that copper(II) carbonate is insoluble in water. Copper(II) carbonate can be made by mixing a solution of *any* soluble copper compound with a solution of *any* soluble carbonate.

Here are examples of solutions which could be mixed to form copper(II) carbonate (the chemical equations are also given for the third example):

copper(II) sulphate solution and sodium carbonate solution
copper(II) nitrate solution and potassium carbonate solution
copper(II) chloride solution and sodium carbonate solution

$$CuCl_2(aq) + Na_2CO_3(aq) \rightarrow CuCO_3(s) + 2NaCl(aq)$$
$$\text{or } Cu^{2+}(aq) + CO_3^{2-}(aq) \rightarrow Cu^{2+}CO_3^{2-}(s)$$

The chloride (Cl^-) and sodium (Na^+) ions remain in solution. They are the spectator ions.

INSOLUBLE SALTS — MAKING PREDICTIONS

The name of the precipitate which is formed when two solutions are mixed can be predicted from a table of solubilities. For example, when calcium chloride solution is mixed with sodium carbonate solution, the possible precipitates are sodium chloride and calcium carbonate. Sodium chloride is 'very soluble' in water. Calcium carbonate is 'insoluble' in water, so the precipitate will be calcium carbonate.

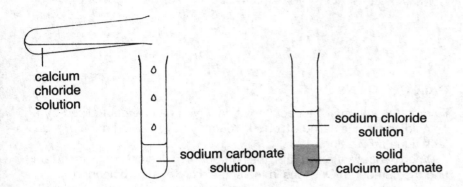

calcium chloride solution

sodium carbonate solution

sodium chloride solution

solid calcium carbonate

▶ FORMULA MASS AND THE MOLE

The **formula mass** (or relative formula mass) of a substance is the total mass of all the atoms in its formula. The formula mass is given the units 'amu', 'atomic mass units'.

Carbon dioxide CO_2 contains 1 carbon atom and 2 oxygen atoms:

$$
\begin{aligned}
\text{carbon} \quad & 1 \times 12 = 12 \\
\text{oxygen} \quad & 2 \times 16 = 32 \\
\text{formula mass} &= 44 \text{ amu}
\end{aligned}
$$

The formula mass expressed in grams is known as 1 **mole**. 1 mole of carbon dioxide weighs 44g.

MEASURING THE CONCENTRATION OF A SOLUTION

The concentration of a solution is given in **mol/l** or **mol/dm³**. This is the 'number of moles' dissolved in '1 litre of solution'. A litre is written as '*l*'. One litre is 1000 cm³.

$$
\begin{aligned}
&\text{sodium carbonate } Na_2CO_3 \\
\text{sodium} \quad & 2 \times 23 = 46 \\
\text{carbon} \quad & 1 \times 12 = 12 \\
\text{oxygen} \quad & 3 \times 16 = 48 \\
\text{formula mass} &= 106 \text{ amu} \\
\text{mass of 1 mole} &= 106 \text{ g}
\end{aligned}
$$

A 1 mol/*l* solution of sodium carbonate contains 106 g/*l*.

The number of moles of a solute in a solution can be calculated if the concentration and volume of the solution are known:

$$
\text{number of moles in solution} = \frac{\text{concentration} \times \text{volume (cm}^3\text{)}}{1000}
$$

1 litre

Example

$$500 \text{ cm}^3 \text{ of a } 0.5 \text{ mol/} l \text{ solution contain } \frac{0.5 \times 500}{1000} \text{ moles}$$
$$= 0.25 \text{ mole}$$

500 cm³ of *any* 0.5 mol/*l* solution will contain 0.25 mole of the solute in 1 litre of the solution.

If this is a solution of sodium hydroxide (NaOH), then
the mass of sodium hydroxide = 0.25 × mass of 1 mole of NaOH
$$= 0.25 \times 40$$
$$= 10 \text{ g}$$

CALCULATIONS

Finding the volume of an acid solution which can be neutralised by an antacid solution is called **titration**. You may have carried out a practical technique on titration.

When neutralisation occurs, the number of moles of H^+ ions in the acid and the number of OH^- ions in the antacid are exactly balanced.

Here are three ways in which sodium hydroxide solution could be neutralised by an acid.

25 cm³ of 1 mol/*l* hydrochloric acid neutralises 25 cm³ of 1 mol/*l* of sodium hydroxide

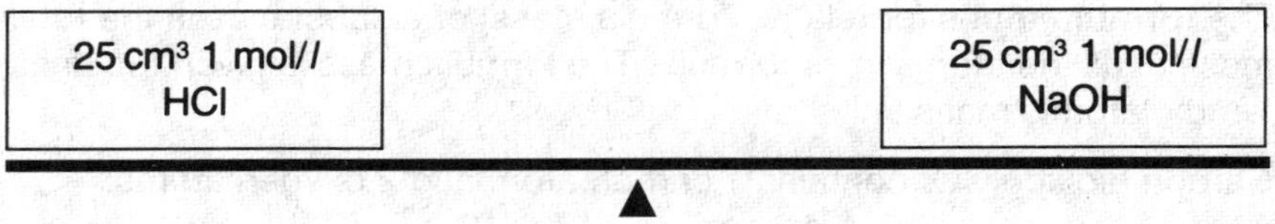

25 cm³ 1 mol/*l* HCl		25 cm³ 1 mol/*l* NaOH

▲

25 cm³ of 1 mol/*l* hydrochloric acid neutralises 50 cm³ of 0.5 mol/*l* of sodium hydroxide

25 cm³ 1 mol/*l* HCl		50 cm³ 0.5 mol/*l* NaOH

▲

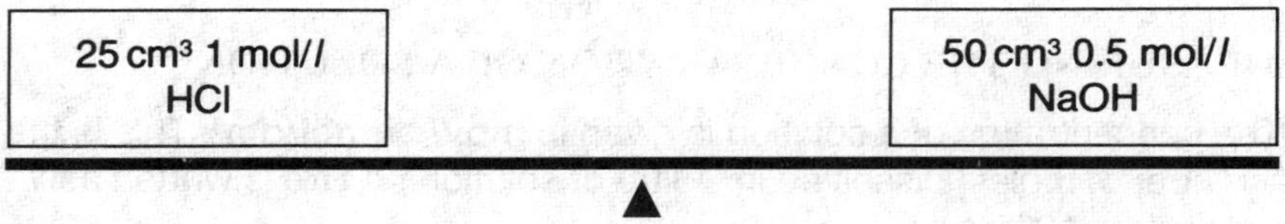

25 cm³ of 1 mol/*l* sulphuric acid neutralises 50 cm³ of 1 mol/*l* of sodium hydroxide

25 cm³ 1 mol/*l* H₂SO₄		50 cm³ 1 mol/*l* NaOH

▲

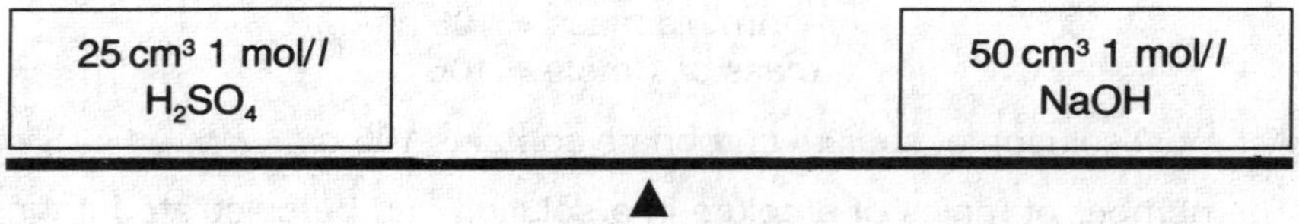

In the last example, sulphuric acid neutralised *more* of the 1 mol/*l* solution of sodium hydroxide than hydrochloric acid of the same concentration did. This is because sulphuric acid (H_2SO_4) contains two H^+ ions. There is only one H^+ ion in hydrochloric acid (HCl).

In general:

[volume] × [concentration] × [number of H⁺ ions] = [volume] × [concentration] × [number of OH⁻ ions]

Here are some examples of calculations on titrations.

Example 1 What volume of 1 mol/l sulphuric acid will neutralise 100 cm³ of 4 mol/l of sodium hydroxide?

[volume] × [concentration] × [number of H⁺ ions] = [volume] × [concentration] × [number of OH⁻ ions]
$$\text{volume} \times 1 \times 2 = 100 \times 4 \times 1$$
$$\text{volume} = 200 \text{ cm}^3$$

Example 2 25 cm³ of hydrochloric acid is neutralised by 50 cm³ of 1 mol/l sodium hydroxide. What is the concentration of the hydrochloric acid?

[volume] × [concentration] × [number of H⁺ ions] = [volume] × [concentration] × [number of OH⁻ ions]
$$25 \times \text{concentration} \times 1 = 50 \times 1 \times 1$$
$$\text{concentration} = 2 \text{ mol/}l$$

These calculations allow the concentration of a solution to be determined. In each case the formula of the acid and antacid (usually an alkali) must be known.

REACTING MASSES

A balanced chemical equation indicates the numbers of moles of reactants and products. For example, this balanced equation for magnesium reacting with hydrochloric acid:

$$Mg + 2HCl \rightarrow H_2 + MgCl_2$$

states that:

'*1 mole of magnesium* reacts with *2 moles of hydrochloric acid* to form *1 mole of hydrogen* and *1 mole of magnesium chloride*'.

The numbers in front of formulae in the equation indicate the numbers of moles. If there is no number this is taken to mean 1 mole.

The mass of each substance which is reacting can be calculated from the balanced equation.

Mg	+	2HCl	→	H₂	+	MgCl₂
1 mole	+	2 moles	→	1 mole	+	1 mole
24 g	+	73 g	→	2 g	+	95 g

- *24 g of magnesium* will react with *73 g of hydrochloric acid* to give *2 g of hydrogen* and *95 g of magnesium chloride*.

24 g of magnesium is an enormous amount. Your chemistry class will not use that much magnesium in a year! It is, however, a simple matter to make calculations for other numbers of moles.

For example if only 2.4 g of magnesium was used:

- *2.4 g of magnesium* will react with *7.3 g of hydrochloric acid* to give *0.2 g of hydrogen* and *9.5 g of magnesium chloride*.

Or if 12 g of magnesium was used:

- *12 g of magnesium* will react with *36.5 g of hydrochloric acid* to give *1 g of hydrogen* and *47.5 g of magnesium chloride*.

Once a balanced equation is written, the quantities of any of the reactants or products can be calculated.

CALCULATIONS WITH MOLES

Here are some examples of calculations of reacting masses.

Example 1 What mass of lithium will react with 16 g of sulphur to form lithium sulphide?

Step 1 Write a balanced equation:

$$2Li + S \rightarrow Li_2S$$

Step 2 In the equation <u>underline</u> the substance whose mass is *given* and the substance whose mass you are asked to *find*.

$$\underline{2Li} + \underline{S} \rightarrow Li_2S$$

Step 3 Underneath the equation write down the numbers of reacting moles of these substances.

2 moles of lithium react with *1 mole of sulphur*.
(There is *no* need to mention lithium sulphide.)

Step 4 Now calculate the masses of the moles you have written down.

2 moles Li   1 mole S = 32 g
$2 \times 7 = 14$ g

14 g of lithium react with 32 g of sulphur,
so 7 g of lithium react with 16g of sulphur.
Answer: 7 g of lithium reacts.

Example 2 What mass of carbon dioxide forms when 5 g of calcium carbonate reacts with hydrochloric acid?

$$\underline{CaCO_3} + 2HCl \rightarrow \underline{CO_2} + H_2O + CaCl_2$$

1 mole of calcium carbonate gives *1 mole of carbon dioxide*.
1 mole $CaCO_3$ 1 mole CO_2
$40 + 12 + (3 \times 16) = 100$ g $12 + (2 \times 16) = 44$ g
100 g of calcium carbonate gives 44 g of carbon dioxide.
5 g of calcium carbonate gives 2.2 g of carbon dioxide.
Answer: 2.2 g of carbon dioxide forms.

Example 3 What mass of nitric acid reacts with copper(II) oxide to form 18.8 g of copper(II) nitrate?

$$CuO + \underline{2HNO_3} \rightarrow H_2O + \underline{Cu(NO_3)_2}$$

2 moles of nitric acid   give   *1 mole of copper(II) nitrate.*
2 moles HNO_3 1 mole $Cu(NO_3)_2$
$2 \times [1 + 14 + (3 \times 16)] = 126$ g $64 + (2 \times 14) + (6 \times 16) = 188$ g
126 g of nitric acid gives 188 g of copper(II) nitrate.
12.6 g of nitric acid gives 18.8 g of copper(II) nitrate.
Answer: 12.6 g of nitric acid reacts.

Calculating reacting masses is not always easy. You must be able to do all of these things.

- Write a balanced chemical equation from information given. (This will often be given.)
- Select the substance whose mass has to be found and the substance whose mass is given.
- Calculate the relative formula mass of the substances.
- Carry out the arithmetic required to get the answer.

A calculator will be required to work out the answer in some Credit questions.

Here is an example in which the arithmetic is more difficult.

Example 4   In an industrial process, ammonia (NH_3) is made by reacting together nitrogen and hydrogen. What mass of ammonia per hour is obtained if 8 kg per hour of nitrogen reacts completely with hydrogen?

$$N_2 + 3H_2 \rightarrow 2NH_3$$

1 mole of nitrogen gives 2 moles of ammonia.

1 mole N_2 2 moles NH_3
$2 \times 14 = 28$ g $2 \times [14 + (3 \times 1)] = 34$ g
28 g of nitrogen gives 34 g of ammonia.

8 kg of nitrogen gives $\dfrac{34}{28} \times 8$ kg.

Answer: 9.71 kg/hour.

PRACTICE QUESTIONS

1. Many acidic, alkaline and neutral substances are to be found about the house as can be seen in this passage.

> Vinegar and lemon juice are acids which will be found in the kitchen. Fizzy drinks such as lemonade are also acids.
> Baking soda is an example of an alkali. Many household cleaners are alkalis. Sodium carbonate is an alkali used for cleaning ovens, and sodium hydroxide (a very strong alkali) is used to clear drains.
> Sulphuric acid, a strong acid, is found in a car battery.
> Tap water is neither acidic nor alkaline; it is neutral. So too is a solution of salt in water.

Present the above information in the form of a table with **three** headings.

2. There are many common acids used in chemistry laboratories.

    Which **one** of the following boxes contains a statement true **only** of hydrochloric acid?

A	It has a pH of less than 7.
B	It forms compounds called chlorides.
C	It contains hydrogen ions, H^+.
D	It gives hydrogen when electrolysed.

3. Potassium hydroxide solution is a common alkali with many uses.

    Which box (or boxes) contains a statement which is **true** about potassium hydroxide solution?

A	It contains more H^+ ions than water.
B	It produces 'acid' rain when dissolved in water.
C	It has a pH of more than 7.
D	It forms when potassium oxide dissolves in water.

4. Neutralisation is a common chemical reaction with many everyday applications.

    Which **two** of the following boxes contain statements referring to neutralisation?

A	Treatment of acid indigestion by antacid.
B	Formation of 'acid' rain in the atmosphere.
C	Treatment of acidic water in a lake by adding lime.
D	Dilution of acid solution by addition of water.

5. Gases form in many chemical reactions.

    Which **two** of the following boxes represent reactions in which a gas forms?

A	Reaction of zinc and hydrochloric acid.
B	Reaction of hydrochloric acid and sodium hydroxide solution.
C	Reaction of sodium sulphate solution and barium chloride solution.
D	Reaction of calcium carbonate and hydrochloric acid.

6. Calculate the formula mass of the following.   ◀SCOTVEC

(a) NaF   (b) CaO   (c) $CaCO_3$
(d) H_2SO_4 (e) nitric acid   (f) sodium hydroxide

7. Name the neutralisation product (salt) formed when each of the following substances react.   ◀SCOTVEC

(a) zinc and sulphuric acid
(b) sodium hydroxide and hydrochloric acid
(c) copper(II) carbonate and sulphuric acid
(d) copper(II) oxide and hydrochloric acid
(e) potassium hydroxide and nitric acid

8. (a) Write balanced state equations for each of the following reactions. **Do not show charges**.
   (i) magnesium and hydrochloric acid
   (ii) sulphuric acid and copper(II) oxide
   (iii) nitric acid and sodium hydroxide
   (iv) hydrochloric acid and calcium carbonate
   (b) Rewrite the above equations as ionic equations omitting the spectator ions.

9. Calculate the mass of each of the following.   ◀SCOTVEC

(a) 1 mole of water
(b) 2 moles of calcium carbonate
(c) 0.5 mole of sulphuric acid
(d) 0.1 mole of nitric acid
(e) 2 moles of sodium hydroxide

10. Calculate the number of moles in each of the following.   ◀SCOTVEC

(a) 10 g of calcium carbonate
(b) 8 g of sulphur
(c) 10.6 g of sodium carbonate
(d) 100 cm³ of 1 mol/l of hydrochloric acid
(e) 2 litres (2000 cm³) of 2 mol/l of sulphuric acid

Ⓟ︎Ⓢ︎ 11. Use the table of solubilities to state the name of any insoluble salts formed when the following solutions are mixed. (Not all of the mixtures of solutions give a precipitate.)

(a) sodium sulphate and copper(II) chloride
(b) barium nitrate and copper(II) sulphate
(c) sodium hydroxide and ammonium nitrate
(d) copper(II) chloride and sodium carbonate
(e) potassium iodide and lead(II) nitrate

12. Lead(II) carbonate is an insoluble compound.

Ⓟ︎Ⓢ︎ (a) Use the table of solubilities to select **two** solutions which could be mixed to make lead(II) carbonate.
(b) Write (i) the state equation for the reaction,
            (ii) the state equation omitting spectator ions (ionic equation).
(c) What name is given to the above reaction?
Ⓟ︎Ⓢ︎ (d) Draw a diagram showing how you would separate the lead(II) carbonate from the solution in the above reaction. Label the 'lead(II) carbonate'.

13. (a) What volume of 2 mol/l hydrochloric acid will neutralise 20 cm³ of 1 mol/l sodium hydroxide? ◀SCOTVEC
   (b) What volume of 1 mol/l sulphuric acid will neutralise 20 cm³ of 1 mol/l potassium hydroxide? ◀SCOTVEC
   (c) 25 cm³ of 1 mol/l sodium hydroxide neutralises 50 cm³ of nitric acid. What is the concentration of the nitric acid? ◀SCOTVEC
   (d) 50 cm³ of sulphuric acid neutralises 25 cm³ of 4 mol/l potassium hydroxide. What is the concentration of the sulphuric acid? ◀SCOTVEC

14. Sodium hydroxide can be neutralised by an acid. ◀SCOTVEC

Which box (or boxes) contains an **incorrect** statement about the amount of acid required to neutralise 50cm³ of 2 mol/l sodium hydroxide?

A	25 cm³ of 4 mol/l hydrochloric acid.
B	100 cm³ of 1 mol/l sulphuric acid.
C	100 cm³ of 1 mol/l nitric acid.
D	50 cm³ of 2 mol/l hydrochloric acid.

15. Sulphur combines directly with many elements when heated. ◀SCOTVEC
   (a) What mass of calcium reacts with 16 g of sulphur?
   (b) What mass of sulphur reacts with 23 g of sodium?
   (c) What mass of iron(II) sulphide forms when 5.6 g of iron are heated with sulphur?

16. Many elements burn in oxygen. ◀SCOTVEC
   (a) Calculate the mass of oxygen needed to burn each of the following.
      (i) 6 g of carbon (ii) 24 g of magnesium (iii) 2.3 g of sodium
   (b) Calculate the mass of the products when each of the following is burned.
      (i) 3 g of carbon (ii) 12 g of magnesium
      (iii) 16 g of sulphur (which forms sulphur dioxide)

17. (a) What mass of hydrogen forms when 6 g of magnesium reacts with hydrochloric acid? ◀SCOTVEC
   (b) What mass of copper(II) carbonate precipitate forms when excess copper(II) sulphate solution is added to a solution containing 10.6 g of sodium carbonate? ◀SCOTVEC
   (c) What mass of carbon dioxide gas is formed when excess nitric acid is added to 10 g of calcium carbonate? ◀SCOTVEC
   (d) What mass of water forms when 4 g of methane (CH_4) is burned in oxygen? ◀SCOTVEC

18. Ethene reacts with bromine to form dibromoethane. ◀SCOTVEC

Calculate the mass of dibromoethane which forms when 1 g of ethene reacts with bromine.

$$\begin{array}{ccc} H & H & \\ | & | & \\ C = C & + Br-Br \rightarrow \end{array} \quad \begin{array}{ccc} H & H & \\ | & | & \\ Br - C - C - Br \\ | & | & \\ H & H \end{array}$$

19. When chalk, calcium carbonate, is roasted it decomposes to form carbon dioxide and calcium oxide.

Calculate the number of moles of chalk which should be roasted to form 0.1 g of carbon dioxide. ◀SCOTVEC

CHAPTER SEVEN

MAKING ELECTRICITY

► ELECTRICITY

Energy changes occur in all chemical reactions.

When magnesium burns **light** is produced.
When an acid is neutralised **heat** is given out.

In certain chemical reactions it is possible for **electrical** energy to form. Electricity is produced by a chemical reaction in a **cell** or **battery**. The words 'cell' and 'battery' are often used as if they were the same thing. In fact a 'battery' is a number of cells joined together.

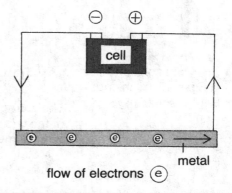

flow of electrons ⓔ

There are two units used to describe electricity: amperes (A) and volts (V). Amperes, or amps, are a measure of the amount of current (electrons) flowing. Volts can be thought of as being the energy which these electrons have.

When a cell is 'done' the chemicals in it have been used up. In the same way a chemical reaction in a beaker or a test tube will come to a halt.

Analogue and digital ammeters, used to measure current

RECHARGEABLE CELLS

Cells in which the chemicals can be regenerated are called **rechargeable**. The most common of these are nickel-cadmium cells and lead-acid batteries used in cars. Here is a model of the lead-acid car battery.

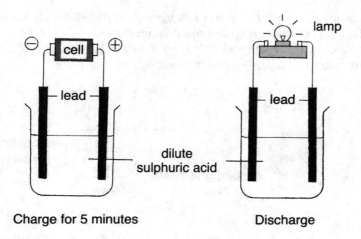

Charge for 5 minutes   Discharge

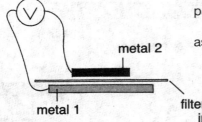

copper | magnesium

salt solution
(e.g. sodium chloride
solution)

metal 2

metal 1

filter paper soaked
in electrolyte

A SIMPLE CELL

A simple cell can be made with two different metals connected by an electrolyte (ionic solution or paste). An electrolyte completes the electrical circuit. It is called a **salt bridge** or **ion bridge**.

Cells which are used for radios, toys, cameras, etc. contain no liquids. They are sometimes called 'dry' cells. The electrolytes in them, for example ammonium chloride, are in the form of pastes. Pastes are used because an entirely 'dry' cell would not conduct electricity.

▶ THE ELECTROCHEMICAL SERIES

The **voltage** of a cell depends on the difference in the chemical reactivity of the two metals inside it. The diagram shows how the voltage between pairs of metals can be measured by a voltmeter (V).

Metal 1 could be copper and a number of other metals can be used in turn as metal 2. This enables the voltages of a number of cells to be measured.

$Na^+(aq)$	+	e	→	$Na(s)$
$Mg^{2+}(aq)$	+	2e	→	$Mg(s)$
$Al^{3+}(aq)$	+	3e	→	$Al(s)$
$Zn^{2+}(aq)$	+	2e	→	$Zn(s)$
$Fe^{2+}(aq)$	+	2e	→	$Fe(s)$
$Sn^{2+}(aq)$	+	2e	→	$Sn(s)$
$Pb^{2+}(aq)$	+	2e	→	$Pb(s)$
$2H^+(aq)$	+	2e	→	$H_2(g)$
$Cu^{2+}(aq)$	+	2e	→	$Cu(s)$
$Ag^+(aq)$	+	e	→	$Ag(s)$
$Au^+(aq)$	+	e	→	$Au(s)$

Metals are listed in order of these voltages in the **electrochemical series**. This series is given in full in the *Data Booklet*. Part of it is shown on the right.

REACTIVITY OF METALS

As well as being arranged in the electrochemical series, the metals can also be arranged in order of their chemical activity. The two orders are almost the same.

Sodium reacts violently with *water*. **Magnesium** reacts quickly with *dilute acids*.
Magnesium reacts slowly with *water*. **Zinc** reacts more slowly with *dilute acids*.
Copper does not react with *water*. **Copper** does not react with *dilute acids*.

DISPLACEMENT REACTIONS

The position of metals in the electrochemical series can be used to explain the results of **displacement reactions**.

As shown in the diagram, *zinc* metal reacts with *copper(II) sulphate* solution to form *copper* metal and *zinc sulphate* solution.

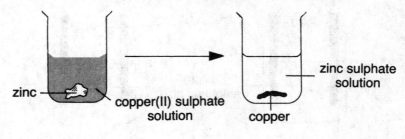

zinc

copper(II) sulphate
solution

zinc sulphate
solution

copper

$$Zn(s) + CuSO_4(aq) \rightarrow Cu(s) + ZnSO_4(aq)$$
$$\text{or} \quad Zn(s) + Cu^{2+}(aq) \rightarrow Cu(s) + Zn^{2+}(aq)$$

Zinc, being more reactive than copper, **displaces** the copper from copper(II) sulphate solution. Any metal in the electrochemical series will displace any other metal, which is less active, in the same way.

THE POSITION OF HYDROGEN

Hydrogen can be given a place in the electrochemical series. This can be shown by using the reactions of copper and lead with acids.

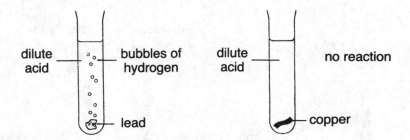

Metals which are more active than **copper** react with dilute acids to displace hydrogen. Metals which are less active than **lead** do *not* react with dilute acids to displace hydrogen.

Hydrogen can be seen to come between lead and copper in the electro-chemical series.

► CONSTRUCTING A CELL

In a **cell** two chemicals react to produce electricity. For example, zinc reacts with copper sulphate solution in a displacement reaction which can form a cell.

Zinc atoms, Zn(s), change from being neutral atoms to become positively charged ions, $Zn^{2+}(aq)$. Two electrons are lost:

$$Zn(s) \rightarrow Zn^{2+}(aq) + 2e$$

Copper ions, $Cu^{2+}(aq)$, gain two electrons to become neutral atoms, Cu(s):

$$Cu^{2+}(aq) + 2e \rightarrow Cu(s)$$

Electrons are transferred from zinc atoms to copper ions. An electric current is produced if the zinc and copper sulphate solution are separated as shown in the diagram. The ion electron equations are given in the *Data Booklet*.

A number of different substances could be used for solution X and metal Y. Solution X could be zinc sulphate solution and metal Y could be copper.

Paper soaked in an electrolyte will act as a **salt** or **ion bridge**. Ions move through the salt bridge to complete the circuit.

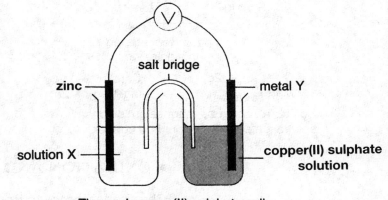

Zinc and copper(II) sulphate cell

59

DESIGNS FOR CELLS

There are many possible designs for cells. What is required is:

- a substance which will *lose* electrons; and
- a substance which will *gain* electrons.

These reactants must be separated from each other and the circuit completed by suitable solutions, electrodes and a salt bridge.
Here are examples of cells.

Cell 1 Copper and silver nitrate solution cell

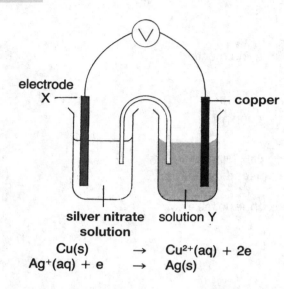

$$Cu(s) \rightarrow Cu^{2+}(aq) + 2e$$
$$Ag^+(aq) + e \rightarrow Ag(s)$$

Electrode X could be silver or carbon; solution Y could be copper(II) nitrate solution.

Cell 2 iron(III) chloride solution and potassium iodide solution cell

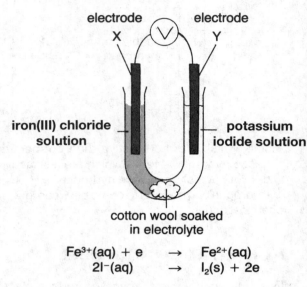

$$Fe^{3+}(aq) + e \rightarrow Fe^{2+}(aq)$$
$$2I^-(aq) \rightarrow I_2(s) + 2e$$

Electrodes X and Y could both be carbon.

Cell 3 Magnesium and copper(II) sulphate solution cell

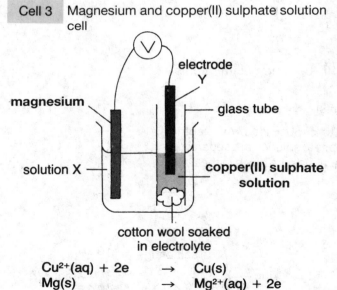

$$Cu^{2+}(aq) + 2e \rightarrow Cu(s)$$
$$Mg(s) \rightarrow Mg^{2+}(aq) + 2e$$

Solution X could be magnesium sulphate solution; electrode Y could be copper.

The salt bridge should *not* react with the contents of either beaker. Filter paper or cotton wool soaked in potassium nitrate solution or sodium nitrate solution is always a convenient salt bridge.

Cells and batteries are both safer and more portable than mains electricity. However, they are expensive, and can wear out at the wrong time!

▶ OXIDATION AND REDUCTION (REDOX)

Chemical reactions which produce electricity are called **redox** (**red**uction and **ox**idation) reactions. One reactant will *lose* electrons and one will *gain* electrons. *Both* reduction *and* oxidation must take place for an electric current to be produced in a cell.

The process of losing electrons is called **oxidation** and that of gaining electrons is called **reduction**.

A way of remembering redox:

Oxidation is loss of electrons.		
O	**i**	**l**
R	**i**	**g**
Reduction is gain of electrons.		

EXAMPLES OF OXIDATION AND REDUCTION

1. When a *metal forms from one of its compounds* the process is called *reduction.* The electrons are always on the **left** of the equation.

   Reduction $\quad Fe^{3+}(aq) + 3e \rightarrow Fe(s)$
   Reduction $\quad Cu^{2+}(aq) + 2e \rightarrow Cu(s)$

2. When a *metal forms a compound or corrodes* the process is called *oxidation.* The electrons are always on the **right** of the equation.

   Oxidation $\quad Mg(s) \rightarrow Mg^{2+}(aq) + 2e$
   Oxidation $\quad Na(s) \rightarrow Na^+(aq) + e$

3. Although you will nearly always encounter metal reactions in redox, it is possible for non-metals to be involved. For example, in Cell 2 iodide ions were oxidised.

   Oxidation $\quad 2I^-(aq) \rightarrow I_2(s) + 2e$

   Non-metals such as chlorine can be reduced.

   Reduction $\quad Cl_2(g) + 2e \rightarrow 2Cl^-(aq)$

4. In some redox reactions it may be harder to spot what is gaining and what is losing electrons.

   Oxidation $\quad SO_3^{2-}(aq) + H_2O(l) \rightarrow SO_4^{2-}(aq) + 2H^+(aq) + 2e$
   Reduction $\quad 2H^+(aq) + NO_3^-(aq) + e \rightarrow NO_2(g) + H_2O(l)$

   These may seem to be very complicated equations. However, electrons are lost and gained in a similar way to the earlier examples. You may be asked to identify an oxidation or reduction reaction. Look it up in the *Data Booklet*. The common reduction reactions are listed.

PRACTICE QUESTIONS

1. Which box represents a statement about a cell which is **untrue**?

A	A chemical reaction inside a cell produces electricity.
B	A cell goes done when the reactants inside are used up.
C	Electricity passing along wires from a cell is a flow of ions.
D	Lead-sulphuric acid batteries are rechargeable.

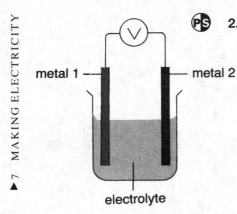

metal 1 — | — metal 2

electrolyte

PS **2.** Which box represents the pair of metals which will give the **greatest** voltage when connected together in the cell illustrated?

	Metal 1	Metal 2
A	zinc	magnesium
B	zinc	copper
C	zinc	iron
D	magnesium	copper

PS **3.** Which **one** box represents the most suitable electrolyte for the cell illustrated in question 2 above?

A	sodium nitrate solution
B	water
C	copper(II) sulphate solution
D	sulphuric acid

PS **4.** In this question the element symbol 'X' does not refer to an actual symbol in the periodic table.
Here is some information about a metal 'X'.

> X reacts with a solution of copper(II) sulphate.
> X reacts with a solution of zinc sulphate.
> Aluminium reacts with a solution of X sulphate.
> Tin does *not* react with a solution of X sulphate.

From the information above which letter indicates the position of X in the reactivity series of metals?

SCOTVEC▶

sodium
magnesium
Ⓐ A
aluminium
Ⓑ B
zinc
iron
Ⓒ C
tin
lead
hydrogen
Ⓓ D
copper
silver

PS **5.** Draw **labelled** diagrams of cells based on the following reactions.

(a) Magnesium reacting with copper(II) sulphate solution.
(b) Iron reacting with silver nitrate solution.
(c) Iron(III) chloride solution reacting with potassium iodide solution.
(d) Zinc reacting with copper(II) nitrate solution.

6. In which of the following reactions is redox occurring?

A	$CH_4(g) + Br_2(g) \rightarrow CH_3Br (l) + HBr(g)$
B	$Ag^+(aq) + Cl^-(aq) \rightarrow Ag^+Cl^-(s)$
C	$Cu(s) + 2Ag^+(aq) \rightarrow Cu^{2+}(aq) + 2Ag(s)$
D	$Al^{3+}(l) + 3e \rightarrow Al(s)$

7. Which box (or boxes) could contain information which is **true** about the cell illustrated?

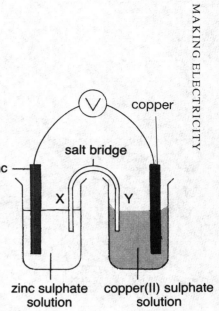

A	Electrons flow from zinc to copper through the meter.
B	Electrons flow through the salt bridge from X to Y.
C	Copper atoms lose electrons in beaker Y.
D	The blue colour in beaker Y will become more intense.
E	The salt bridge completes the circuit.

8. Here is the chemical equation showing how iron(III) chloride solution reacts with potassium iodide solution in a redox reaction.

$$2FeCl_3 + 2KI \rightarrow I_2 + 2KCl + 2FeCl_2$$

Which **one** of the following represents the reduction step?

SCOTVEC▶

A	$Fe^{3+}(aq) + e \rightarrow Fe^{2+}(aq)$
B	$I_2(aq) + 2e \rightarrow 2I^-(aq)$
C	$K^+(aq) + e \rightarrow K(s)$
D	$Cl_2(g) + 2e \rightarrow 2Cl^-(aq)$

9. 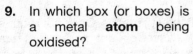 In which box (or boxes) is a metal **atom** being oxidised?

SCOTVEC▶

A	$Fe^{3+}(aq) + e \rightarrow Fe^{2+}(aq)$
B	$2Cl^-(aq) + Cl_2(g) + 2e$
C	$Mg(s) \rightarrow Mg^{2+}(aq) + 2e$
D	$Cu^+(aq) \rightarrow Cu^{2+}(aq) + e$
E	$Ag^+(aq) + e \rightarrow Ag(s)$
F	$Zn(s) \rightarrow Zn^{2+}(aq) + 2e$

10. Rewrite each of the following equations to show the reduction and oxidation steps. **◀SCOTVEC**

(a) $Mg + Cu^{2+}(Cl^-)_2 \rightarrow Mg^{2+}(Cl^-)_2 + Cu$

(b) $Zn + 2H^+Cl^- \rightarrow Zn^{2+}(Cl^-)_2 + H_2$

(c) $Zn + Cu^{2+}SO_4{}^{2-} \rightarrow Zn^{2+}SO_4{}^{2-} + Cu$

(d) $2Fe^{3+}(Cl^-)_3 + 2K^+I^- \rightarrow I_2 + 2K^+Cl^- + 2Fe^{2+}(Cl^-)_2$

(e) $Cl_2 + 2K^+Br^- \rightarrow 2K^+Cl^- + Br_2$

CHAPTER EIGHT

METALS

Metals are amongst the most versatile of materials. The choice of a metal for a particular purpose depends on its **properties**. The properties of metals can be altered by mixing them with other metals or non-metals. Such mixtures are called **alloys**.

Metals
- conduct electricity,
- conduct heat,
- can be hammered (malleable),
- can be twisted, bent, stretched (ductile),
- can be mixed to form alloys,
- are extracted from ores,
- may corrode.

► SOME NOTES ON COMMON METALS

Copper   Good electrical and thermal conductivity. Because it is fairly unreactive it can be used for water pipes and tanks. Alloys include bronze (with tin) and brass (with zinc). Used for making coins.

Iron   Usually found in the form of alloys which are called 'steels'. Steels often contain carbon and small amounts of other metals to increase strength, hardness or rust resistance. Stainless steels contain chromium and are resistant to corrosion. Iron and steel are widely used for car and lorry bodies, ships, and girders for the construction industry.

Zinc   Protects steel (called galvanising) and is used as an electrode in cells and batteries.

Aluminium   One of the least dense ('lightest') metals. Does not require protection from corrosion. Used for light garden furniture and kitchen utensils. Overhead power lines are made from aluminium rather than copper. A major use is in making cooking foil and what is called 'silver paper'.

Tin   A soft metal. Expensive compared with others mentioned. Main use is in coating steel to form 'tin' cans. Tin cans are *not* made from pure tin but from steel coated with tin. Tin mixed with lead gives the low melting alloy called solder which is used for electrical connections.

Lead   Soft dense metal. Used in car batteries, in solder (see above) and as shielding in work involving X-rays and radioactive material.

METAL ORES

Reserves of metals are limited. Metals are **finite resources**. Apart from a few unreactive metals, such as gold and silver, metals occur combined with other elements in the earth's crust. These compounds are called **ores** and include oxides, sulphides and carbonates.

Geologists have their own names for metal ores, for example:

bauxite	aluminium ore
haematite	iron ore
cerussite	lead ore
pyrites	forms of iron sulphide, called 'fool's gold'.

PRECIOUS METALS

Precious metals occur uncombined in the earth. Although they do form compounds they are very resistant to corrosion. They are bought and sold for their own value or made into jewelry. They also have important uses in science and industry.

Silver Extremely good electrical conductor. Main component of photographic films and papers. Also used in dentistry.

Gold Mainly used for ornamental purposes. Rather soft on its own, it is alloyed with silver or copper to make it more wear resistant. Like silver it can be used in dentistry.

Platinum Used for making jewelry, and in chemistry for special crucibles for use with very corrosive reactants. One of a group of transition metals which includes iridium and palladium which are catalysts. Used in catalytic convertors in car exhausts.

Mercury The only liquid metal. Used in mercury vapour lamps, thermometers and in small batteries. Has the property of being a solvent for other metals, forming an alloy called an amalgam.

Because of the finite nature of metal resources it is becoming more and more important that methods of **recycling** be developed. Aluminium is an example of a metal which can be recycled.

▶ REACTIONS OF METALS

Metals react with a whole variety of substances to form compounds. Some metals react more readily than others. The extent to which different metals react is given by their **reactivity**. The order of their reactivity is very similar to the electrochemical series which was described in Chapter Seven.

REACTION OF METALS AND OXYGEN

Many metals, such as magnesium, burn in oxygen. Oxygen can be made by heating potassium permanganate. The reactivity of a series of metals with oxygen can be seen by burning the metals in gas jars of oxygen or as shown in the diagram. The most reactive metals burn most brightly.

Magnesium burns brightly $2Mg + O_2 \rightarrow 2MgO$
Copper burns feebly $\quad\quad 2Cu + O_2 \rightarrow 2CuO$

REACTION OF METALS AND WATER

When iron becomes wet it rusts. Many other metals react with water. Some metals such as sodium and potassium react violently and must be stored under oil.

When metals react with water they form metal hydroxides (alkalis) and hydrogen.

Sodium reacts violently $2Na + 2H_2O \rightarrow 2NaOH + H_2$
Calcium reacts quickly $Ca + 2H_2O \rightarrow Ca(OH)_2 + H_2$

REACTION OF METALS WITH ACIDS

Metals also react with acids. The most reactive metals, sodium and potassium, react with acids almost explosively. Magnesium, aluminium, zinc, iron and tin react increasingly slowly. Lead hardly reacts with acids, while the other metals, from copper to the least reactive, do not react at all.

In each case hydrogen forms. The other compound formed is a salt.

Magnesium	$Mg + H_2SO_4 \rightarrow MgSO_4 + H_2$	
Zinc	$Zn + 2HCl \rightarrow ZnCl_2 + H_2$	

Metals lose electrons in the reactions described above. The metal atoms are oxidised.

▶ REDUCTION OF METAL ORES

The precious metals do not usually require a chemical process for their extraction. A gold mine, for example, produces gold which is uncombined with other elements.

Most metals, however, do require to be separated from the other elements with which they are combined in their ores. The process of making a metal from its ore is called **reduction**. A substance which removes the other elements from the ores is called a **reducing agent**.

A metal may be displaced from its ore by a more active metal. This, however, can be an expensive process. Carbon, carbon monoxide and hydrogen are much cheaper reducing agents.

Here are some examples of reducing agents in action:

carbon	$2Pb^{2+}O^{2-} + C \rightarrow 2Pb + CO_2$
carbon monoxide	$Fe^{2+}O^{2-} + CO \rightarrow Fe + CO_2$
hydrogen	$Cu^{2+}O^{2-} + H_2 \rightarrow Cu + H_2O$

The reduction of metal ores can be demonstrated in the laboratory in two ways.

1. Carbon
Powdered metal oxides are reduced to metal when roasted with carbon powder.

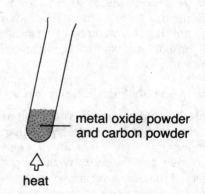

metal oxide powder and carbon powder

heat

2. Hydrogen or carbon monoxide
A method of reducing a metal oxide with a gas is as follows:

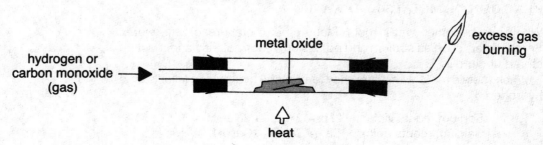

hydrogen or carbon monoxide (gas)

metal oxide

excess gas burning

heat

DISCOVERY OF METALS

As chemists have learned more about reduction, they have been able to make the more active metals such as sodium and potassium from their ores. The discovery of metals has occurred through the ages almost in the order of their chemical reactivity. Here are some examples.

Gold and silver	Occur naturally. No need for chemical reduction. Mentioned in the *Bible*.
Copper	Easily extracted from ore. *Bronze Age*.
Iron	Higher temperatures needed for reduction. *Iron Age*.
Zinc and nickel	Extracted from their ores for about *250 years*.
Aluminium, sodium and calcium	Have to be extracted by electricity. Made in *modern times*.

IRON

It is not easy to make iron from iron(III) oxide in a school chemistry laboratory. A much higher temperature is required to reduce iron ore than is required for lead or copper ores.

Iron is made in industry in a blast furnace. The 'blast' refers to blasts of air which, together with the reducing agent, enable the high temperature to be attained.

The blast furnace is loaded with *iron ore* (Fe_2O_3), *coke* (carbon, the reducing agent) and *limestone*. It is heated and air is blown into the hot mixture. Near the bottom of the furnace carbon burns, forming carbon dioxide. This further increases the temperature.

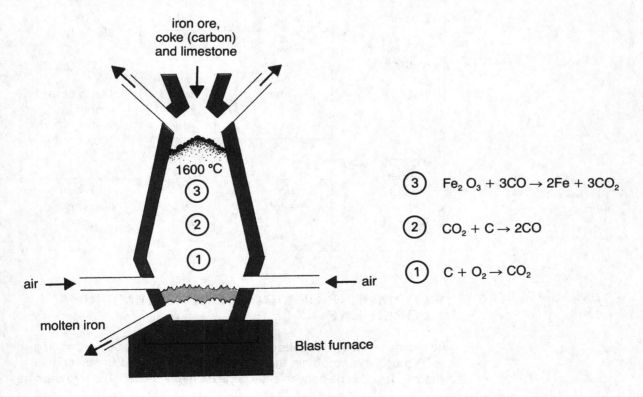

iron ore, coke (carbon) and limestone

1600 °C

③ $Fe_2O_3 + 3CO \rightarrow 2Fe + 3CO_2$

② $CO_2 + C \rightarrow 2CO$

① $C + O_2 \rightarrow CO_2$

air   air

molten iron

Blast furnace

Carbon burns: $C + O_2 \rightarrow CO_2$
The carbon dioxide rises and reacts with more carbon to form carbon monoxide.

Carbon monoxide forms: $CO_2 + C \rightarrow 2CO$
Carbon monoxide is the main reducing agent. Being a gas it reacts more effectively with the iron ore than lumps of carbon can.

Iron oxide is reduced: $Fe_2O_3 + 3CO \rightarrow 2Fe + 3CO_2$

In time all of the iron ore in the furnace is reduced to molten iron. Since it is molten it can be easily run off or 'tapped'.

Having been dug out of the earth, iron ore contains many impurities. These combine with limestone to form a 'slag' which floats on top of the molten iron.

Zinc, tin, lead and copper are other metals which can be made by reducing their oxides with carbon or carbon monoxide.

OTHER METHODS OF REDUCTION

Oxides of precious metals such as silver or mercury decompose when heated. The products are the metal and oxygen:

$$2Ag_2O \rightarrow 4Ag + O_2$$

Metals which are more active than zinc are made by electrolysis of their molten ores. This method is described later.

Metals can also be made by heating their oxides with a more active metal.

A SUMMARY OF THE PROPERTIES OF COMMON METALS

Potassium Sodium Lithium Calcium	React with cold water	React violently with acid	Made from ores by electrolysis
Magnesium Aluminium Zinc Iron Tin Lead	React slowly with water	React with acids to give hydrogen	Made from ores by heating with carbon
(Hydrogen) Copper Mercury Platinum Silver Gold	Do not react with water	Do not react with acids	Oxides decompose on heating

▶ FORMULAE OF METAL OXIDES (EMPIRICAL FORMULAE)

The formulae of compounds can be written from the 'rules' for bonding. It is also possible to obtain the formula of a compound by experimental means. This can be conveniently done for metal oxides. The formula of a compound obtained from experiments in this way is called the **empirical formula**.

The empirical formula of magnesium oxide can be found by burning magnesium, and that of copper oxide by reducing copper oxide.

EMPIRICAL FORMULA OF MAGNESIUM OXIDE

Magnesium ribbon is weighed in a crucible with a loose-fitting lid. When the crucible is roasted for a time, the magnesium burns and forms magnesium oxide. The mass will increase.

Here is a set of results obtained in this experiment.

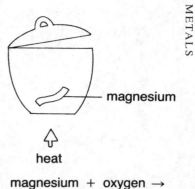

magnesium + oxygen →

magnesium oxide

Example

A   Mass of crucible + lid   =   53.16 g
B   Mass of crucible + lid + magnesium   =   53.40 g
C   Mass of crucible + lid + magnesium oxide   =   53.56 g
    Mass of magnesium (B – A)   =   *0.24 g*
    Mass of oxygen (C – B)   =   *0.16 g*

The formula of magnesium oxide is, however, *not* $Mg_{0.24}O_{0.16}$.
The formula of a compound is the ratio of the *numbers* of atoms or ions and not of their *masses*.
To calculate the numbers of ions their masses are divided by their relative atomic masses.
Ratio of moles of magnesium : moles of oxygen

$$= \frac{0.24}{24} : \frac{0.16}{16}$$
$$= 0.01 : 0.01$$

Magnesium oxide can be seen from these results to contain equal numbers of moles of magnesium and oxygen.

The empirical formula of magnesium oxide is MgO, the same as the formula obtained from the rules of bonding.

EMPIRICAL FORMULA OF COPPER OXIDE

Copper oxide can be reduced to copper by using hydrogen or carbon monoxide. The mass becomes less in this experiment.

Here are sample results.

Example

A   Mass of test tube   =   29.65 g
B   Mass of test tube + copper oxide   =   30.37 g
C   Mass of test tube + copper   =   30.29 g
    Mass of copper (C – A)   =   *0.64 g*
    Mass of oxygen (B – C)   =   *0.08 g*

Ratio of moles of copper : moles of oxygen in copper oxide

$$= \frac{0.64}{64} : \frac{0.08}{16}$$
$$= 0.01 : 0.005$$
$$= \quad 2 : 1$$

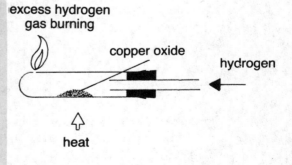

This shows that copper oxide contains two ions of copper to one ion of oxygen. The empirical formula of copper oxide is Cu_2O.

The name of this compound is copper(I) oxide. You have already met another oxide of copper, copper(II) oxide (CuO).

EMPIRICAL FORMULA FROM PERCENTAGE COMPOSITION

It is not necessary to know the masses of the elements making up a compound. The percentage composition will allow the empirical formula to be calculated.

> **Example** A compound has the composition by mass:
> 52% carbon
> 13% hydrogen
> 35% oxygen.
> What is the empirical formula of the compound?
>
> The masses of the elements in 100 g are:
> 52 g carbon; 13 g hydrogen; 35 g oxygen.
>
> Ratio of C : H : O $= \dfrac{52}{12} : \dfrac{13}{1} : \dfrac{35}{16}$
> $= 4.33 : 13 : 2.19$
>
> The simplest ratio is most easily found by *dividing by the smallest number.*
> $= 2 : 6 : 1$
> The empirical formula of the compound is C_2H_6O.

To find the empirical formula of a compound:
- the mass of all the elements in the compound must be known;
- the mass of each element is divided by its relative atomic mass;
- each of the numbers obtained is divided by the smallest number.

For ionic compounds the empirical formula and the formula obtained from the 'rules' are usually the same.

PRACTICE QUESTIONS

1. Use the information in the table below to draw a **bar chart** showing the price of some common metals.

Metal	Price per tonne (£) in 1990
Aluminium	1145
Copper	810
Lead	250
Nickel	5500
Tin	2950
Zinc	770

2. Metals are some of the most useful and versatile materials used today.

A	B	C
brass	copper	mercury
D	**E**	**F**
aluminium	zinc	tin
G	**H**	**I**
gold	magnesium	sodium

Which metal: ◀ **SCOTVEC**

(a) is used to galvanise steel?
(b) is a liquid at room temperature?
(c) occurs uncombined in the earth?
(d) is an alloy?
(e) is stored under oil?

3. Metals and their compounds react with a wide range of substances.

A	B	C
zinc	sodium	potassium oxide
D	**E**	**F**
hydrogen	carbon monoxide	carbon dioxide
G	**H**	**I**
potassium hydroxide	potassium carbonate	oxygen

Which box refers to:

(a) a reducing agent which is used in the blast furnace?
(b) the compound formed when potassium reacts with water?
(c) the gas formed when magnesium reacts with dilute sulphuric acid?
(d) a metal which reacts with cold water?

4. Metals occur naturally as ores. Many of these ores are oxides.

A	B
aluminium oxide	iron(III) oxide
C	D
potassium oxide	mercury(II) oxide
E	F
silver oxide	copper(II) oxide

Which box (or boxes) could refer to metal oxides which are normally reduced to the metal by:

(a) electrolysis when molten?
(b) heat alone?
(c) heating with carbon?

5.

> **Aluminium**
>
> Aluminium is made by the electrolysis of molten aluminium oxide. This is an expensive process which uses a great deal of energy.
>
>   Aluminium has many properties which make it suitable for a wide range of uses. It is an excellent conductor of both heat and electricity. It is light, strong and does not require protection against corrosion.

(a) Give the formula for aluminium oxide.
(b) Suggest **two** reasons why aluminium is used to make overhead electric power lines.
(c) From your knowledge of the activity of aluminium, explain why it is unusual that aluminium 'does not require protection against corrosion'.

6. Use the information below to make a **table** with appropriate headings of the amounts of metals thought to be available in the earth's crust. Use the **names** of the elements in the table.

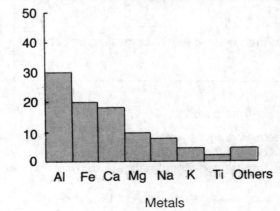

7. Use the *Data Booklet* to complete the table below.

Metal	Symbol	Melting point (°C)	Density (g/cm³)	Relative atomic mass
Aluminium	Al	660	2.7	27
Copper				
Iron				
	Pt			
		328	11.3	207

8.

> ### Recycling Aluminium Cans
>
> Aluminium is one of the easiest metals to recycle. Aluminium cans, not being magnetic, are quickly separated from 'tin' cans. They are also easy to crush which makes them convenient for storage in large quantities. It is even possible to get paid for handing in aluminium cans at some collection centres!
>
> Melting scrap aluminium needs only about half the energy required to make aluminium from its ore. However, although aluminium is a finite resource, only about 30% of the aluminium manufactured is recycled. As aluminium cans are made of unalloyed aluminium, little additional treatment is required to make new cans.

 (a) Which property enables aluminium cans to be separated from 'tin' cans?

(b) What is meant by a 'finite' resource?

(c) (i) (Refer to the *Data Booklet*.) State the melting points of aluminium, copper and iron.

     (ii) Use your answer to (i) above to suggest a reason why 'aluminium is one of the easiest metals to recycle'.

(d) What is an alloy?

 9. Metals can exist in many forms such as lumps, foils, powders or wires.

Explain how a fair test of three metals, magnesium, zinc and iron, could be carried out in order to arrange them in order of their activity.

10. Many chemical reactions produce gases. State the name of the **gas** produced in each of the following reactions.

(a) Heating potassium permanganate.
(b) Heating carbon with carbon dioxide.
(c) Zinc reacting with dilute hydrochloric acid.
(d) Burning carbon in a plentiful supply of oxygen.
(e) Heating copper(II) oxide with carbon.

11. Metal compounds can be reduced in a number of ways. State the names of the products in each of the following reactions.

(a) copper(II) oxide + hydrogen $\rightarrow$

(b) lead(II) oxide + carbon $\rightarrow$

(c) copper(II) chloride + zinc $\rightarrow$

(d) iron(III) oxide + aluminium $\rightarrow$

(e) iron(III) oxide + carbon monoxide $\rightarrow$

12. A compound of calcium has the following composition: 40% calcium; 48% oxygen; 12% carbon. ◄SCOTVEC

Calculate its empirical formula. (Use the *Data Booklet* for atomic masses in this and the following questions.)

13. A compound of sodium has the following composition: 57.5% sodium; 40% oxygen; 2.5% hydrogen.

Calculate its empirical formula. ◄SCOTVEC

14. A compound has the following composition: 40% carbon; 6.6% hydrogen; 53.4% oxygen. ◄SCOTVEC

Calculate its empirical formula.

15. Silica is an oxide of silicon. It contains 46.6% silicon. What is its empirical formula? ◄SCOTVEC

MORE ABOUT METALS

Unprotected metals corrode when they react with oxygen and water in the atmosphere. The reaction is speeded up by the presence of polluted air or by sea water. The **corrosion** of a metal is an oxidation process.

metal $\rightarrow$ metal compound **oxidation**

Metals which are high in the activity or electrochemical series corrode most quickly.

Unprotected iron corrodes on the surface in a day or two. The product formed when iron corrodes is given a special name: **rust**.

Copper takes much longer to corrode than iron. When copper corrodes the corrosion product is green in colour. Lead pipes from Roman forts often show very little sign of corrosion even after nearly 2000 years, while objects made of gold are unlikely ever to corrode.

▶ RUSTING OF IRON

Iron is one of the commonest metals and rusts quickly. The term 'rusting' is *not* applied to any other metals. For iron to rust *both water and oxygen (air)* are needed as the following experiments demonstrate.

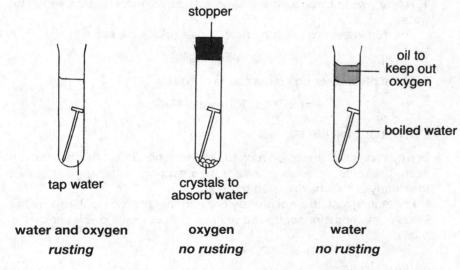

water and oxygen

rusting

oxygen

no rusting

water

no rusting

Evidence of the corrosion of iron can be seen in a day or so with the formation of rust. However, an indicator (**ferroxyl indicator**) will show in only a few minutes if iron is rusting.

Ferroxyl indicator turns:
- *blue* when Fe^{2+} (aq) ions are forming;
- *red* when OH^- (aq) ions are forming.

The rusting of iron is a redox reaction. Fe^{2+} (aq) ions are the result of *oxidation* and OH^- (aq) ions are the result of *reduction*.

Iron oxidises in two stages:

Stage 1 $Fe(s) \rightarrow Fe^{2+}(aq) + 2e$

Stage 2 $Fe^{2+}(aq) \rightarrow Fe^{3+}(aq) + e$

The reduction step in the rusting of iron involves both water and oxygen.

$$2H_2O(l) + O_2(g) + 4e \rightarrow 4OH^-(aq)$$

Water contains very few ions and the presence of any extra ions in water will greatly accelerate corrosion.

The presence of the ions in salt (sodium chloride) accelerates corrosion. Salt may come from sea spray in coastal areas or from grit for roads in winter.

RUSTING OF IRON: A CELL

The rusting of iron can be represented as a cell.

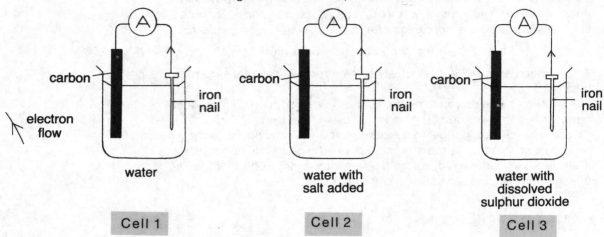

The direction of the electron flow indicates if rusting is taking place. If *electrons flow away from iron* then *rusting is occurring*. The current obtained in each of the cells 2 and 3 will be *greater* than the current in cell 1. This shows that iron rusts faster when there are more ions present in the water.

The iron in the nail in each of the above cells is *oxidised*:

$$Fe(s) \rightarrow Fe^{2+}(aq) + 2e$$

At the other electrode *reduction* is occurring:

$$2H_2O(l) + O_2(g) + 4e^- \rightarrow 4OH^-(aq)$$

CONTROLLING RUSTING

The cost of metal corrosion runs to billions of pounds to the nation every year. Often cars, whose engines are still operating, are scrapped because their body panels have rusted through.

Preventing rusting is not an easy or a permanent process. There are two kinds of methods for controlling rusting: surface coating and using electricity.

Surface Coating

Iron can be completely sealed off from air and water by a surface coating. Here are some examples:

- a plastic coating;
- a plating with another metal;
- painting;
- the coating of moving parts by grease or oil;
- galvanising.

Coating iron by dipping in molten zinc is called **galvanising**. Articles made of galvanised iron may not look very attractive but they do not need to be painted.

Tin-plated iron is used to make 'tin' cans. Tin does not taint food and it is not poisonous.

Iron can also be plated with precious metals such as gold and silver to make attractive and expensive looking trophies. The expensive metal is only a thin coating.

Most methods of protection which are based on coating will eventually fail when the coating barrier is broken.

Using Electricity

Using electricity offers another solution to the problem of rusting. Making an iron object negatively charged makes it more difficult for it to lose electrons and corrode. This is called **cathodic protection**.

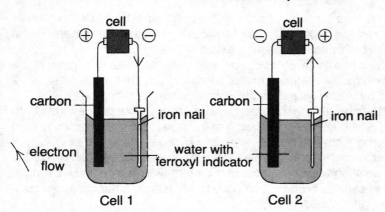

In cell 1 there will be no sign of iron rusting. In cell 2, however, a blue colour will quickly form around the iron, indicating that rusting is taking place. The negative terminal of the battery pushes electrons on to the iron nail in cell 1. This makes it more difficult for the iron to lose electrons. In a car, the negative terminal of the battery is connected to the body to help reduce rusting.

Instead of the negative terminal of a battery, a more active metal can be attached to iron. This also protects the iron.

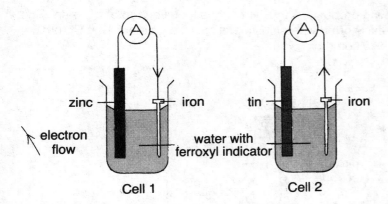

In cell 1 *no* rusting takes place. Electrons flow from the zinc to the iron, making it more difficult for the iron to lose electrons. Because zinc is above iron in the electrochemical series, it is zinc which corrodes rather than iron.

$$Zn(s) \rightarrow Zn^{2+}(aq) + 2e$$

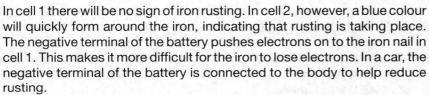

Zinc is 'sacrificed' to protect the iron. This is called **sacrificial protection**. *Any* metal more active than iron will protect iron in the same way.

In cell 2 severe rusting takes place. Tin does *not* protect iron. The electrons flow from iron to tin. In this cell iron is rusting and the iron is protecting the tin.

77

The difference between zinc and tin coating can be seen from the two cells. An iron structure which is protected by zinc (galvanised) should not rust even if the zinc coating is damaged. However, a tin-coated object, such as a 'tin' can, will rust very quickly when the tin coating is broken.

There are other methods of sacrificial protection apart from galvanising. Iron or steel structures, pipelines or boats can be protected from rusting by being connected by a wire to scrap zinc or magnesium.

► EXTRACTION OF METALS BY ELECTROLYSIS

Aluminium is one of the more active metals. It cannot be made from its ore by using reducing agents such as carbon. It has to be made by the **electrolysis** of molten aluminium oxide.

When a molten metal compound is electrolysed, the metal forms at the negative electrode. Aluminium, calcium, sodium and potassium are all extracted by electrolysis of molten compounds.

The extraction of active metals requires large amounts of energy, both electricity and heat. For this reason extraction is carried out most economically where cheap electricity (usually hydroelectricity) is available.

Less active metals can also be extracted by electrolysis. In their cases, aqueous solutions can be used rather than molten compounds. Even so, this is an expensive process compared with using a reducing agent such as carbon, and is seldom used.

► ELECTROPLATING

When one metal is coated with another metal in electrolysis the process is called **electroplating**. The diagram shows how a piece of copper can be electroplated with nickel.

$Ni^{2+}(aq)$ ions gain electrons at the copper electrode and are reduced.

$$Ni^{2+}(aq) + 2e \rightarrow Ni(s)$$

Electroplating produces a thin film of one metal on top of the other. The plating metal is often a precious metal such as gold or silver. Chromium plating is also common.

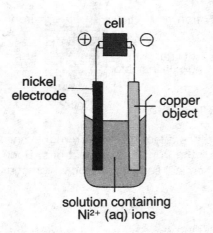

cell

nickel electrode

copper object

solution containing Ni^{2+} (aq) ions

PRACTICE QUESTIONS

1. Preventing rusting is an important process. In the following experiments the rate of rusting of an iron nail is being investigated.

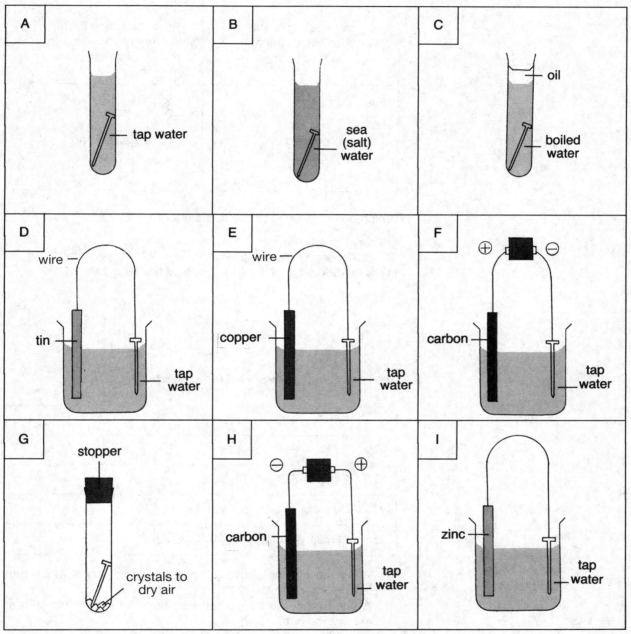

 (a) In which boxes will there be **no** rusting of the iron nail?

(b) Which **three** boxes are needed to demonstrate that 'both water and oxygen are required for iron to rust'?

(c) Which box shows iron being protected by sacrificial protection?

 (d) In which boxes will iron rust at a **greater** rate than A?

2. Prevention of the corrosion of metals is of the greatest importance.

A		B	
tinplating		connecting iron to scrap magnesium	
C		D	
connecting to the positive terminal of a battery		connecting to the negative terminal of a battery	
E		F	
coating in plastic		galvanising iron	

Which box (or boxes) above could refer to:

(a) sacrificial protection?
(b) protecting **without** a physical barrier?
(c) a method which fails if the physical barrier is broken?

3. The rusting of iron involves a redox reaction.

A	$Fe^{2+}(aq) + 2e \rightarrow Fe(s)$
B	$Fe(s) \rightarrow Fe^{2+}(aq) + 2e$
C	$Fe(s) \rightarrow Fe^{3+}(aq) \rightarrow 3e$
D	$Fe^{2+}(aq) \rightarrow Fe^{3+}(aq) + e$
E	$2H_2O(l) + O_2(g) + 4e \rightarrow 4OH^-(aq)$

(a) Which **one** of the above half reactions forms ions which turn ferroxyl indicator blue?
(b) Which **one** of the above half equations forms ions which turn ferroxyl indicator red?
(c) In which box (or boxes) is reduction occurring?

4. Explain why iron coated with zinc does **not** rust even when the coating is damaged, whereas iron coated with tin rusts very badly when the tin coating is damaged.

5.

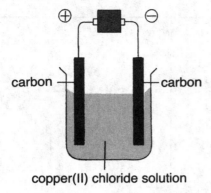

carbon ――| |――carbon

copper(II) chloride solution

Copper(II) chloride solution contains ions and conducts electricity.

A synthesis	B decomposition
C water	D chlorine
E copper	F oxidation
G electrolyte	H reduction

(a) Which box refers to the copper(II) chloride solution?
(b) Which box refers to the substance forming at the **negative** electrode?
(c) Which box refers to the process occurring at the **negative** electrode?
(d) Which box refers to what is happening in a solution during electrolysis?

6. Write ion electron equations for each of the following.

(a) Molten aluminium being formed from molten aluminium oxide.
(b) Solid copper forming from copper(II) sulphate solution.
(c) Hydrogen gas forming in the electrolysis of an acid.
(d) Solid copper oxidising to form copper(II) ions in solution.

PS 7. Draw a **labelled** diagram to show a method of testing to find if a solution conducts electricity.

8. It is very common for electricity to be used in chemistry.

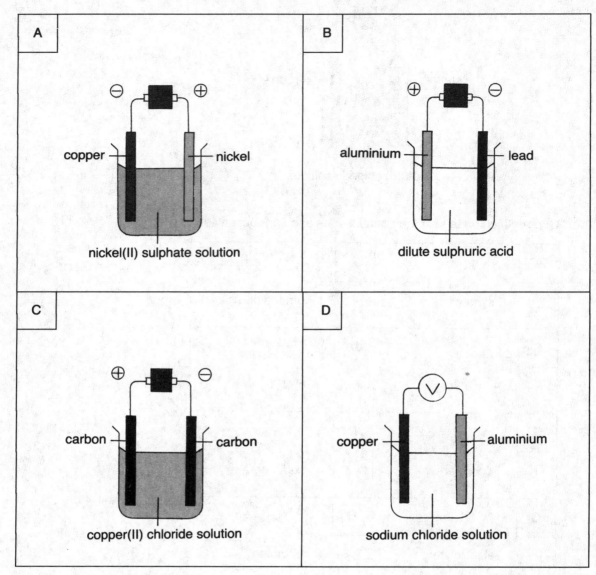

In which box (or boxes) above is the reduction of metal ions in solution taking place?

9. Write the ion electron equations for the reactions at the **negative** and **positive** electrodes in the electrolysis of each of the following.

(a) molten aluminium oxide
(b) molten lead(II) bromide
(c) copper(II) chloride solution
(d) hydrochloric acid
(e) nickel(II) chloride solution

CHAPTER TEN
PLASTICS AND SYNTHETIC FIBRES

▶ NATURAL AND SYNTHETIC MATERIALS

Materials can be grouped as natural and **synthetic**. Natural materials come from plants and animals, from farms, forests and quarries. Synthetic materials are made in factories.

Natural materials have been in use for thousands of years. Here are some examples:

- *wool* from sheep and goats;
- *leather* from animal skins;
- *wood* from trees;
- *silk* from silk worms;
- *stone* from rocks;
- *cotton* from plants.

Fabrics have always been made from natural fibres such as wool and cotton. Wool feels warm as it has good insulating properties. Cotton is still used for light summer wear. There are, however, drawbacks to all natural materials. Woollen garments are liable to shrink or stretch if not washed correctly; cotton is difficult to iron; wood requires protection against decay. All natural materials are liable to decompose in certain conditions and may be attacked by bacteria or eaten by certain types of insects. This means, however, that natural materials rot away when they are discarded. They are **biodegradable**.

It is impossible to satisfy the material demands of modern consumer society with natural materials alone. Over the last fifty years an increasing number of synthetic materials have been developed. Most of these are derived from raw materials made from oil. They include **plastics** and **synthetic fibres**.

PROPERTIES OF SYNTHETIC MATERIALS

Synthetic fibres and plastics have many properties which enable them to take over from natural materials in many areas. They are light, are good thermal and electrical insulators and are not prone to deterioration from dampness.

Plastics are generally resistant to attack by common acids and alkalis as well as not being affected by water. Plastic (PVC) window frames do not require painting. Nylon shirts are 'non-iron'. Plastic kitchen utensils are lighter than their metal counterparts and do not need protection from corrosion. Plastics are ideal as electrical insulators, both as sheathing for wires and as casings for tools and switches.

There are drawbacks, however. This durability means that many plastics are to all extents and purposes indestructible. They are non-biodegradable. Plastic litter does not disintegrate when wet as paper and cardboard do. Plastic rubbish can only be buried out of sight.

A house fire

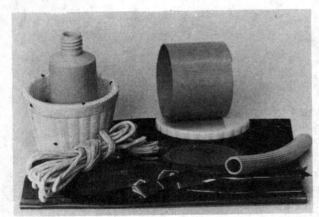

Thermoplastic polymers

There are other problems. For example, like all chemicals derived from oil, plastics burn. This limits their use in the kitchen — no plastic frying pans or plastic oven-ware are possible.

Some plastics contain elements other than carbon and hydrogen. When these burn, they give off a cocktail of poisonous gases such as carbon monoxide, hydrogen cyanide and hydrogen chloride. Most people who die in house fires nowadays die from poisoning rather than from burns.

▶ POLYMERS

'Plastic' is the word by which the new synthetic materials have come to be known. They are referred to as **polymers** by chemists.

TYPES OF POLYMERS

There are two types of polymers: **thermoplastic** and **thermosetting**.

Thermoplastic polymers soften and melt when heated. They can be moulded into a variety of shapes and can be spun into fibres. Most polymers are thermoplastic. Polythene and nylon are common examples.

Thermosetting polymers do not melt when heated. They may be made from liquids which harden when heated. Many glues are in this category, and the casings for electrical fittings are made from thermosetting polymers.

MONOMERS AND POLYMERISATION

Polymers are long chain molecules which are made by the joining together or **polymerisation** of small molecules called **monomers**. The simplest model of polymerisation is a chain of paper clips. Each paper clip is a 'monomer' and the chain is a 'polymer'.

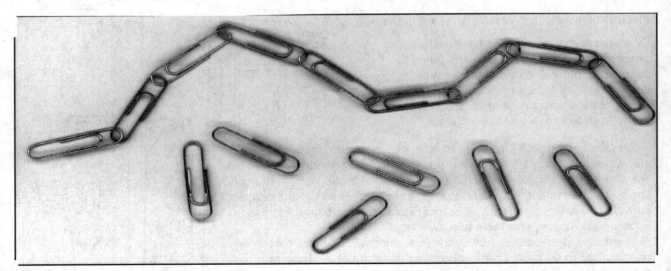

Polymerisation model

One of the first polymers was made by joining together ethene molecules to form poly(ethene), commonly known as polythene. Here is how ethene molecules polymerise:

$$
\begin{array}{cccccc}
H & H & H & H & H & H \\
| & | & | & | & | & | \\
C & = C & C & = C & C & = C \\
| & | & | & | & | & | \\
H & H & H & H & H & H
\end{array}
$$

high pressure and catalyst   polymerises

$$
\begin{array}{cccccc}
H & H & H & H & H & H \\
| & | & | & | & | & | \\
-C & -C & -C & -C & -C & -C- \\
| & | & | & | & | & | \\
H & H & H & H & H & H
\end{array}
$$

Writing out polymer structures in this way takes a long time! Structures of polymers are usually written showing only the **repeating unit**. For poly(ethene) this is:

$$
\begin{array}{cc}
H & H \\
| & | \\
-C & -C- \\
| & | \\
H & H
\end{array}
$$

The structural formula of poly(ethene) can also be written in the following shortened way.

$$
\left(
\begin{array}{cc}
H & H \\
| & | \\
-C & -C- \\
| & | \\
H & H
\end{array}
\right)_n
$$

In this structural formula 'n' is a very large number. It can be many thousands of units.

This process continues as many thousands of ethene molecules join together and the *polymer* called *poly(ethene)* results. In the same way other types of alkene monomers can join together to form other types of polymers.

A polymer which is formed from alkene monomers is called a **polyalkene**. Each alkene molecule contains a double bond. Alkenes are unsaturated hydrocarbons. The polymers formed are saturated hydrocarbons. This type of polmerisation is called **addition polymerisation**.

Here is a small part of the polymerisation of *monochloroethene* (vinyl chloride) monomers to form *poly(monochloroethene)* or PVC.

$$
\begin{array}{cccccc}
H & H & H & H & H & H \\
| & | & | & | & | & | \\
C & = C & C & = C & C & = C \\
| & | & | & | & | & | \\
H & Cl & H & Cl & H & Cl
\end{array}
$$

high pressure and catalyst   polymerises

$$
\begin{array}{cccccc}
H & H & H & H & H & H \\
| & | & | & | & | & | \\
-C & -C & -C & -C & -C & -C- \\
| & | & | & | & | & | \\
H & Cl & H & Cl & H & Cl
\end{array}
$$

The repeating unit of PVC is:

$$- \overset{\displaystyle \overset{H}{|}}{\underset{\displaystyle \underset{H}{|}}{C}} - \overset{\displaystyle \overset{H}{|}}{\underset{\displaystyle \underset{Cl}{|}}{C}} -$$

The usual way of representing PVC is to write the structural formula as:

$$\left(- \overset{\displaystyle \overset{H}{|}}{\underset{\displaystyle \underset{H}{|}}{C}} - \overset{\displaystyle \overset{H}{|}}{\underset{\displaystyle \underset{Cl}{|}}{C}} - \right)_n$$

Many other polyalkenes are known. Most are known by their trade names rather than their chemical names. Here are some examples.

Monomer	Polymer	Other names	Uses
ethene	poly(ethene)	polythene	packaging
monochloroethene	poly(monochloroethene)	PVC	gutters, rainware
propene	poly(propene)	polypropylene	buckets, kitchenware
styrene	poly(styrene)		packing
tetrafluoroethene	poly(tetrafluoroethene)	PTFE, Teflon, Fluon	non-stick linings
methylmethacrylate	poly(methylmethacrylate)	Perspex	glass substitute

Polyalkenes are thermoplastic. The monomers, alkenes, are made from the products of cracking oil. There are a few naturally occurring poly-alkenes, the best known of which is rubber.

PRACTICE QUESTIONS

1. Name the polymers made from the following monomers.
   (a) ethene
   (b) propene
   (c) tetrafluoroethene
   (d) styrene
   (e) monochloroethene

2. Polymers occur in many forms and have a wide variety of everyday uses. The grid below includes some common polymers.

A oil	B wool	C silk
D cotton	E poly(ethene)	F PVC

(a) Which box contains the source of most synthetic addition polymers?

(b) Which **three** boxes contain natural polymers?

(c) Which **two** boxes contain polymers made from alkenes?

3. Polymers are compounds which are made from monomers. The grid below includes some examples of monomers.

A	B	C
H H I I C = C I I H H ethene	H H I I H – C – C – H I I H H ethane	O = C = O carbon dioxide

D	E	F
H H I I C = C I I H Cl monochloroethene (vinyl chloride)	H – Cl hydrogen chloride	H I H – C – H I H methane

(a) Which box (or boxes) contains compounds which will polymerise?

(b) Which **two** boxes contain compounds which are produced when PVC, poly(monochloroethene), burns?

(c) Which box (or boxes) could contain **hydrocarbons** which do **not** polymerise?

4. (a) State if you would use a **thermoplastic** polymer or a **thermosetting** polymer to manufacture each of the following.
   (i) ashtray   (ii) washing-up basin   (iii) electric switch casing
   (iv) drinking cup   (v) handle of a frying pan   (vi) drain pipe

(b) Explain your answer to (v) above.

5. The chemical name of the polymer Perspex is poly(methyl meth-acrylate). It is a thermoplastic polymer made from the monomer with the structure:

$$
\begin{array}{cc}
\text{H} & \text{CH}_3 \\
| & | \\
\text{C} & = \text{C} \\
| & | \\
\text{H} & \text{COOCH}_3
\end{array}
\qquad \text{methyl methacrylate}
$$

(a) Explain what 'thermoplastic' means.

(b) To which series of compounds does the monomer shown above belong?

(c) What is the formula mass of methyl methacrylate?

(d) Draw the polymer Perspex showing **three** monomers polymerised.

6.

Plastics

Many fractions obtained from crude oil can be used as fuels. Some fractions, however, are turned into compounds which are then used to make plastics.

These plastics are buried in rubbish tips when they are discarded. However, they *could* be effectively used as fuels. Most plastics give out a great deal of heat when they burn, Poly(ethene), for example, gives out more than twice as much energy in burning as wood does!

Burning plastics requires great care for not all plastics are simple hydrocarbons.

(a) Name **three** uses of fractions obtained from the fractional distillation of crude oil.

(b) Name the series of monomers used to make plastics which are called addition polymers.

(c) Name the process used to make the monomers for addition polymerisation.

(d) Why do plastics not rot away in rubbish tips?

 (e) Why is it said that the use of plastics as fuels requires 'great care for not all plastics are simple hydrocarbons'?

CHAPTER ELEVEN

FERTILISERS

Growing plants require food in the same way that animals do. The 'food' needed for their growth must contain a number of essential elements, of which the most important are *nitrogen, phosphorus* and *potassium*. The exact proportions of the three elements depend on the plants and the stages of their growth.

▶ TYPES OF FERTILISERS

Fertilisers contain compounds which are necessary for the growth of plants. These compounds are often salts containing nitrogen, phosphorus and potassium. Examples of fertilisers are:

- potassium sulphate;
- ammonium sulphate;
- calcium phosphate;
- ammonium nitrate;
- urea.

The effectiveness of fertilisers can be estimated from the percentage composition of the essential elements.

The example gives a comparison of two fertilisers.

Example

Which contains more nitrogen: ammonium phosphate or ammonium sulphate?

$(NH_4)_3PO_4$

nitrogen	$3 \times 14 =$	42
hydrogen	$12 \times 1 =$	12
phosphorus	$1 \times 31 =$	31
oxygen	$4 \times 16 =$	64
relative formula mass		$= 149$

$(NH_4)_2SO_4$

nitrogen	$2 \times 14 =$	28
hydrogen	$8 \times 1 =$	8
sulphur	$1 \times 32 =$	32
oxygen	$4 \times 16 =$	64
relative formula mass		$= 132$

$$\text{percentage nitrogen} = \frac{42}{149} \times 100 \qquad \text{percentage nitrogen} = \frac{28}{132} \times 100$$

$$= 28\% \qquad\qquad\qquad = 21\%$$

Ammonium phosphate contains more nitrogen than ammonium sulphate.

SOLUBILITY OF FERTILISERS

The mass of essential elements is not the only factor that makes a fertiliser an effective one. After being added to the soil, the fertiliser must then dissolve in water before it can be taken up by the roots of the plant. The compound magnesium phosphate may contain the essential element phosphorus, but the table of solubilities shows that magnesium phosphate is insoluble in water. This means that it is less effective as a fertiliser than soluble compounds of phosphorus.

There is a danger that, in areas of high rainfall or flooding, highly soluble ionic compounds will simply be washed out of the soil. For this reason less soluble fertilisers such as urea (CH_4N_2O), which is not ionic, are often used. Urea dissolves in water more slowly than other fertilisers.

NATURAL FERTILISERS

Plants grew successfully long before artificial fertilisers were developed. Essential elements are taken into plants *naturally* in different ways.

After death an animal or plant decays and the compounds within it break down into simpler compounds which contain the essential elements. Today this process only occurs in primitive forests or in wilderness areas. In our gardens and public parks dead animals, fallen leaves and rotting plants are quickly removed long before they have a chance to decay.

Plant remains which are used as fertilisers are called *compost*. Animal remains include bone meal, dried blood, manure and processed sewage.

There is a move today to make more use of natural fertiliser and compost in gardening. For example, rather than putting leaves into a dustbin they can be allowed to rot down in a container and then be dug back into the soil.

Natural fertilisers are sometimes used in preference to artificial fertilisers and may be cheaper. In this case the essential elements such as nitrogen are being recycled. Natural fertilisers avoid problems caused when very soluble fertilisers such as nitrates are washed into rivers and reservoirs. The presence of nitrates in rivers and reservoirs is harmful to both animals and humans.

However, it is now impossible to rely on natural fertilisers alone to sustain the increasing world population. Artificial fertilisers are needed and their use in agriculture has to be controlled.

Fixing Nitrogen

Nitrogen is essential for the synthesis of **proteins**, chemicals which are present in all living things. However, most living things are unable to absorb this nitrogen from the air. The process of turning 'free' nitrogen in air into nitrogen compounds is called **fixation**.

Some plants such as peas, beans, lupins and clover contain bacteria called **nitrifying bacteria** in their root nodules which can fix nitrogen. These plants increase the fertility of the soil in which they are growing. This was known for a long time before the chemistry of the process was understood. Farmers often allowed a field to remain uncultivated for a year in a rotation of crops. In that year the clover which grew restored nitrogen to the soil. Plants like peas and beans which can fix atmospheric nitrogen are in the *leguminosae* family.

► MAKING FERTILISERS

The fixation of atmospheric nitrogen is the first and most important step in the manufacture of artificial fertilisers. **Ammonia** (NH_3) which is formed in fixation is then oxidised to make oxides of nitrogen and finally **nitric acid** (HNO_3). From these two compounds, ammonia and nitric acid, a whole range of fertilisers can be manufactured.

The fixation of nitrogen and hydrogen to form ammonia is called the **Haber process**. Nitric acid is produced from the **Ostwald process**.

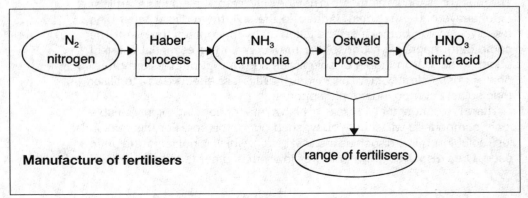

Manufacture of fertilisers

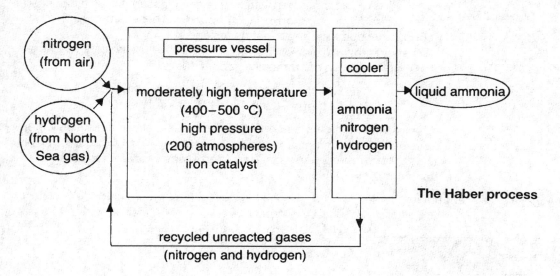

The Haber process

The pressure referred to in the diagram, '200 atmospheres', means 200 times normal air pressure. The higher the pressure, the more ammonia forms.

The reaction of nitrogen and hydrogen is a reversible reaction in which the sign $\rightleftharpoons$ is used instead of the normal $\rightarrow$ sign:

$$N_2(g) + 3H_2(g) \rightleftharpoons 2NH_3(g)$$

The rate of the *reverse* reaction increases at high temperatures; compounds normally decompose at high temperatures. In spite of this, the reaction is carried out at a 'moderately high temperature'.

The following table indicates how the choice of temperature used in the Haber process is made.

Low temperature	High temperature
slow reaction	fast reaction
high percentage of ammonia	low percentage of ammonia

or

A moderately high temperature is a compromise condition which produces a reasonable yield of ammonia at a moderate rate.

Not all of the hydrogen and nitrogen used in the Haber process is converted into ammonia. This does not matter as ammonia gas liquefies in the cooler and separates as a liquid from the nitrogen and hydrogen gases. The nitrogen and hydrogen can then be recycled.

MAKING AMMONIA IN THE LABORATORY

Ammonia can also be made in the laboratory from ammonium compounds. Ammonia gas is produced when *any ammonium compound* is heated with *any alkali*.

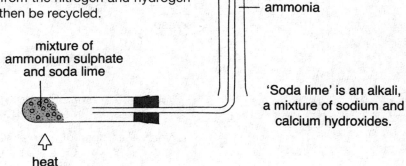

'Soda lime' is an alkali, a mixture of sodium and calcium hydroxides.

$$(NH_4)_2SO_4(s) + 2NaOH(s) \rightarrow Na_2SO_4(s) + 2H_2O(l) + 2NH_3(g)$$

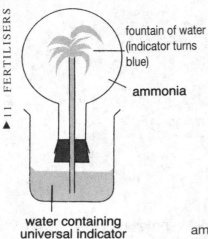

fountain of water (indicator turns blue)

ammonia

water containing universal indicator

AMMONIUM COMPOUNDS

Ammonia is a poisonous gas with a strong unpleasant smell. It can easily be converted into ammonium compounds. These ammonium compounds are especially important as fertilisers.

When ammonia dissolves in water it forms an alkaline solution. The pH of a 1 mol/l solution of ammonia is about 12.

$$\text{ammonia} + \text{water} \rightarrow \text{ammonium hydroxide}$$
$$NH_3(g) + H_2O(l) \rightarrow NH_4^+(aq) + OH^-(aq)$$

The experiment shown demonstrates how soluble ammonia is in water.

A solution of ammonia in water, ammonium hydroxide, neutralises acids to form ammonium salts. Here is an example of ammonium hydroxide neutralising an acid.

$$\text{ammonium hydroxide} + \text{hydrochloric acid} \rightarrow \text{ammonium chloride} + \text{water}$$
$$\text{(alkali)} \qquad \text{(acid)} \qquad \text{(salt)}$$
$$NH_4OH(aq) + HCl(aq) \rightarrow NH_4Cl(aq) + H_2O(l)$$

NITRIC ACID

Nitric acid forms when nitrogen dioxide is dissolved in water. Nitrogen dioxide *cannot* be made by burning either nitrogen or ammonia.

Nitrogen dioxide forms when a spark is passed through air. This happens during thunderstorms.

The small amounts of nitrogen dioxide produced find their way into the soil as nitrates.

THE OSTWALD PROCESS (MANUFACTURE OF NITRIC ACID)

Nitrogen dioxide is made industrially by the catalytic oxidation of ammonia in the **Ostwald** process.

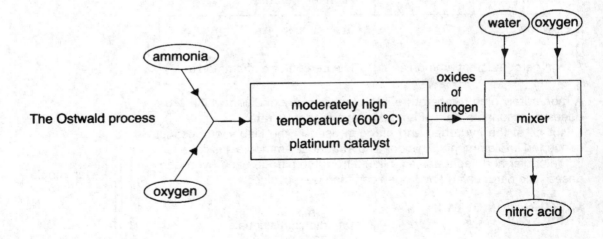

The Ostwald process

ammonia

oxygen

moderately high temperature (600 °C)

platinum catalyst

oxides of nitrogen

water   oxygen

mixer

nitric acid

$$\text{ammonia} + \text{oxygen} \rightarrow \text{nitrogen dioxide} + \text{water}$$
$$NH_3 + O_2 \rightarrow NO_2 + H_2O \quad \text{(unbalanced)}$$

$$\text{oxygen} + \text{nitrogen dioxide} + \text{water} \rightarrow \text{nitric acid}$$
$$O_2 + NO_2 + H_2O \rightarrow HNO_3 \quad \text{(unbalanced)}$$

This process can be carried out in a laboratory as shown in the diagram.

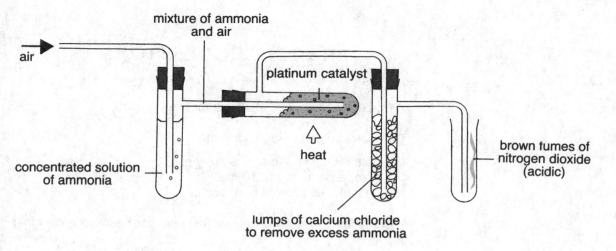

The reaction of ammonia and oxygen (or air) is exothermic. After a time the platinum catalyst can be seen to glow red hot. Even when the source of heat is removed the catalyst will continue to glow.

▶ THE NITROGEN CYCLE

Nitrogen makes up the greater part of air. It can be fixed in the root nodules of plants of the *leguminosae* family or, industrially, by the Haber process. Finding its way into animals which feed on plants, it will eventually return to the atmosphere in some form when the animals die or the plants decay. This interchange of nitrogen between living things and the air is summarised in the **nitrogen cycle**.

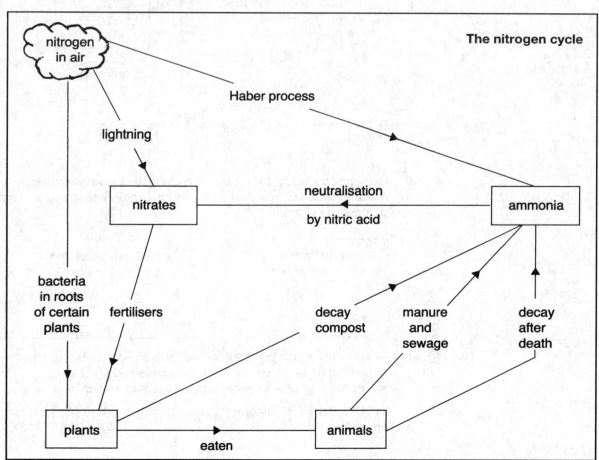

The nitrogen cycle

PRACTICE QUESTIONS

1. Name **three** 'essential' elements for plant growth.

 2. Calculate the percentage mass of:

    (a) potassium in potassium sulphate.
    (b) nitrogen in ammonium nitrate.
    (c) phosphorus in calcium phosphate.

3. Explain how nitrogen from the atmosphere can be taken into certain plants. ◀ S C O T V E C

4. Explain why the solubility of a fertiliser in water is important.

5. The flow diagram represents the Haber process. ◀ S C O T V E C

    (a) Name substances A and B.
    (b) Name the catalyst used in the reactor.
    (c) Name the 'recycled gases'.
    (d) Why is the reaction carried out at a 'moderately high temperature'?

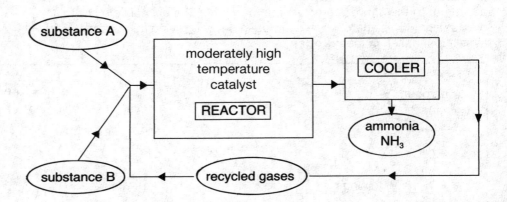

6. Copy and complete the table below using the following entries: slow reaction rate; fast reaction rate; low percentage of ammonia; high percentage of ammonia.

Low temperature	High temperature

 7. Ammonia gas can be made in the laboratory by heating together powdered ammonium sulphate and powdered soda lime.
Ammonia is soluble in water and is collected in a dry test tube.

Draw a **labelled** diagram showing this method of preparing ammonia.

8. **Name** the main substance formed when:

(a) ammonia dissolves in water
(b) nitrogen reacts with hydrogen in the Haber process
(c) potassium hydroxide reacts with nitric acid
(d) ammonium sulphate is heated with sodium hydroxide
(e) ammonium hydroxide neutralises nitric acid.

9. Write the formulae for each of the following.　◀ S C O T V E C

(a) ammonia   (b) nitrogen
(c) ammonium hydroxide   (d) ammonium chloride
(e) ammonium nitrate   (f) ammonium sulphate
(g) nitric acid   (h) calcium nitrate

10. Describe how you could demonstrate that ammonia gas was soluble in water.

11. The flow diagram illustrates the process used to make nitric acid.　◀ S C O T V E C

(a) What is the name of the process illustrated?
(b) What is the source of ammonia for this process?
(c) Why is oxygen not directly combined with nitrogen?
(d) Heat is given out in the reaction. What is such a reaction called?

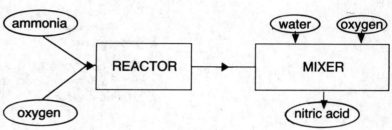

12. Write **balanced** chemical equations for the reactions of:　◀ S C O T V E C

(a) potassium hydroxide and nitric acid
(b) magnesium carbonate and nitric acid
(c) copper(II) oxide and nitric acid
(d) ammonium hydroxide and nitric acid

13. Decribe how to make a pure dry sample of calcium nitrate starting from calcium carbonate and dilute nitric acid.

14.

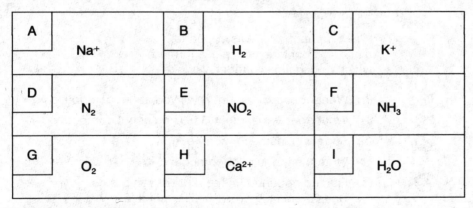

Identify the substance(s) which:

(a) is taken in by nitrifying bacteria
(b) forms an acid solution
(c) gives a lilac flame colour
(d) forms an alkaline solution
(e) is formed in the Haber process
(f) are reactants in the Ostwald process.

PS 15. Use the table of solubilities to answer this question.

(a) Make a table with the headings '**soluble**' and '**insoluble**' and enter in it the following compounds:
ammonium nitrate; calcium carbonate; calcium phosphate; ammonium sulphate; magnesium phosphate; ammonium phosphate; potassium nitrate.

(b) What do you notice, in general, about the solubility of nitrogen compounds?

16.

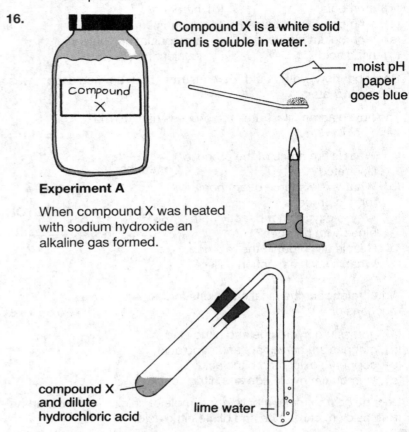

Compound X is a white solid and is soluble in water.

moist pH paper goes blue

Experiment A

When compound X was heated with sodium hydroxide an alkaline gas formed.

compound X and dilute hydrochloric acid

lime water

Experiment B

When compound X was added to dilute hydrochloric acid a gas formed which turned lime water chalky.

PS (a) What does experiment **A** tell you about compound X?

PS (b) What does experiment **B** tell you about compound X?

PS (c) Suggest a name for compound X.

(d) Write the formula for compound X.

PS (e) Find compound X in the table of solubilities.
Does the entry agree that it is 'soluble in water'?

CHAPTER TWELVE

CARBOHYDRATES AND RELATED SUBSTANCES

▶ CARBOHYDRATES

Carbohydrates are naturally occurring compounds which contain carbon, hydrogen and oxygen.

PHOTOSYNTHESIS

Carbohydrates are formed when carbon dioxide and water react in the leaves of plants in a process called **photosynthesis**. Oxygen is also produced in the reaction. Photosynthesis is activated by the sun's light energy which is absorbed by chlorophyll, a green substance present in the leaves of plants.

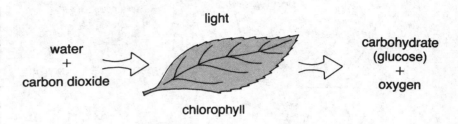

RESPIRATION

Carbohydrates can be thought of as having 'trapped' energy from the sun. This energy can be used again by plants and also by animals which have eaten the plants. When plants and animals utilise carbohydrates to produce energy the process is called **respiration**. Respiration is the opposite of photosynthesis.

Energy is released in respiration.

carbohydrate + oxygen → carbon dioxide + water + (energy)

Carbohydrates ('food') are to animals and plants what oil products ('fuel') are to machines.

The formation of carbon dioxide and water in respiration shows that carbohydrates contain carbon and hydrogen.

The products of respiration

Although we usually think of our body's 'energy' in terms of movement, this is only one form of energy which is produced. Heat energy is also produced, as is sound, and even, in some living creatures, light. Energy is also needed in living organisms for growth.

THE CARBON CYCLE

Photosynthesis uses up carbon dioxide from the air and produces oxygen. Respiration does the opposite. As the level of these gases remains fairly constant in the atmosphere, there is clearly a balance between the two processes.

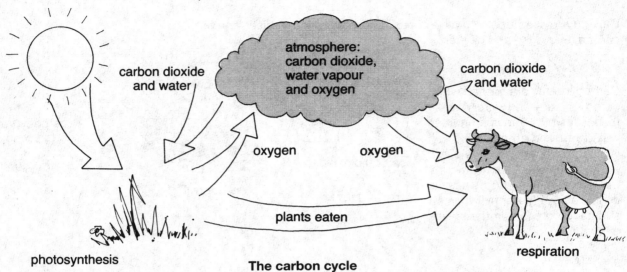

The carbon cycle

Recently concern has been expressed at activities which threaten to upset the balance of this cycle. Extra amounts of carbon dioxide have been produced by the burning of hydrocarbon fuels in the last hundred years. The growth in the world's population has also contributed to this increase. At the same time, extensive clearing of forests has taken place.

The effect of these activities over a long period of time will be to increase the proportion of carbon dioxide in the atmosphere. Most scientists agree that this will cause the temperatures on earth to rise. This will result in what has been called the 'greenhouse effect'.

COMMON CARBOHYDRATES

The carbohydrate which is formed in plants in photosynthesis is **glucose**. However, glucose is only one of a number of carbohydrates.

Fructose is an isomer of glucose. Carbohydrates such as glucose and fructose have the same molecular formulae but different structural formulae.

Here are some common carbohydrates.

Carbohydrate	Molecular formula
glucose	$C_6H_{12}O_6$
fructose	$C_6H_{12}O_6$
maltose	$C_{12}H_{22}O_{11}$
sucrose	$C_{12}H_{22}O_{11}$
starch	polymer
cellulose	polymer

Carbohydrates such as glucose and fructose with six carbon atoms in their molecules are called **monosaccharides**. Maltose and sucrose molecules with twelve carbon atoms are double the length of those of glucose and fructose and are called **disaccharides**. Starch is a **polysaccharide**. Starch molecules contain hundreds of carbon atoms.

Disaccharides and polysaccharides form when the simpler monosaccharides join together with the loss of water.

$$2C_6H_{12}O_6 \quad \rightarrow \quad C_{12}H_{22}O_{11} \quad + \quad H_2O$$
monosaccharide   disaccharide

$$nC_6H_{12}O_6 \quad \rightarrow \quad \text{polysaccharide} \quad + \quad nH_2O$$
monosaccharide

In the second example 'n' is a large number.

The formation of a polysaccharide such as starch from a monosaccharide such as glucose is an example of **condensation polymerisation**. Plants contain starch which forms when glucose molecules polymerise.

Mono, di, and polysaccharides differ in their chain length and also in some of their chemical properties. The short chain molecules are soluble in water. The longer chained molecules are less soluble. Some carbohydrates such as glucose and sucrose have a sweet taste.

Two Chemical Tests

1. A blue solution called **Benedict's reagent** turns a *red colour* when heated with glucose, fructose or maltose. Carbohydrates which give a positive test with Benedict's reagent are called **reducing sugars**.

    Sucrose and the polysaccharides such as starch do not affect Benedict's reagent.
2. When yellow iodine solution is added to starch solution a black colour is formed. The other carbohydrates do not affect iodine solution.

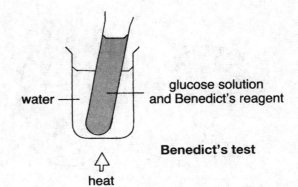

water — glucose solution and Benedict's reagent

Benedict's test

heat

A summary of the properties of some common carbohydrates is given in the table.

Carbohydrate	Type	Formula	Notes
glucose	monosaccharide	$C_6H_{12}O_6$	soluble, sweet, turns Benedict's reagent red
fructose	monosaccharide	$C_6H_{12}O_6$	soluble, sweet, turns Benedict's reagent red
maltose	disaccharide	$C_{12}H_{22}O_{11}$	soluble, turns Benedict's reagent red
sucrose	disaccharide	$C_{12}H_{22}O_{11}$	soluble, sweet
starch	polysaccharide	polymer	slightly 'soluble', turns iodine solution black

Tyndall Beam

There is another way of distinguishing between the monosaccharides and the polysaccharide starch. If a beam of light is shone through water containing starch, it will show an intense beam. A glucose solution will have no such beam.

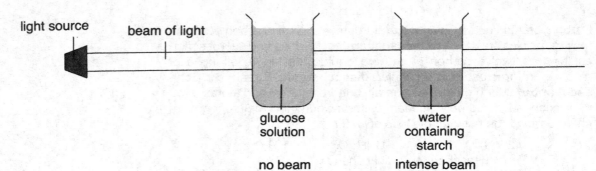

light source · beam of light · glucose solution · no beam · water containing starch · intense beam

The effect in the starch is called the **Tyndall beam**. The intense beam is caused by the reflection of the light by large groups of starch molecules. Starch does not really dissolve in water. This is why it is described as 'water containing starch' rather than a solution of starch. Starch forms a suspension of large particles in water which is known as a **colloid**.

DIGESTION

Carbohydrates and other foods are carried round the body in the bloodstream. To pass into the bloodstream molecules of carbohydrates have to pass through the wall of the gut. In the digestive system large starch molecules are broken down into smaller glucose molecules which are soluble in water. This process is called **digestion**.

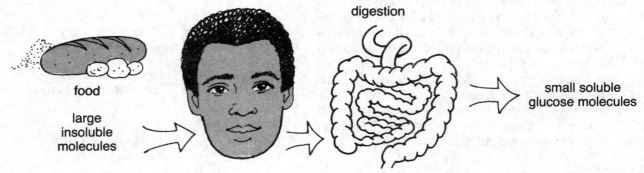

food · large insoluble molecules · digestion · small soluble glucose molecules

Starch molecules are broken down in the digestive system by the addition of water and the effect of both acid and biological catalysts called **enzymes**. Amylase is an example of an enzyme.

$$starch + water \rightarrow glucose$$

The breaking down of long chain molecules by the addition of water is called **hydrolysis**. Hydrolysis is the opposite of condensation, in which water is eliminated.

Glucose is carred around the body in the bloodstream. It reacts with oxygen in the cells of the body in the process of respiration.

Oxygen and the products of respiration, carbon dioxide and water, are also carried in the bloodstream. Oxygen, carbon dioxide and water vapour all enter and leave the body through the lungs.

▶ FERMENTATION

Fruits and vegetables which contain starch or glucose are the source of alcoholic drinks. The type of drink varies with the plant source as shown in the table.

Drink	Source
wine	grapes
beer	hops
cider	apples
whisky	barley
vodka	potatoes
brandy	grapes

What is described as 'alcohol' is called **ethanol** and is one of the members of a series of compounds called **alkanols**.

Ethanol forms from carbohydrates in a process called **fermentation**. An enzyme called zymase present in yeast, a living organism, acts as a catalyst for this reaction.

$$C_6H_{12}O_6 \quad \rightarrow \quad 2C_2H_5OH \quad + \quad 2CO_2$$

ethanol 'alcohol'

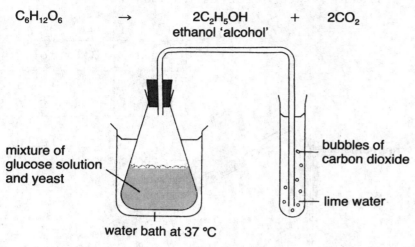

ethanol

mixture of glucose solution and yeast

bubbles of carbon dioxide

lime water

water bath at 37 °C

Fermentation

Carbon dioxide is a byproduct of this reaction. Fermentation is an important source of carbon dioxide.

Conditions must be controlled in the large scale production of alcoholic drinks. The enzymes in yeast are complex compounds which are sensitive to changes in both temperature and pH. They cannot tolerate high concentrations of alcohol and are killed off when the concentration of alcohol exceeds a certain point.

STRENGTH OF ALCOHOLIC DRINKS

After a few days of fermentation the rate will slow down and carbon dioxide will stop bubbling. There may still be glucose left in the solution but, as the concentration of alcohol increases, the effectiveness of the enzyme is reduced. The alcohol 'poisons' the yeast cells.

Drinks made by fermentation alone include beer, cider and wine. The concentration of alcohol in wines is around 10%.

Drinks which contain larger amounts of alcohol, for example whisky or brandy, are made by distillation. They have alcohol concentrations of over 40%.

DISTILLATION

Distillation increases the alcohol concentration of the fermentation products.

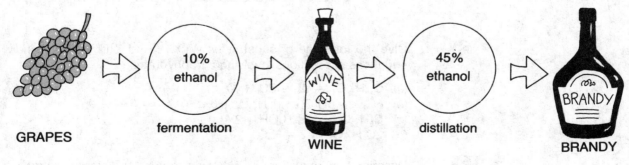

GRAPES → 10% ethanol (fermentation) → WINE → 45% ethanol (distillation) → BRANDY

Making brandy

When a mixture of liquids is heated, the one with the lowest boiling point boils off first. The liquid which boils first in the distillation illustrated is ethanol. The temperature when this happens will be about 78°C. Ethanol can be separated from water by using distillation.

Liquid	Boiling point (°C)
water	100
ethanol	78

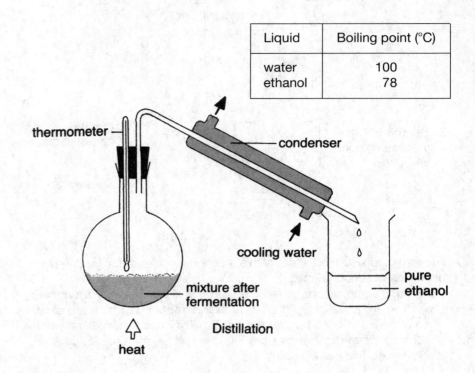

Distillation

PRACTICE QUESTIONS

1. Give the formulae of substances W, X, Y and Z in the following equations of reactions involving carbohydrates.

   (a) $C_{12}H_{22}O_{11} + W \rightarrow 2C_6H_{12}O_6$
   (b) $6CO_2 + 6H_2O \rightarrow C_6H_{12}O_6 + 6X$
   (c) $C_6H_{12}O_6 \rightarrow 2C_2H_5OH + 2Y$
   (d) $2C_6H_{12}O_6 \rightarrow Z + H_2O$

2. Describe how to distinguish between glucose and starch using:
   (a) Benedicts' reagent
   (b) iodine solution
   (c) a Tyndall beam.

3. Photosynthesis is a process which takes place in plants. Respiration takes place in both plants and animals and is the opposite process to photosynthesis.

   The grid shows some of the substances which are involved in these processes.

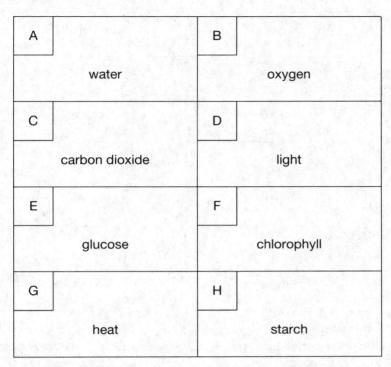

A water	B oxygen
C carbon dioxide	D light
E glucose	F chlorophyll
G heat	H starch

   (a) Which **two** boxes contain the products of photosynthesis?
   (b) Which box contains a chemical which traps light energy?
   (c) Which box contains a polymer?
   (d) Which **two** boxes contain the products of respiration?

4. Give **two** reasons why the level of carbon dioxide in the atmosphere has risen in recent years.

5. Carbohydrates are transported through the bloodstream.

   Give **two** reasons why starch must be hydrolysed to glucose before this can happen.

6. Ethanol (alcohol) and carbon dioxide form when glucose solution is fermented.

$$C_6H_{12}O_6 \rightarrow 2C_2H_5OH + 2CO_2$$

   (a) State **two** conditions which must be controlled in the fermentation of glucose.
   (b) What is the mass of
      (i) 1 mole of glucose?
      (ii) 2 moles of carbon dioxide?
   (c) What mass of gas forms in the above reaction when 9 g of glucose is used, and fermentation stops when 40% of the glucose has reacted?
   (d) Give the test for carbon dioxide.

7. Consult the *Data Booklet* for this question.

   (a) What are the boiling points of (i) octane, (ii) cyclohexane?
   (b) Explain why a mixture of these two liquids can be separated by distillation.

8. Carbohydrates are naturally occurring compounds which are also called saccharides.

A		B	
glucose		chlorophyll	
C		D	
maltose		sucrose	
E		F	
starch		fructose	
G		H	
iodine		water	

(a) Which box (or boxes) refer to monosaccharides?

(b) Which **two** boxes refer to substances which form when glucose polymerises?

(c) Which **two** substances react to give a black colour?

(d) Which substance always forms in a condensation reaction?

(e) Which substance has a sweet taste but does **not** react with Benedict's reagent?

9. Here is the structural formula of the compound known as 'alcohol' which is found in alcoholic drinks.

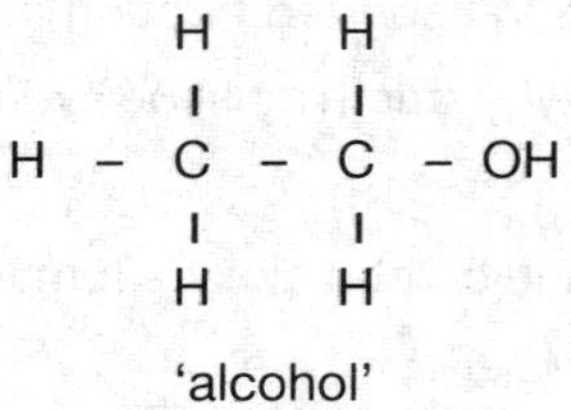

$$
\begin{array}{ccc}
 & H & H \\
 & | & | \\
H - & C - C & - OH \\
 & | & | \\
 & H & H \\
\end{array}
$$

'alcohol'

(a) Copy and complete these sentences:
'Alcohol' is a member of the alkanol family and is called _____. It is made by the _____ of glucose by _____.

(b) Calculate the relative formula mass of 'alcohol'.

(c) Some alcoholic drinks have alcohol concentrations of about 10%. In others the concentration is about 40%.
Explain how 40% concentration is achieved.

CHAPTER THIRTEEN

PROBLEM SOLVING

Half of the questions in the written exams in Standard Grade Chemistry are tests of 'problem solving'. You may think it strange that only one chapter of this book is devoted to problem solving. Many problem solving questions are, however, applications of knowledge and understanding. There are many questions on problem solving in earlier chapters. Many of these questions are about applications of knowledge as well as, for example, selecting and presenting information.

Here are the areas of problem solving which you should practise.

- Selecting information
- Presenting information
- Selecting procedures
- Concluding and explaining
- Predicting and generalising

You may find selecting and presenting information to be the most straightforward areas to master. Success in other areas may depend on your knowledge and understanding. Many of the problem solving questions in exams will be about concluding, explaining and predicting.

Several experiments and substances mentioned in the questions which follow will be unfamiliar to you. If the chemistry is not contained in the earlier chapters, then it is *not* part of the learning outcomes for Standard Grade Chemistry and you do not need to know them.

Parts of some of the questions which follow also test knowledge and understanding. You must expect to cope with both areas within one question.

The questions have been arranged under each of the five areas listed above. However, usually only one part of each question is about the area described in the title of the section. A question about selecting information may also contain parts about several other problem solving areas. This is what you must expect in a Standard Grade Chemistry exam.

PRACTICE QUESTIONS

► SELECTING INFORMATION

Questions in which you are asked to select information are usually straightforward. You may be asked to select information from sources such as the *Data Booklet*, line and bar graphs, picture keys, flowcharts, pie charts, diagrams, passages of writing, word or chemical equations.

1. Use the *Data Booklet* to find the following:

   (a) the melting point of sodium;
   (b) the boiling point of cyclohexane;
   (c) the date of the discovery of phosphorus;

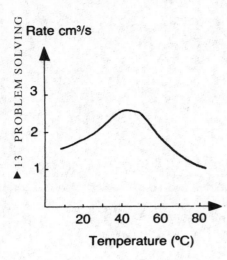

Rate cm³/s

Temperature (°C)

(d) the flame colour of the barium ion;
(e) the density of silicon;
(f) the solubility of magnesium phosphate;
(g) the electron arrangement of sulphur;
(h) the formula of the nitrate ion.

2. The graph shows the rate of a chemical reaction at different temperatures.

(a) Normally the rate of a chemical reaction increases with temperature.
What is unusual about the rate of this reaction?
(b) At what temperature is the reaction rate **greatest**?

3. Here is a diagram of the apparatus used to make carbon monoxide gas. The carbon monoxide produced in the flask may be contaminated with carbon dioxide.

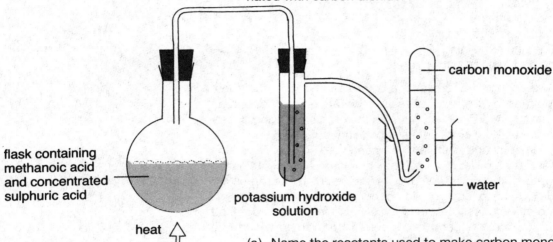

flask containing methanoic acid and concentrated sulphuric acid

carbon monoxide

potassium hydroxide solution

water

heat

(a) Name the reactants used to make carbon monoxide.
(b) A solution of carbon dioxide is acidic. Carbon monoxide does not form an acidic solution. Explain how this enables the two gases to be separated in the experiment above.
(c) Here is the chemical equation for the reaction.

$$2H_2CO_2 \rightarrow 2CO + 2X$$

State the formula of compound X.

4. Nickel forms many alloys. The following pie charts show the composition of some of the common alloys.

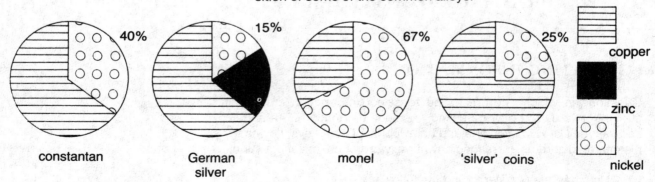

constantan   German silver   monel   'silver' coins

copper

zinc

nickel

(a) What is an alloy?
(b) Draw a **table** with appropriate headings to show the amount of nickel in each of the four alloys.
(c) Name the metals which are present in monel.

13 PROBLEM SOLVING

106

5. The flowchart shows the manufacture of sulphuric acid.

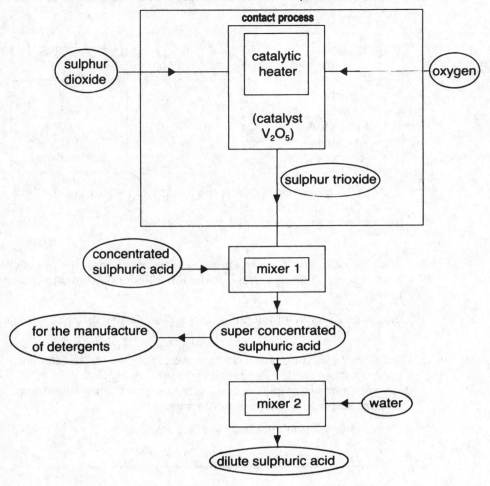

(a) What are the **reactants** for the contact process?
(b) What is the **product** of the contact process?
(c) What are **two** uses of super concentrated sulphuric acid?
(d) How is super concentrated sulphuric acid made?
(e) Write the formula for sulphur trioxide.

▶ PRESENTING INFORMATION

You may be asked to present information as tables, bar and line graphs. You may also be asked to select your own method of presenting information. Whichever method you choose must be easy to understand and accurate. In the Credit paper the data which you have to handle will be more complex than in the General paper.

1. (a) Construct a table showing the boiling points of the following compounds: **ethane**, **butane**, **propane**, **pentane** and **methane**. The information will be found in the *Data Booklet*.
(b) Draw a **bar chart** of the boiling point against the number of carbon atoms in each compound.
(c) State which of the compounds is/are liquid at 10°C.

2. A glaze for pottery consists of 40% lead oxide, 30% fine sand, 25% soda and 5% cobalt salt.

Present this information in a suitable way.

3. The table gives the boiling points of **four** members of the cycloalkane series.

Cycloalkane	Number of carbon atoms	Boiling point (°C)
cyclopentane	5	49
cyclohexane	6	81
cycloheptane	7	119
cyclooctane	8	151
cyclononane	9	not available

(a) Draw a **bar chart** showing the information about the first **four** compounds above.

(b) Estimate the boiling point of cyclononane.

4. Sulphur dioxide can be made by adding concentrated sulphuric acid to copper turnings. Water and copper(II) sulphate solution also form.

Choose a suitable format and present this information.

5. Substances can be classified as compounds or elements. Elements can be further divided into metals and non-metals.
Here are some examples of such substances: **ethane**, **aluminium**, **silicon**, **sulphur**, **water**, **ammonia**, **zinc**.

Present the information above in a suitable way.

6.

Aluminium compounds have many everyday uses.
Aluminium oxide is an abrasive used in sandpaper, and aluminium sulphate is used to settle solids in water treatment. Aluminium hydroxide is an effective antacid for treating indigestion. Both aluminium sodium silicate and sodium aluminium phosphate have uses as food additives.

Present this information as a **table** with suitable headings.

7. Lorna added 5 g of powdered iron to 100 cm^3 of copper(II) sulphate solution. She measured the temperature every minute and recorded the results.

Temperature (°C)	Time (minutes)
22	0
24	2
28	4
32	6
31	8
29	10
28	12

Draw a **line graph** of the temperature against time for her results.

▶SELECTING PROCEDURES

You may be asked to select a method of carrying out an experiment, or how you would carry out a procedure. A labelled diagram will often be your best method of explanation.

You are also expected to have some idea of what is termed *fairness*. When an investigation is carried out the result must be conclusive. There are several comparisons in the questions that are clearly 'unfair'.

1. Making and using electricity are important processes in chemistry.

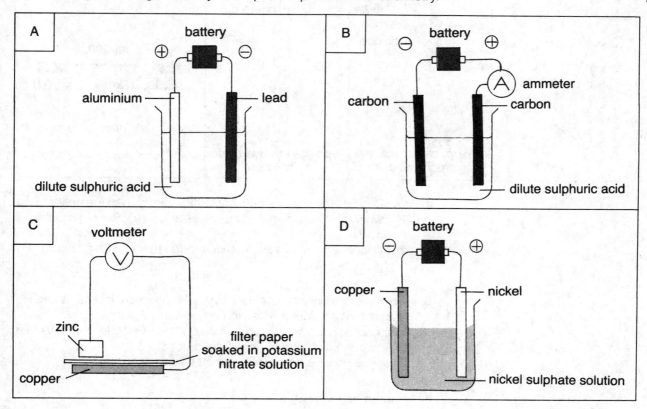

Which box (or boxes) could be used to measure:

(a) the position of metals in the electrochemical series?
(b) the conductivity of a solution?

2. Copper(II) sulphate crystals can be made by the reaction of copper (II) carbonate powder and dilute sulphuric acid.

Write down **all** the letters from the grid below to show the order you would use to make copper(II) sulphate crystals.

A	Continue to add copper(II) carbonate until no more reacts.
B	Allow the solution to evaporate to dryness.
C	Measure 100 cm³ of dilute sulphuric acid into a beaker.
D	Filter the solution to remove excess copper(II) carbonate.
E	Add copper(II) carbonate powder to the sulphuric acid.

3. Carbon monoxide can be made by passing carbon dioxide over red hot carbon.
    Unreacted carbon dioxide can be removed by passing the gas formed through potassium hydroxide solution.
    Carbon monoxide is insoluble in water.

    Write down **all** of the letters from the grid below in the correct order to prepare carbon monoxide.

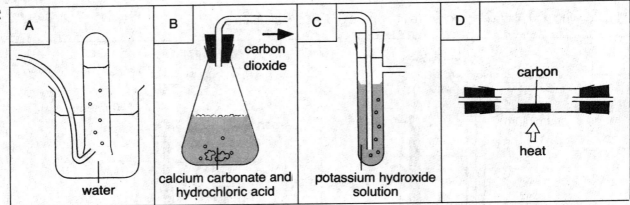

A water

B calcium carbonate and hydrochloric acid   carbon dioxide

C potassium hydroxide solution

D carbon   heat

4. (a) Describe how you would show that carbon dioxide gas formed when zinc carbonate powder was added to dilute hydrochloric acid.
    (b) Describe how you would test a toffee to show that it contained glucose.

5. Colin requires dry alcohol to carry out a practical investigation. He knows that calcium reacts with water but not with alcohol.
    His teacher supplies him with three bottles of alcohol and asks him to find out which one contains **dry** alcohol.
    Describe how he determines which bottle to use.

6. Naeem has recorded in his chemistry note-book the approximate pH of some 1 mol/l solutions.

Solution (1 mol/l)	pH
sodium chloride	7
sulphuric acid	0.5
ammonium hydroxide	12
potassium hydroxide	14
potassium nitrate	7
ammonium sulphate	4
hydrochloric acid	1

    (a) In what way has it been made certain that this is a fair comparison?
    (b) When Naeem was revising his chemistry notes he told his dad
        'All salts have a pH of 7.'
        Which **one** of the solutions above is **an exception** to this statement?
    (c) 25 cm³ of 1 mol/l hydrochloric acid (HCl) was added to 30 cm³ of 1 mol/l potassium hydroxide.
        Which **one** of the following will be the pH of the resulting solution?

        A more than 7   B exactly 7   C less than 7

7.

> ### *Manganese dioxide — a catalyst*
>
> A catalyst speeds up a chemical reaction but is not used up. When lumps of manganese dioxide, a catalyst, were added to hydrogen peroxide solution, oxygen gas formed. There appeared to be as much manganese dioxide at the end of the reaction as there was at the start.

Describe how you would show that the manganese dioxide was **not** used up.

8. The rate of rusting of an iron nail can be slowed down by connecting the iron nail by a wire to a more active metal. Here are some experiments concerned with this process.

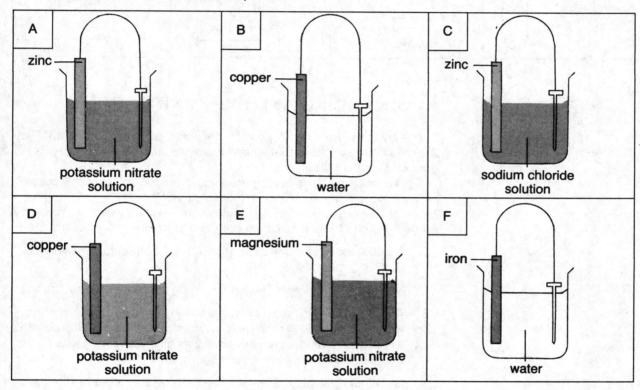

A — zinc — potassium nitrate solution

B — copper — water

C — zinc — sodium chloride solution

D — copper — potassium nitrate solution

E — magnesium — potassium nitrate solution

F — iron — water

(a) Select the **three** experiments which show **fairly** that the rusting of iron 'can be slowed down by connecting the iron nail to a more active metal'.

(b) Which **two** experiments show **fairly** that the presence of an ionic solution affects the rate of rusting on an iron nail?

9. Kim and Ali were asked to carry out a practical investigation to compare two types of yeast.

The effectiveness of the yeast was measured by the rate of production of carbon dioxide gas in fermentation.
The apparatus is shown in the diagram.

State **four** things that Kim and Ali could control in order to make the comparison a **fair** one.

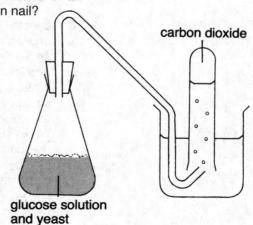

carbon dioxide

glucose solution and yeast

10. Ammonia is less dense than air and is soluble in water but insoluble in paraffin.

Which box (or boxes) in the grid could be used to enable a **full** test tube of ammonia to be collected?

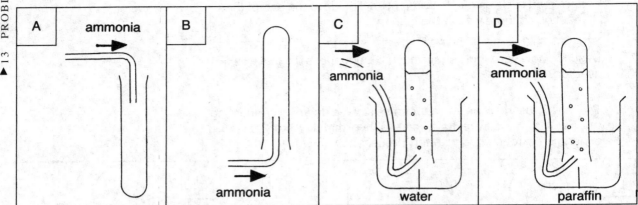

▶ CONCLUDING AND EXPLAINING

These are the commonest types of questions that you will be asked. They are the kind of questions that your teacher probably asks you every day of your chemistry course:

   'This substance turns pH paper a blue colour. What does this mean?'
   'Why did this metal react with this solution?'

Most of the questions are applications of your knowledge. You may sometimes find that calculations are needed to draw conclusions.

1. A substance reacts with water forming **only** calcium hydroxide, $Ca(OH)_2$, and ethyne, C_2H_2.

Name the **two** elements which must be present in the substance.

2. A white powder dissolved in water to form a solution which conducted electricity. When dilute sulphuric acid was added to the solution which had formed, carbon dioxide was given off. When a flame test was carried out a yellow colour was seen.

(a) What does the evidence above tell you about the kind of bonding in the compound?
(b) Which types of compounds give off carbon dioxide when an acid is added?
(c) Use information in the *Data Booklet* to help you deduce the name of the compound.

3. Lynsey was carrying out a practical investigation with a black powder. She was told that it was a mixture of **two** substances, one an element and the other a compound.
She found that **neither** substance dissolved in water.
When she heated them both with dilute sulphuric acid, **one** of the substances produced a blue solution. The other did not react with the acid.
When she heated the mixture of the two substances she noticed that carbon dioxide and a brown metal formed.
Lynsey suggested that the black powder was a mixture of copper(II) oxide and carbon. Her teacher agreed.

Explain how she had arrived at her conclusion.

4. The table lists the boiling points of a number of liquids.

Liquid	Boiling point (°C)
ethanol	78
propanone	56
hexane	69
heptane	98
octane	—

(a) Use the *Data Booklet* to find the boiling point of octane.
(b) Which of the three hydrocarbons shown will boil first when heated?
(c) Name the method used to separate a mixture of liquids.
(d) Explain why the boiling point of heptane is between those of hexane and octane.

5. The table gives the formulae of some compounds of metals.

Compound	Formula
(a) cadmium oxide	CdO
(b) mercury chloride	$HgCl$
(c) thorium chloride	$ThCl_2$
(d) chromium oxide	Cr_2O_3
(e) manganese sulphate	$MnSO_4$
(f) iron nitrate	$Fe(NO_3)_3$

Write the name of each compound, indicating the valency of the metal. For example, cadmium oxide is written **cadmium(II) oxide**.

6. Some substances are made by dehydration. Dehydration means the removal of water. For example, carbon monoxide can be made by dehydrating oxalic acid.

$$H_2C_2O_4 \rightarrow CO + CO_2 + H_2O$$

State the formulae of **X**, **Y** and **Z** in each of the following dehydration reactions.
(a) **X** $\rightarrow H_2O + CO$
(b) $C_3H_6O_3 \rightarrow 3\textbf{Y} + 3H_2O$
(c) $C_2H_6O \rightarrow \textbf{Z} + H_2O$

7. The presence of mercury in mercury chloride solution can be detected by adding copper foil.

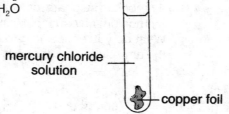

Mercury will be deposited as a grey layer on the copper. The grey coated copper is then removed from the test tube, put into a second dry test tube and warmed.
The mercury will vaporise and be seen to condense in droplets at the mouth of the test tube.

(a) Why does copper react with a compound of mercury?
(b) What would be the result of adding copper foil to a solution of zinc chloride?
(c) Soluble silver compounds react with copper in exactly the same ways as soluble mercury compounds.

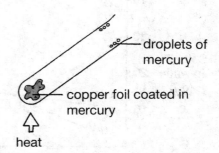

113

Use the table of melting and boiling points in the *Data Booklet* to explain how the **second** part of the experiment could be used to distinguish them.

▶ PREDICTING AND GENERALISING

Predicting is not the same as guessing! Once you have a certain amount of knowledge, it is possible to predict what may happen in a situation which is unfamiliar to you. You may deduce from a graph, for instance, what will happen between the points which are drawn. Or you may spot a trend in results and be able to predict what will happen next.

Although you may meet someone who claims that it once snowed in June you would know yourself that that was very unusual weather! *In general* the weather is very pleasant in June. When you look at the results of a series of experiments you may be able to make a 'generalisation'. You are stating what *usually* happens in a given situation.

Solution	Product at the negative electrode	Product at the positive electrode
sodium chloride	hydrogen	chlorine
potassium chloride	hydrogen	chlorine
zinc chloride	hydrogen	chlorine
copper(II) chloride	copper	chlorine
sodium fluoride	hydrogen	oxygen
silver nitrate	silver	oxygen
copper(II) sulphate	copper	oxygen

1. Here is a summary of the results of a number of experiments in which solutions were electrolysed.

The products at the electrodes are given.

Give the correct words for (a) to (d) in the following statement.

'When a solution is electrolysed _____ (a) _____ always forms at the negative electrode unless a very _____ (b) _____ metal is present. When a solution of calcium nitrate is electrolysed _____ (c) _____ will form at the negative electrode and _____ (d) _____ will form at the positive electrode.'

2. Use information in the *Data Booklet* to answer this question.

(a) Construct a table with suitable headings showing the solubility of the following compounds: ammonium carbonate; ammonium sulphate; calcium carbonate; aluminium carbonate; ammonium chloride; calcium phosphate.

(b) What do you notice, in general, about the solubility in water of the ammonium compounds?

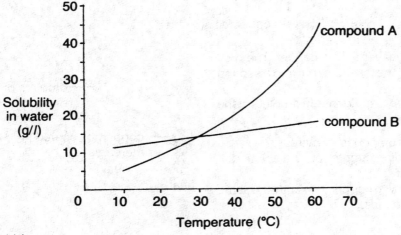

3. The graph shows the solubility of two compounds in water at different temperatures.

(a) Give a general rule about the solubility of the compounds in water at different temperatures.

(b) What is the solubility of compound **A** in water at 60°C?

(c) At what temperature are both compounds equally soluble?

(d) 1 litre of a solution of compound **A** is cooled down from 60°C to 40°C. What mass of compound **A** will crystallise?

4. The change in mass which may take place during a chemical reaction can be measured by putting the reaction flask on a balance as shown.

State whether the reading of mass on the balance will **increase**, **decrease** or **remain the same** during the reactions described by the following chemical equations.

(a) $Mg(s) + 2HCl(aq) \rightarrow MgCl_2(aq) + H_2(g)$
(b) $CaCO_3(s) + 2HCl(aq) \rightarrow CaCl_2(aq) + CO_2(g) + H_2O(l)$
(c) $Zn(s) + CuCl_2(aq) \rightarrow ZnCl_2(aq) + Cu(s)$
(d) $2Fe(s) + O_2(g) + 2H_2O(l) \rightarrow 2Fe(OH)_3(s)$

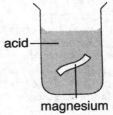

reaction mixture

59.53 g

5. When metal carbonates are heated, they often decompose forming the metal oxide and carbon dioxide gas.
The carbonates of the **least active metals** decompose **most easily**. The carbonates of the **most active metals** such as sodium and potassium **do not decompose** on heating.

(a) Describe how the above procedure could be used to place **sodium, copper** and **zinc** in the order of their reactivity.
(b) From the information above, write a **word** equation showing the effect of heat on zinc carbonate.
(c) Suggest what you would observe if you compared the rate of decomposition of copper and zinc carbonates.

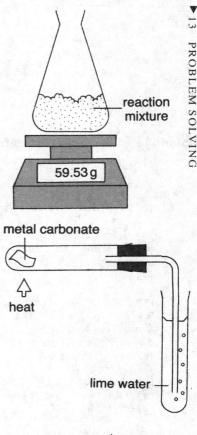

metal carbonate

heat

lime water

6. Here are the results of an experiment in which equal volumes of different concentrations of an acid were added to magnesium.

Experiment	Concentration of acid (mol/l)	Time for magnesium to react (minutes)
1	1.00	2
2	0.10	14
3	0.01	79
4	0.001	192

acid

magnesium

(a) In which experiment was the **most** concentrated acid used?
(b) In which experiment was the rate **greatest**?
(c) Predict what the time would be for the magnesium to react if acid of concentration 2 mol/l was used.
(d) Suggest **two** ways in which the rate of reaction in experiment 4 could be increased **without** altering the concentration.
(e) Why were equal volumes of the acid used in each experiment?

7. Inflated balloons go down after a time, even though they do not leak. Balloons containing hydrogen go down more quickly than balloons filled with oxygen. It is thought that the different sizes of the gas molecules can explain this observation.

(a) Suggest a reason why balloons go down after a time.
(b) Use your answer to (a) to explain why balloons filled with hydrogen go down more quickly than balloons filled with oxygen.
(c) Predict the rate at which a balloon filled with xenon gas would go down. Give a reason for your answer.

ANSWERS TO
PRACTICE QUESTIONS

Note to teachers.   See note about grid questions below Introduction.

CHAPTER ONE

1. (a) A, D, F, H   *In each case a new substance forms.*
    (b) B, E
    (c) F   *Water is a compound of hydrogen and oxygen.*
    (d) G

2. (a) C   (b) Ne   (c) Fe   (d) Cl
    (e) Na   (f) Cr   (g) Cu   (h) W   (i) He
    Consult the periodic table.
    The first letter of a symbol is always a capital letter, the second one a small letter.

3. (a) phosphorus   (b) nitrogen   (c) argon
    (d) potassium   (e) platinum   (f) bromine
    (g) calcium   (h) gold   (i) boron

4. (a) magnesium and oxygen
    (b) zinc and chlorine
    (c) potassium, hydrogen and oxygen
    (d) copper, carbon and oxygen
    (e) barium and iodine
    (f) potassium, sulphur and oxygen
    (g) calcium, hydrogen and oxygen
    (h) sodium and sulphur

5. (a) zinc chloride   (b) iron oxide
    (c) sodium fluoride   (d) copper sulphate
    (e) hydrogen oxide   (f) magnesium nitride

6. The mixture of iron and sulphur can be separated into iron and sulphur. For example, iron could be removed with a magnet. Iron sulphide, on the other hand, is a compound in which the atoms of the elements iron and sulphur are joined together. Iron sulphide cannot be separated by a magnet.

7. The mixture of sand and salt should be added to water in a beaker, then stirred until all the salt has dissolved. The sand can be separated from the salt solution by filtration. The sand left behind in the filter paper should then be dried. The salt can be obtained by boiling the salt solution dry in an evaporating dish.

8. (a) Solute: copper sulphate; solvent: water.
    (b) Label: copper sulphate solution.

9. (a) A   *D would also work but would require heating.*

(b) B   *(salt in water)* and E   *(gas, etc. in water)*
(c) C

10.

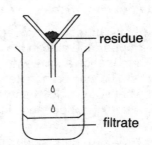

residue

filtrate

Ruler or stencil. Accurate labels. No 'art' work required. Items like 'bench' or 'stand' are not required.

11. (a) H   *Concentrated, high temperature and powder.*
    (b) A   *Dilute, low temperature and lump.*
    (c) A and G or B and D or C and E or F and H   *Only one variable, the concentration of acid, changes.*

12. Adding ice cools the acid and slows the rate of the reaction. Ice will also melt and dilute the acid which will also slow down the reacton rate.

13. (a) Two beakers are required with equal volumes of water at the same temperature in each. Add the same mass of sugar to each, one in lump form, the other powdered. Stir each in the same way. Make a note of the times required for the sugar to dissolve in each.
    (b) The variables are: volume of water, temperature of water, rate or method of stirring.

14. (a) A   (b) F   (c) D

15. (a) The formation of a new substance, a gas, is evidence of a chemical reaction.
    (b) It slowed down when hydrogen peroxide was being used up, and so its concentration was reducing.
    (c) Manganese dioxide
    A catalyst is unchanged in a reaction.
    (d) 2.00 g of manganese dioxide. As the catalyst is unchanged, the mass at the end will be the same as at the start.

1. (a) C *Group 0*
    (b) A and F *Group I*
    (c) B and H
    (d) D and E *Group VII*
    (e) C, D, E and G

2. (a)
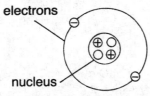

    (b) It has the same number of protons (positive charge) and electrons (negative charge).
    (c) helium *(2 protons so atomic number of 2, He)*

3. Both elements have one electron in their outer shells and so belong to the same group.

4.

Particle	Charge	Mass	Where particle found in atom
proton	+	1	in nucleus
neutron	0	1	in nucleus
electron	–	almost 0	outside nucleus

5.

Atom	Number of protons	Number of neutrons	Number of electrons
$^{4}_{2}He$	2	2	2
$^{19}_{9}F$	9	10	9
$^{27}_{13}Al$	13	14	13
$^{31}_{15}P$	15	16	15

6.

Ion	Number of protons	Number of neutrons	Number of electrons
$^{23}_{11}Na^+$	11	12	10
$^{19}_{9}F^-$	9	10	10
$^{24}_{12}Mg^{2+}$	12	12	10
$^{32}_{16}S^{2-}$	16	16	18

Positive ions have fewer electrons than protons. Negative ions have more electrons than protons.

7. (a) (i) 2, 8   (ii) 2, 8   (iii) 2, 8   (iv) 2, 8
    Remember that electron arrangements of all the elements are given in the Data Booklet.
    (b) When an atom forms an ion, it obtains the same electron structure as a noble gas. Metals lose electrons and non-metals gain electrons to achieve this.

8. (a) $^{35}_{17}Cl$ and $^{37}_{17}Cl$ are described as isotopes. Although they both have the same atomic number, their mass numbers differ. $^{35}_{17}Cl$ has 18 neutrons in its nucleus whereas $^{37}_{17}Cl$ has 20 neutrons.
    (b) The relative atomic mass of an element is the average mass number of all the isotopes. Chlorine is made up of some $^{35}_{17}Cl$ and some $^{37}_{17}Cl$ and has an average mass number of 35.5.

9. (a) CH_4 (b) CCl_4 (c) HF   (d) H_2
    (e) NH_3 (f) H_2S (g) PH_3 (h) CCl_2F_2

10. (a) H – F   (b) F – O – F

    (c) H – N – H   (d)   H
              | |
              H   H – C – H
                                   |
                                   H

11. (a) H ÷ F̈:   (b) F̈ ÷ Ö ÷ F̈:

    (c) H ÷ N̈ ÷ H   (d)   H
              ·|·   ·|·
              H   H ÷ C ÷ H
                                   ·|·
                                   H

Hydrogen is unique in that it has only two electrons in its outer level when it forms bonds, whereas the other non-metals have eight.

CHAPTER THREE

1. (a) NaCl   (b) F_2O
    (c) MgS   (d) Al_2O_3
    (e) CO   (f) CS_2
    (g) N_2O_4 (h) $CuCl_2$
    (i) Fe_2O_3 (j) $HgBr_2$

2.

	Reactants	Products
(a)	sodium, chlorine	sodium chloride
(b)	magnesium, copper(II) bromide	copper, magnesium bromide
(c)	magnesium, oxygen	magnesium oxide
(d)	chlorine, sodium iodide	iodine, sodium chloride
(e)	calcium carbonate	calcium oxide, carbon dioxide

When a substance 'burns', oxygen is added. Decomposing means breaking down into simpler substances.

3. (a) sodium + chlorine → sodium chloride
    (b) magnesium + copper(II) bromide → magnesium bromide + copper
    (c) magnesium + oxygen → magnesium oxide
    (d) chlorine + sodium iodide → sodium chloride + iodine
    (e) calcium carbonate → calcium oxide + carbon dioxide

4. (a) aluminium + chlorine → **aluminium chloride**
    (b) zinc + hydrochloric acid → zinc chloride + **hydrogen**

(c) lead(II) nitrate + potassium iodide → potassium nitrate + **lead(II) iodide**
(d) sodium + **oxygen** → sodium oxide
(e) **iron** + copper(II) chloride → iron(II) chloride + copper
In (b) 'hydrochloric acid' is also called 'hydrogen chloride'.
You should write equations in one line only.

5. (a) Zn + S → ZnS
    (b) Fe + $CuCl_2$ → $FeCl_2$ + Cu
    (c) Ca + Cl_2 → $CaCl_2$
    (d) C + O_2 → CO_2
    (e) 2Na + S → Na_2S
    (f) 2Al + 3S → Al_2S_3
    (g) 2Mg + O_2 → 2MgO
    (h) $2H_2$ + O_2 → $2H_2O$
    (i) H_2 + Cl_2 → 2HCl
    (j) Mg + 2HCl → $MgCl_2$ + H_2

In 5 (a), (b), (c) and (d), no balancing is required. Simply writing the formulae gives a balanced equation. Do not always rush into balancing equations. Often it will not be necessary.

6. (a) CH_4 + $2O_2$ → CO_2 + $2H_2O$
    (b) H_2 + F_2 → 2HF
    (c) 2Mg + CO_2 → 2MgO + C
    (d) 2Al + Fe_2O_3 → Al_2O_3 + 2Fe
    (e) Fe + 2HCl → $FeCl_2$ + H_2

7. (a) Mg(s) + H_2O(g) → MgO(s) + H_2(g)
    (b) Fe(s) + S(s) → FeS(s)
    (c) $CuCl_2$(aq) + Mg(s) → $MgCl_2$(aq) + Cu(s)
    (d) CaO(s) + 2HCl(aq) → $CaCl_2$(aq) + H_2O(l)

CHAPTER FOUR

1. (a) A   (b) E and F   (c) F   (d) B
    The more carbon atoms there are in a hydrocarbon molecule the heavier the molecule is. This makes the liquid more difficult to boil, less flammable and more viscous.

2.

Gas	Percentage in air	Chemical test
nitrogen	79%	largely unreactive
oxygen	20%	relights a glowing splinter
argon	less than 1%	totally unreactive
carbon dioxide	traces	turns lime water chalky

3.

Fuel	Combustion products
hydrogen	**water**
carbon	**carbon dioxide**
carbon monoxide	**carbon dioxide**
methane	**carbon dioxide and water**
ethene	**carbon dioxide and water**

A hydrocarbon burns to produce both carbon dioxide and water.

4. (a) B, E   (b) D, G   (c) D, E
    (d) F   (e) C

5. (a) A, C and D
    (b) E   *Not B, which is a molecular formula, or F, which is a name.*
    (c) C   *Not A, which is a structural formula, or D, which is a name.*
    (d) F
    (e) B, E and F

6. (a) butene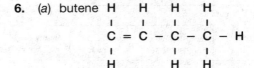

    You might also have written:

    H   H   H   H
    | | | |
    H – C – C = C – C – H
        | |
        H   H

    (b) (i) C_5H_{10} pentene
        (ii)

    (cyclopentane)

7. (a) A is butene; B is cyclobutane.
    (b) Add bromine solution (bromine 'water') to each in turn. The one in which the bromine is decolourised is butene, the one which is unaffected is cyclobutane.
    When you are asked to 'distinguish' between two substances you should give the effect of the test on both of them.
    The bromine is 'decolourised'. Do not say it goes 'clear'. Bromine water is clear. You can see through something which is clear even although it may be coloured. Substances like water, which have no colour, are described as being 'colourless'.
    (c) isomers

8.

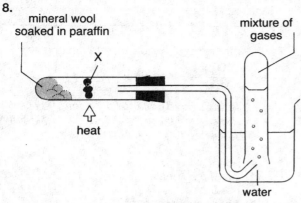

mineral wool
soaked in paraffin

X

heat

mixture of
gases

water

X = steel wool or broken pottery or catalyst

*Instead of showing a Bunsen burner, an arrow
with the word 'heat' will do. Heat is applied to X
and not to the paraffin.*

9. (a) C_2H_4 ethene (*substraction:*
$C_4H_{10} - C_2H_6 = C_2H_4$)

(b) (i)

$$H - \underset{\underset{H}{|}}{\overset{\overset{H}{|}}{C}} - \underset{\underset{H}{|}}{\overset{\overset{H}{|}}{C}} - H$$

(ii)

$$H - \underset{\underset{Br}{|}}{\overset{\overset{H}{|}}{C}} - \underset{\underset{Br}{|}}{\overset{\overset{H}{|}}{C}} - H$$

*In (ii) the position of the bromine atoms is not
important so long as one is on each carbon atom.*

(c) addition reaction

CHAPTER FIVE

1. (a) A, B and I   *All metals and carbon in the form
of graphite conduct electricity.*
(b) G and H   *D contains ions but does not conduct as it is in the solid state.*
(c) C
(d) D

2. Each carbon dioxide molecule, CO_2, is
separate from all the others. There are no
charges on covalent molecules to attract
adjacent molecules.
Magnesium oxide is a network solid made up
of many millions of positive and negative ions.
Each is strongly attracted to its neighbours of
the opposite charge, thus making the compound a solid.

3.

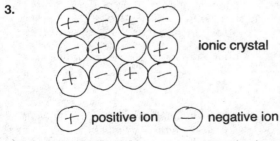

ionic crystal

⊕ positive ion   ⊖ negative ion

positive ion   negative ion

Each positive and negative ion is attracted to
its oppositely charged neighbours and is
tightly held by them. When melted or dissolved
in water this network breaks down and the ions
become free to move.

4. (a) $Cu^{2+}(Cl^-)_2$
(b) (i) $Cu^{2+} + 2e \rightarrow Cu$ (ii) $2Cl^- \rightarrow Cl_2 + 2e$

5. (a) Copper ions have a positive charge,
dichromate ions have a negative charge.
(b) Copper ions, Cu^{2+}, are attracted to the
negative charge at A. Opposite charges
attract.
(c) In a direct current the electrons always
move in the same direction. If this were not
the case the blue colour, for example,
would move in both directions.
(d) An electrolyte is a better conductor of
electricity than water.

6. (a) $NaNO_3$ (b) KOH
(c) NH_4Cl (d) NH_4OH
(e) $CuSO_4$ (f) Na_2CO_3
(g) Li_2CO_3 (h) $(NH_4)_2SO_4$
(i) $Fe(NO_3)_3$ (j) $Al_2(SO_4)_3$

7. (a) $Na^+(NO_3^-)$ (b) $K^+(OH^-)$
(c) $(NH_4^+)Cl^-$ (d) $(NH_4^+)(OH^-)$
(e) $Cu^{2+}(SO_4^{2-})$ (f) $(Na^+)_2(CO_3^{2-})$
(g) $(Li^+)_2(CO_3^{2-})$ (h) $(NH_4^+)_2(SO_4^{2-})$
(i) $Fe^{3+}(NO_3^-)_3$ (j) $(Al^{3+})_2(SO_4^{2-})_3$

1.

Acid	Alkali	Neutral
vinegar lemon juice lemonade sulphuric acid	baking soda sodium carbonate sodium hydroxide	tap water salt solution

The headings 'Substance', 'pH' and 'Use' would also be acceptable.

2. B

All acids have a pH of less than 7. (A)
All acids produce H⁺ ions. (C)
All acids give hydrogen when electrolysed. (D)

3. C and D
Potassium hydroxide solution is an alkali. Only acidic solutions contain more H⁺ ions than water. (A)
Oxides of sulphur are part of the cause of 'acid' rain. (B)

4. A and C *Dilution of acid by water does not neutralise it. (D)*

5. A *(hydrogen)* and D *(carbon dioxide)*

6. (a) 42 amu (b) 56 amu (c) 100 amu
(d) 98 amu (e) 63 amu (f) 40 amu

7. (a) zinc sulphate
(b) sodium chloride
(c) copper(II) sulphate
(d) copper(II) chloride
(e) potassium nitrate

8. (a) (i) $Mg(s) + 2HCl(aq) \rightarrow H_2(g) + MgCl_2(aq)$
(ii) $H_2SO_4(aq) + CuO(s) \rightarrow CuSO_4(aq) + H_2O(l)$
(iii) $HNO_3(aq) + NaOH(aq) \rightarrow H_2O(l) + NaNO_3(aq)$
(iv) $2HCl(aq) + CaCO_3(s) \rightarrow CaCl_2(aq) + H_2O(l) + CO_2(g)$
(b) (i) $Mg(s) + 2H^+(aq) \rightarrow Mg^{2+}(aq) + H_2(g)$
(ii) $2H^+(aq) + O^{2-}(s) \rightarrow H_2O(l)$
(iii) $H^+(aq) + OH^-(aq) \rightarrow H_2O(l)$
(iv) $2H^+(aq) + CO_3^{2-}(s) \rightarrow H_2O(l) + CO_2(g)$

9. (a) H_2O = 18 g
(b) $CaCO_3$ 100 × 2 = 200 g
(c) H_2SO_4 98 × 0.5 = 49 g
(d) HNO_3 63 × 0.1 = 6.3 g
(e) $NaOH$ 40 × 2 = 80 g

10. (a) $CaCO_3$ 1 mole is 100 g; 10 g contain **0.1 mole**.
(b) S   1 mole is 32 g; 8 g contain **0.25 mole**.
(c) Na_2CO_3 1 mole is 106 g; 10.6 g contain **0.1 mole**.
(d) 100 cm³ of 1 mol/*l* of solution contains
$$\frac{100 \times 1}{1000} = \textbf{0.1 mole}.$$

(e) 2000 cm³ of 2 mol/*l* of solution contains
$$\frac{2000 \times 2}{1000} = \textbf{4 moles}.$$

In answers (d) and (e) the name of the substance is not important. 100 cm³ of any 1 mol/l solution contains 0.1 mole.

11. (a) none
(b) barium sulphate
(c) none
(d) copper(II) carbonate
(e) lead(II) iodide

12. (a) lead(II) nitrate solution and sodium carbonate solution
The Data Booklet lists many 'soluble' or 'very soluble' lead compounds and carbonate compounds which would do equally well.
(b) (i) $Pb(NO_3)_2(aq) + Na_2CO_3(aq) \rightarrow PbCO_3(s) + 2NaNO_3(aq)$
(ii) $Pb^{2+}(aq) + CO_3^{2-}(aq) \rightarrow Pb^{2+}CO_3^{2-}(s)$
(c) precipitation
(d)

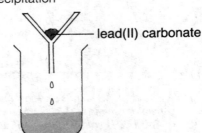

— lead(II) carbonate

13. *In the calculations involving neutralisation it is essential to know the formulae of the common acids and alkalis.*
(a) Acid HCl   Alkali NaOH
volume × concentration × no. of H⁺ ions = volume × concentration × no. of OH⁻ ions
volume × 2 ×1 = 20 × 1 × 1
volume of hydrochloric acid = 10 cm³
(b) Acid H_2SO_4 Alkali KOH
volume × 1 × 2 = 20 × 1 × 1
volume of sulphuric acid = 10 cm³
(c) Acid HNO_3 Alkali NaOH
50 × concentration × 1 = 25 × 1 × 1
concentration of nitric acid = 0.5 mol/*l*
(d) Acid H_2SO_4 Alkali KOH
50 × concentration × 2 = 25 × 4 × 1
$$\text{concentration} = \frac{25 \times 4}{50 \times 2} = 1 \text{ mol/}l$$

14. B

Remember in all the calculations which follow:
- *write a balanced equation;*
- *underline what is to be calculated;*
- *underline what is given;*
- *write the numbers of reacting moles (ignore the other substances);*
- *calculate the masses of the substances underlined;*
- *calculate the answer.*

15. (a) $Ca + S \rightarrow CaS$
1 mole of calcium reacts with 1 mole of sulphur.
40 g of calcium react with 32 g of sulphur, so **20 g of calcium** react with 16 g of sulphur.
(b) $2Na + S \rightarrow Na_2S$
23 g of sodium react with **16 g of sulphur.**
(c) $Fe + S \rightarrow FeS$
5.6 g of iron react to form **8.8 g of iron(II) sulphide.**

16. (a) (i) $C + O_2 \rightarrow CO_2$
6 g of carbon react with **16 g of oxygen.**
(ii) $2Mg + O_2 \rightarrow 2MgO$
24 g of carbon react with **16 g of oxygen.**
(iii) $4Na + O_2 \rightarrow 2Na_2O$
2.3 g of sodium react with **0.8 g of oxygen.**
(b) (i) $C + O_2 \rightarrow CO_2$
3 g of carbon form **11 g of carbon dioxide.**
(ii) $2Mg + O_2 \rightarrow 2MgO$
12 g of magnesium form **20 g of magnesium oxide.**
(iii) $S + O_2 \rightarrow SO_2$
16 g of sulphur form **32 g of sulphur dioxide.**

17. (a) $Mg + 2HCl \rightarrow MgCl_2 + H_2$
6 g of magnesium form **0.5 g of hydrogen.**
(b) $CuSO_4 + Na_2CO_3 \rightarrow CuCO_3 + Na_2SO_4$
10.6 g of sodium carbonate form **12.4 g of copper(II) carbonate.**
(c) $CaCO_3 + 2HNO_3 \rightarrow H_2O + CO_2 + Ca(NO_3)_2$
10 g of calcium carbonate form **4.4 g of carbon dioxide.**
(d) $CH_4 + 2O_2 \rightarrow CO_2 + 2H_2O$
4 g of methane form **9 g of water.**

18.

$$
\begin{array}{ccccc}
H \;\; H & & & H \;\; H \\
| \;\;\; | & & & | \;\;\; | \\
C = C & + & Br_2 & \rightarrow & Br - C - C - Br \\
| \;\;\; | & & & | \;\;\; | \\
H \;\; H & & & H \;\; H \\
\end{array}
$$

1 mole of ethene forms 1 mole of dibromoethane. 28 g of ethene form 188 g of dibromoethane, so 1 g of ethene forms **6.71 g of dibromoethane.**

19. $CaCO_3 \rightarrow CaO + CO_2$
1 mole of calcium carbonate forms 1 mole of carbon dioxide.
100 g calcium carbonate form 44 g of carbon dioxide.
$\dfrac{100}{44} \times 0.1$ g of calcium carbonate form 0.1 g of carbon dioxide.
0.23 g of calcium carbonate gives 0.1 g of carbon dioxide when roasted.
As 1 mole of calcium carbonate is 100 g, then the number of moles = 0.23/100 = **0.0023.**

The last questions involve an understanding of the chemistry learned in several chapters. This enables, for example, the correct equations to be written.
A calculator may be needed in some of the questions. You will also require to make use of what you have learned in your maths course to calculate some of the answers. Maths is not confined to the Maths Department!
You may feel that you can do some chemical calculations in your head and simply put down the answer. The problem about this is that if you make a mistake you will get no marks at all! If you set out your answers as shown above, long winded though it is, it will enable the marker to give you some marks. 1½ marks out of 2 is better than 0 out of 2.

CHAPTER SEVEN

1. C *Electrons (not ions) flow along a metal wire.*

2. D *Consult the electrochemical series. The greatest voltage is given by the metals which are furthest apart.*

3. A *Water is not a good enough conductor. Copper (II) sulphate solution and sulphuric acid both react with iron, zinc and magnesium.*

4. B *'X' is more reactive than all the metals except aluminium which displaces it.*

5. (a)

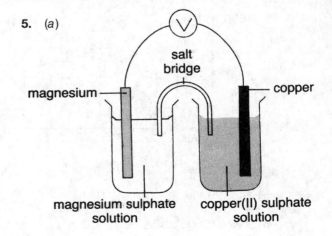

(b)

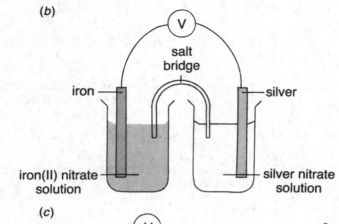

iron — iron(II) nitrate solution

silver — silver nitrate solution

(d)

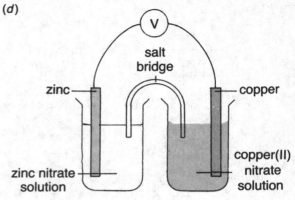

zinc — zinc nitrate solution

copper — copper(II) nitrate solution

(c)

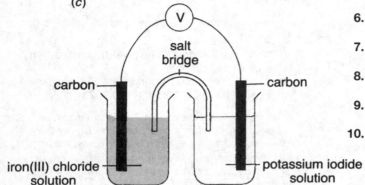

carbon — iron(III) chloride solution

carbon — potassium iodide solution

In each of the cells (a) to (d), the salt bridge can be filter paper soaked in any one of a number of electrolytes. Solutions of potassium nitrate or of sodium nitrate are best as they react with so few other ionic solutions.

6. C   *(A neither, B neither, D reduction only.)*

7. A and E

8. A

9. C and F

10. (a) Reduction $Cu^{2+}(aq) + 2e \rightarrow Cu(s)$
    Oxidation $Mg(s) \rightarrow Mg^{2+}(aq) + 2e$
   (b) Reduction $2H^+(aq) + 2e \rightarrow H_2(g)$
    Oxidation $Zn(s) \rightarrow Zn^{2+}(aq) + 2e$
   (c) Reduction $Cu^{2+}(aq) + 2e \rightarrow Cu(s)$
    Oxidation $Zn(s) \rightarrow Zn^{2+}(aq) + 2e$
   (d) Reduction $Fe^{3+}(aq) + e \rightarrow Fe^{2+}(aq)$
    Oxidation $2I^-(aq) \rightarrow I_2(s) + 2e$
   (e) Reduction $Cl_2(g) + 2e \rightarrow 2Cl^-(aq)$
    Oxidation $2Br^-(aq) \rightarrow Br_2(l) + 2e$

Reduction: electrons on left
Oxidation: electrons on right

CHAPTER EIGHT

1.

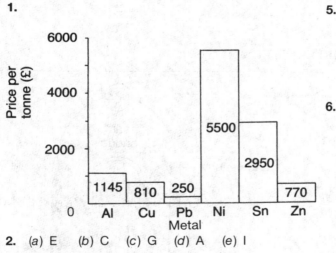

2. (a) E   (b) C   (c) G   (d) A   (e) I

3. (a) E   (b) G   (c) D   (d) B

4. (a) A and C   (b) D and E   (c) B and F

5. (a) Al_2O_3
   (b) Aluminium is light and a good conductor of electricity.
   (c) Aluminium comes just below magnesium which reacts quickly with acids and burns violently.

6.

Metal	Percentage available in earth's crust
Aluminium	30
Iron	20
Calcium	18
Magnesium	10
Sodium	8
Potassium	6
Titanium	3
Other metals	6

You will be allowed a small error in these values.

7.

Metal	Symbol	Melting point (°C)	Density (g/cm³)	Relative atomic mass
Aluminium	Al	660	2.7	27
Copper	Cu	1083	8.92	64
Iron	Fe	1535	7.86	56
Platinum	Pt	1770	21.5	195
Lead	Pb	328	11.3	207

8. (a) Aluminium is not magnetic; 'tin' cans are.
   (b) A finite resource is a resource whose reserves are limited. Oil, coal, gas and metal ores are finite resources.
   (c) (i) Aluminium 600°C; copper 1083°C; iron 1535°C.
       (ii) Aluminium requires less heat to melt it down again than either copper or iron.
   (d) An alloy is a mixture of metals.

9. For a 'fair' test the three metals should all be in the same form, for example all in the form of lumps. Equal weights of each should be added to equal volumes of, say, dilute sulphuric acid. The rate at which hydrogen is produced should then be measured.
   In this investigation there are a number of variables: form and mass of metal; concentration and temperature of acid; the same acid should also be used for each metal.
   Burning the metals in oxygen is also possible. In this case powdered metals would be essential. The reaction with water would not be satisfactory.

10. (a) oxygen
    (b) carbon monoxide
    (c) hydrogen
    (d) carbon dioxide
    (e) carbon dioxide

11. (a) copper + water
    (b) lead + carbon dioxide
    (c) copper + zinc chloride
    (d) iron + aluminium oxide
    (e) iron + carbon dioxide

12. *The percentage composition gives the mass of each element in 100 g.*
    Divide each by its atomic mass to get the number of moles of each.

calcium	:	carbon	:	oxygen
40	:	12	:	48

    mole ratio $\dfrac{40}{40}$: $\dfrac{12}{12}$: $\dfrac{48}{16}$

    1 : 1 : 3

    The empirical formula is $CaCO_3$.

13.

sodium	:	oxygen	:	hydrogen
57.5	:	40	:	2.5

    mole ratio $\dfrac{57.5}{23}$: $\dfrac{40}{16}$: $\dfrac{2.5}{1}$

    2.5 : 2.5 : 2.5

    The empirical formula is NaOH.

14.

carbon	:	hydrogen	:	oxygen
40	:	6.6	:	53.4

    mole ratio $\dfrac{40}{12}$: $\dfrac{6.6}{1}$: $\dfrac{53.4}{16}$

    3.3 : 6.6 : 3.3

    Dividing by the smallest, the empirical formula is CH_2O.

    It will often be the case that the empirical formula does not seem to obey rules you have learned.

15. The mass of oxygen in 100 g is 100 − 46.6 = 53.4 g.

silicon	:	oxygen
46.6	:	53.4

    mole ratio $\dfrac{46.6}{28}$: $\dfrac{53.4}{16}$

    1.6 : 3.3

    Dividing by the smallest, the empirical formula is SiO_2.

CHAPTER NINE

1. (a) C *(no oxygen)*, F *(connected to negative terminal)*, G *(no water)*, I *(sacrificial protection)*.
   (b) A *(water and oxygen)*, C *(no oxygen)*, G *(no water)*
   (c) I *(zinc is more active than iron)*
   (d) B *(ions in the water)*, D and E *(in both cases the iron will sacrificially protect the other metal)*, and H *(the positive electrode will encourage the loss of electrons)*

2. (a) B and F   (b) B and D
   (c) A and E *(B and D will also fail if the connection is broken.)*

3. (a) B   (b) E   (c) A and E *(electrons on left)*

4. If the coating is broken in either case a cell is set up. In the case of the zinc the electrons flow to the iron protecting it. With tin the electrons flow from the iron, causing rusting.

5. (a) G   (b) E   (c) H   (d) B

6. (a) $Al^{3+}(l) + 3e \rightarrow Al(l)$
   (b) $Cu^{2+}(aq) + 2e \rightarrow Cu(s)$
   (c) $2H^+(aq) + 2e \rightarrow H_2(g)$
   (d) $Cu(s) \rightarrow Cu^{2+}(aq) + 2e$

7.

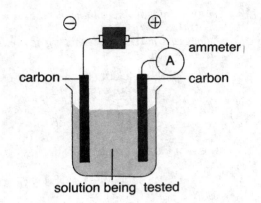

solution being tested

8. A and C

9.

Negative electrode	Positive electrode
(a) $Al^{3+}(l) + 3e \rightarrow Al(l)$	$2O^{2-}(l) \rightarrow O_2(g) + 4e$
(b) $Pb^{2+}(l) + 2e \rightarrow Pb(l)$	$2Br^-(l) \rightarrow Br_2(g) + 2e$
(c) $Cu^{2+}(aq) + 2e \rightarrow Cu(s)$	$2Cl^-(aq) \rightarrow Cl_2(g) + 2e$
(d) $2H^+(aq) + 2e \rightarrow H_2(g)$	$2Cl^-(aq) \rightarrow Cl_2(g) + 2e$
(e) $Ni^{2+}(aq) + 2e \rightarrow Ni(s)$	$2Cl^-(aq) \rightarrow Cl_2(g) + 2e$

Each of the reactions at the negative electrode (reductions) is found in the electrochemical series in the Data Booklet. The reactions at the positive electrode are also found there but must be reversed.

CHAPTER TEN

1. (a) poly(ethene)
(b) poly(propene)
(c) poly(tetrafluoroethene)
(d) poly(styrene)
(e) poly(monochloroethene)

2. (a) A
(b) B, C and D
(c) E and F

3. (a) A and D   *(alkenes)*
(b) C and E   *(water will also form)*
(c) B and F

4. (a) (i) thermosetting
(ii) thermoplastic
(iii) thermosetting
(iv) thermoplastic
(v) thermosetting
(vi) thermoplastic
(b) A thermoplastic polymer softens when heated. The handle of a frying pan should be made of a thermosetting polymer.

5. (a) Thermoplastic means that the polymer will soften and melt when heated.
(b) Alkene
(c) The molecular formula of methyl methacrylate is $C_5H_8O_2$. This is written by examining the structural formula which is given.

$C_5H_8O_2$
carbon $5 \times 12 = 60$
hydrogen $8 \times 1 = 8$
oxygen $2 \times 16 = 32$
formula mass $= 100$ amu

It may seem unfair to be asked a question about formula mass in a topic concerning plastics! You must be ready to deal with any questions in exams.

(d)

```
    H  CH₃      H  CH₃      H  CH₃
    |  |        |  |        |  |
  - C - C ───── C - C ───── C - C -
    |  |        |  |        |  |
    C  COOCH₃  H  COOCH₃  H  COOCH₃
```

Although you are not asked for it the repeating unit is:

```
    H   CH₃
    |   |
  - C - C -
    |   |
    H   COOCH₃
```

6. (a) Choose three names from fuel gas, petrol, kerosine, diesel, lubricating oil, bitumen.
When you are asked to state a certain number of answers do not give more than this. If you give a greater number of answers including some which are incorrect you may lose marks.
(b) alkenes
(c) cracking
(d) Most plastics are not biodegradable.
(e) If a plastic is a hydrocarbon, then it will burn (in a plentiful supply of air) to form carbon dioxide and water vapour.
If other elements such as nitrogen or chlorine are present then poisonous gases will form.

CHAPTER ELEVEN

1. Nitrogen, phosphorus and potassium (N, P, K)

2. *It is essential to write the formula for each compound.*
   (a) potassium sulphate K_2SO_4
   formula mass (fm)

   $$K\ 2 \times 39 = 78$$
   $$S\ 1 \times 32 = 32$$
   $$O\ 4 \times 16 = 64$$
   $$fm\ \ = 174\ amu$$

   percentage potassium $= \dfrac{78}{176} \times 100 = \mathbf{44.3\%}$

   The other parts of the question are answered in the same way.
   (b) ammonium nitrate $NH_4NO_3 = \mathbf{35\%}$
   (c) calcium phosphate $Ca_3(PO_4)_2 = \mathbf{20\%}$

3. Nitrogen can be absorbed by nitrifying bacteria in the roots of plants such as peas, beans or clover.

4. For a fertiliser to be absorbed by the roots of plants it must dissolve in water and be carried through the soil. High solubility may be a disadvantage because very soluble compounds may be washed out of the soil and so pollute lakes and rivers.

5. (a) nitrogen and hydrogen
   (b) iron
   (c) nitrogen and hydrogen
   (d) The process is carried out at a moderately high temperature because: too low a temperature and the reaction is slow; too high a temperature and the ammonia decomposes.

6.

Low temperature	High temperature
slow reaction rate high percentage of ammonia	fast reaction rate low percentage of ammonia

7. **ammonium sulphate and soda lime**

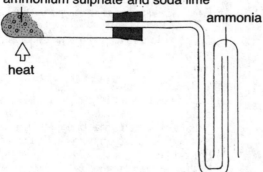

Ammonia is less dense than air so an inverted test tube can be used.

8. (a) ammonium hydroxide
   (b) ammonia
   (c) potassium nitrate   *(and water)*
   (d) ammonia   *(and water and sodium sulphate)*
   (e) ammonium nitrate   *(and water)*

9. (a) NH_3 (b) N_2
   (c) NH_4OH (d) NH_4Cl
   (e) NH_4NO_3 (f) $(NH_4)_2SO_4$
   (g) HNO_3 (h) $Ca(NO_3)_2$

10. Fill a dry test tube with ammonia, then invert it in a beaker of water.

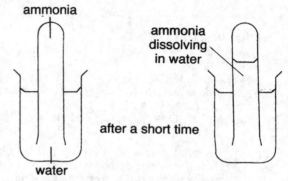

Alternatively, test ammonia gas with wet pH paper. The pH paper will turn blue showing that ammonia is dissolving in the water to form an alkaline solution.

11. (a) Ostwald process
    (b) Ammonia is made in the Haber process.
    (c) Nitrogen is a very inactive gas. *The only way to combine nitrogen and oxygen is to spark air, a mixture of oxygen and nitrogen. This is a dangerous, expensive and slow process.*
    (d) When energy is given out in a reaction, the reaction is called exothermic.

12. (a) $KOH + HNO_3 \rightarrow H_2O + KNO_3$
    (b) $MgCO_3 + 2HNO_3 \rightarrow 2H_2O + CO_2 + Mg(NO_3)_2$
    (c) $CuO + 2HNO_3 \rightarrow H_2O + Cu(NO_3)_2$
    (d) $NH_4OH + HNO_3 \rightarrow H_2O + NH_4NO_3$

13. Put dilute nitric acid into a beaker and then add calcium carbonate. The mixture will fizz as carbon dioxide gas is given off.
    Continue to add calcium carbonate until the fizzing stops. Filter the mixture to remove excess calcium carbonate.
    The solution of calcium nitrate should be left to evaporate and crystals of pure dry calcium nitrate will form after a few days.

14. (a) D
    (b) E   *(produces nitric acid)*
    (c) C   *(see table of flame colours)*
    (d) F   *(gives ammonium hydroxide)*
    (e) F
    (f) F and G

15. (a)

Soluble	Insoluble
ammonium nitrate	calcium carbonate
ammonium sulphate	calcium phosphate
ammonium phosphate	magnesium phosphate
potassium nitrate	

(b) Nitrogen compounds are, in general, soluble in water.

16. (a) Experiment A shows compound X contains the ammonium ion.
(b) Experiment B shows compound X contains the carbonate ion CO_3^{2-}.
(c) Compound X is ammonium carbonate.
(d) $(NH_4)_2CO_3$
(e) Yes! Ammonium carbonate *is* soluble in water as the question suggests.

CHAPTER TWELVE

1. (a) W is H_2O
(b) X is O_2
(c) Y is CO_2
(d) Z is $C_{12}H_{22}O_{11}$

All of these formulae can be obtained by subtraction, for example in (a)
$$W = 2C_6H_{12}O_6 - C_{12}H_{22}O_{11} = H_2O$$

2. (a) Benedict's reagent turns from a blue colour to a red colour when heated with glucose solution. Starch has no effect on Benedict's reagent.
(b) Iodine solution turns from yellow to black when added to starch. Glucose solution has no effect on iodine solution.
(c) When a beam of light is shone through water containing starch, it shows up as an intense beam (Tyndall beam). With glucose solution no Tyndall beam is produced.

When you are asked for a colour change you should give the colours before and after.
When asked to distinguish between two substances, you should state the effect of the reagent on both of them. This may mean simply saying that the second substance gives 'no effect'.

3. (a) B and E
(b) F
(c) H
(d) A and C

4. The level of carbon dioxide in the atmosphere has risen in recent years owing to:
large increases in hydrocarbon fuels being burned;
large scale felling of forests.
The first factor produces extra carbon dioxide. The second factor means that less carbon dioxide is being removed from the atmosphere.

You were asked for two reasons — so you should only give two reasons. Do not get into the habit of simply writing down all you know in questions like this. If part of your answer is wrong or contradicts another part, then you may lose marks.

5. Starch is almost insoluble in water, and starch molecules are too large to be able to diffuse through the wall of the gut.

6. (a) In fermentation the temperature and pH must be controlled. In addition the concentration of alcohol produced affects the yeast. Above about 15% alcohol the yeast cells cease to be able to cause fermentation.
(b) (i) $C_6H_{12}O_6$

	carbon	$6 \times 12 =$	72
	hydrogen	$12 \times 1 =$	12
	oxygen	$6 \times 16 =$	96
	fm		= 180 amu
	mass of 1 mole		= 180 g

(ii) CO_2

	carbon	$1 \times 12 =$	12
	oxygen	$2 \times 16 =$	32
	fm		= 44 amu
	mass of 1 mole		= 44 g
	mass of 2 moles		= 88 g

(c) $C_6H_{12}O_6 \rightarrow 2C_2H_5OH + 2CO_2$
1 mole of glucose produces 2 moles of carbon dioxide.
180 g of glucose produce 88 g of carbon dioxide *(see (b) above)*, so 9 g of glucose produce $\dfrac{88 \times 9}{180}$ = 4.4 g of carbon dioxide.
If only 40% of the glucose reacts, then the mass of carbon dioxide formed is
$$\dfrac{4.4 \times 40}{100} = \textbf{1.76 g}$$

Chemical calculations are to be found in Chapter Six.
(d) Carbon dioxide turns lime water chalky (or milky).

7. (a) (i) 126 °C   (ii) 81 °C
(b) Liquids with different boiling points can be separated by distillation. When the two liquids are heated, the one with the lower boiling point, cyclohexane in this case, will boil off first.

Boiling means turning into a gas. In distillation the gas produced is turned back into a liquid by a condenser.

8. (a) A and F
   (b) E and H
   (c) E and G
   (d) H
   (e) D

9. (a) 'Alcohol' is a member of the alkanol family and is called **ethanol**. It is made by the **fermentation** of glucose by **yeast**.

(b) The formula of 'alcohol' is C_2H_5OH or C_2H_6O.

carbon	$2 \times 12 = 24$
hydrogen	$6 \times 1 = 6$
oxygen	$1 \times 16 = \underline{16}$
formula mass	$= \textbf{46 amu}$

(c) The concentration or strength of alcohol can be increased by distillation.

CHAPTER THIRTEEN

► SELECTING INFORMATION

1. (a) 98°C   *(remember units)*
   (b) 81°C
   (c) 1669
   (d) green
   (e) 2.33 g/cm³
   (f) insoluble
   (g) 2, 8, 6
   (h) NO_3^-

2. (a) What is unusual about this reaction is that the temperature increases for a time but then it *decreases*.
   (b) about 40°C

3. (a) methanoic acid and concentrated sulphuric acid
   (b) Potassium hydroxide solution is an alkali which will react with the carbon dioxide and remove it from the mixture.
   Carbon monoxide gas will pass through the solution unaffected.
   (c) X is H_2O
   Find X by subtraction: $2H_2CO_2 - 2CO$
   $(H_4C_2O_4 - C_2O_2)$
   $= 2H_2O$

4. (a) An alloy is a mixture of a metal and other substances, usually other metals.
   (b)

Alloy	Percentage of nickel
constantan	40
German silver	15
monel	67
'silver' coins	25

   (c) copper and nickel

5. (a) sulphur dioxide and oxygen
   (b) sulphur trioxide
   (c) It is used in the manufacture of detergents and in the manufacture of sulphuric acid.
   (d) Super concentrated sulphuric acid is made by mixing sulphur trioxide and concentrated sulphuric acid.
   (e) SO_3

► PRESENTING INFORMATION

1. (a)

Compound	Boiling point (°C)
ethane	−88
butane	0
propane	−42
pentane	36
methane	−164

(b)

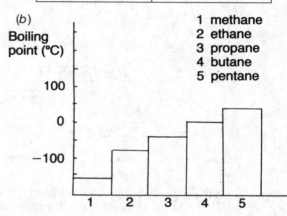

1 methane
2 ethane
3 propane
4 butane
5 pentane

Number of carbon atoms

(c) Pentane is a liquid at 10°C.
A substance is a liquid above its melting point and below its boiling point.
In this question the boiling points scale includes numbers greater than and also less than zero.

2. *A table is the obvious way to present this information.*

Components of glaze	Percentage amount
lead oxide	40
fine sand	30
soda	25
cobalt salt	5

A properly labelled pie chart or a bar chart would also be acceptable.

3. *(a)*

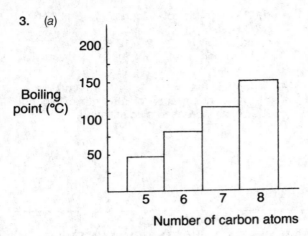

You will be awarded marks for the correct axes, labels and units. You will also get marks for accurately drawing the 'points' in the graph. Be sure to read the question carefully and determine if it is a bar or line graph that has to be drawn.
(b) about 180°C

4. *A word equation could be used to present this information.*

copper + sulphuric acid → sulphuric dioxide + water + copper(II) sulphate

A table with the headings 'Reactants' and 'Products' would also do.

5. *A key or flowchart is one way to present the information.*

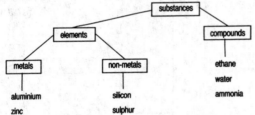

A table with the headings 'Metal elements', 'Non-metal elements' and 'Compounds' is another way to present this information.

6.

Aluminium compound	Use
aluminium oxide	abrasive in sandpaper
aluminium sulphate	water treatment
aluminium hydroxide	antacid
aluminium sodium silicate	food additive
sodium aluminium phosphate	food additive

7.

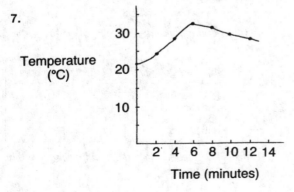

Marks will be deducted if the points which you draw are not accurate. The graph paper provided will be convenient for the figures which are given. Make use of most of the graph paper and take care in choosing the scale.

▶ SELECTING PROCEDURES

1. *(a)* C *The values of the voltages give the position of metals in the electrochemical series.*
(b) B *The meter indicates if the solution is conducting electricity or not.*

2. C, E, A, D and B

3. B, D, C and A

4. *(a)* Use a test tube with a stopper or side arm fitted with a rubber tube. Add zinc carbonate powder to dilute hydrochloric acid in the test tube. Bubble the gas which forms through lime water. The lime water will turn chalky.

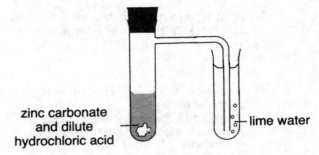

When describing an experiment or drawing a diagram the important question is 'will it work?' Learn to draw real pieces of equipment. A stencil may help you. You will see examples of diagrams all through this book. Lines from labels should be drawn with a ruler, and should touch the part of the experiment to which they refer. Remember that there are no square-shaped test tubes or pear-shaped beakers manufactured!
(b) Add the toffee to water so that some of it dissolves. Test the solution formed by heating it with Benedict's reagent. If the mixture turns a red colour, this shows that the toffee contains glucose.

5. Colin should put samples from the three bottles into three separate dry test tubes. A little piece of calcium should be added to each liquid. The one(s) which gave off bubbles (of hydrogen) contained some water. The one(s) which gave no bubbles should be used.

6. (a) Equal concentrations of each solution were used.
    (b) Ammonium sulphate is a salt (made from ammonium hydroxide and sulphuric acid) and does not have a pH of 7.
    (c) For neutralisation:
    volume × concentration × no. of H⁺ ions = volume × concentration × no. of OH⁻ ions
    25 × 1 × 1 is *not* equal to 30 × 1 × 1
    There is too much potassium hydroxide and so the solution will not be neutral, the pH will be greater than 7. The answer is **A**.
    Perhaps you were able to answer this just by looking at the question.

7. The manganese dioxide should be weighed before starting the experiment and its mass noted. After the experiment the remaining solution should be filtered, the recovered manganese dioxide left in the filter paper to dry and then reweighed. The mass will, of course, be the same as it was at the start.

8. (a) A, D and E
    Each has potassium nitrate solution, and there are two metals more active than iron and one metal less active.
    (b) B and D
    Same metal, copper, in each experiment. One contains water and the other potassium nitrate solution (an ionic solution).

9. Mass of glucose (or concentration of glucose solution), mass of yeast, volume of water and temperature of water.

10. D *Much of the ammonia will escape from A. In B you cannot be sure that the test tube will be full of ammonia. C will not be very effective because a lot of the ammonia will dissolve in the water. D is the correct, but messy, method!*

► CONCLUDING AND EXPLAINING

1. calcium and carbon *Look at the names of the elements in the reactants and products.*

2. (a) Substances which dissolve in water and conduct electricity have ionic bonding.
    (b) carbonates
    (c) sodium carbonate *Sodium ions in a compound give a yellow flame colour.*

3. Copper(II) oxide reacts with dilute sulphuric acid to give a copper(II) sulphate solution which is blue. *Carbon electrodes are used in electrolysis, so you may have guessed that carbon does not react with dilute sulphuric acid.*
    If the mixture of copper(II) oxide and carbon is roasted, it will react to form copper and carbon dioxide. The copper(II) oxide is 'reduced' by the carbon, as many metal oxides are.

4. (a) 126°C
    (b) hexane *(ethanol and propanone are not hydrocarbons)*
    (c) fractional distillation
    (d) The boiling points of the alkanes depends on their formula masses. The fm of heptane comes between those of hexane and octane. This means that its boiling point comes between those of the two alkanes.

5. (a) cadmium(II) oxide
    (b) mercury(I) chloride
    (c) thorium(II) chloride
    (d) chromium(III) oxide
    (e) manganese(II) sulphate
    (f) iron(III) nitrate
    In each compound the valency of the second part in the name is known. This allows the valency of the metal to be found.

6. (a) H_2CO_2
    (b) C
    (c) C_2H_4
    Each answer is found by subtraction.

7. (a) Copper reacts with mercury because copper is more active than mercury.
    (b) Nothing would happen. *Copper is less active than zinc.*
    (c) The boiling point of mercury is so low that it will easily boil when heated. The boiling point of silver is much too high for it to boil when heated.

► PREDICTING AND GENERALISING

1. (a) hydrogen   (b) inactive
    (c) hydrogen   (d) oxygen

2. (a)

Soluble in water	Insoluble in water
ammonium carbonate	calcium carbonate
ammonium sulphate	aluminium carbonate
ammonium chloride	calcium phosphate

    (b) In general, ammonium compounds are soluble in water.

3. (a) In general, the solubility of compounds in water increases as the temperature rises.
    (b) 40 g/l
    (c) 29°C
    (d) Solubility at 60°C is 40 g/l. At 40°C it is 20 g/l. The mass of crystals forming is 40 − 20 = 20 g.

4. (a) Decrease. *A gas, hydrogen, is being given off.*
   (b) Decrease. *A gas, carbon dioxide, is being given off.*
   (c) Remain the same. *Nothing is being added or given off.*
   (d) Increase. *Oxygen from the air is being added.*

5. (a) The carbonates of the three metals should be heated in turn in separate test tubes. The carbonate which gave off carbon dioxide most quickly was the carbonate of the least active metal, etc.
   (b) zinc carbonate → zinc oxide + carbon dioxide
   (c) Copper carbonate would decompose more quickly than zinc carbonate.

6. (a) Experiment 1
   (b) Experiment 1

   (c) It would be less than 2 minutes.
   (d) By heating the acid or by using powdered magnesium.
   (e) Equal volumes ensured a fair comparison.

7. (a) There may be microscopic holes in the skin of the balloon between the molecules or rubber.
   In a question of this nature any scientific answer which is relevant will be acceptable. Answers such as 'The balloon was faulty' will not be acceptable.
   (b) The smaller hydrogen molecules will be able to escape through the skin of the balloon more quickly than the larger oxygen molecules.
   (c) A balloon filled with xenon would go down very slowly because the large xenon molecules would have difficulty in escaping.

The Periodic Table

Showing symbol, relative atomic mass and atomic number (of selected elements)

Group I	Group II				Transition metals									Group III	Group IV	Group V	Group VI	Group VII	Group 0
										1 H 1 Hydrogen									4 He 2 Helium
7 Li 3 Lithium	9 Be 4 Beryllium													11 B 5 Boron	12 C 6 Carbon	14 N 7 Nitrogen	16 O 8 Oxygen	19 F 9 Fluorine	20 Ne 10 Neon
23 Na 11 Sodium	24 Mg 12 Magnesium													27 Al 13 Aluminium	28 Si 14 Silicon	31 P 15 Phosphorus	32 S 16 Sulphur	35·5 Cl 17 Chlorine	40 Ar 18 Argon
39 K 19 Potassium	40 Ca 20 Calcium	Sc 21 Scandium	Ti 22 Titanium	V 23 Vanadium	Cr 24 Chromium	Mn 25 Manganese	56 Fe 26 Iron	Co 27 Cobalt	59 Ni 28 Nickel	64 Cu 29 Copper	65 Zn 30 Zinc	Ga 31 Gallium	Ge 32 Germanium	As 33 Arsenic	Se 34 Selenium	80 Br 35 Bromine	Kr 36 Krypton
Rb 37 Rubidium	Sr 38 Strontium	Y 39 Yttrium	Zr 40 Zirconium	Nb 41 Niobium	Mo 42 Molybdenum	Tc 43 Technetium	Ru 44 Ruthenium	Rh 45 Rhodium	Pd 46 Palladium	108 Ag 47 Silver	Cd 48 Cadmium	In 49 Indium	119 Sn 50 Tin	Sb 51 Antimony	Te 52 Tellurium	127 I 53 Iodine	Xe 54 Xenon
Cs 55 Caesium	Ba 56 Barium	La 57 Lanthanium	Hf 72 Hafnium	Ta 73 Tantalum	W 74 Tungsten	Re 75 Rhenium	Os 76 Osmium	Ir 77 Iridium	195 Pt 78 Platinum	197 Au 79 Gold	201 Hg 80 Mercury	207 Tl 81 Thallium	207 Pb 82 Lead	Bi 83 Bismuth	Po 84 Polonium	At* 85 Astatine	Rn 86 Radon
Fr 87 Francium	Ra 88 Radium	Ac 89 Actinium															

Lanthanides

Ce 58 Cerium	Pr 59 Praseodymium	Nd 60 Neodymium	Pm 61 Promethium	Sm 62 Samarium	Eu 63 Europium	Gd 64 Gadolinium	Tb 65 Terbium	Dy 66 Dysprosium	Ho 67 Holmium	Er 68 Erbium	Tm 69 Thulium	Yb 70 Ytterbium	Lu 71 Lutetium

Actinides

Th 90 Thorium	Pa 91 Protactinium	U 92 Uranium	Np* 93 Neptunium	Pu* 94 Plutonium	Am* 95 Americium	Cm* 96 Curium	Bk* 97 Berkelium	Cf* 98 Californium	Es* 99 Einsteinium	Fm* 100 Fermium	Md* 101 Mendelevium	No* 102 Nobelium	Lr* 103 Lawrencium

Man-made elements

Relative atomic mass (simplified for calculations)

Symbol

Atomic number

Name

INDEX

edexcel
advancing learning, changing lives

Edexcel GCSE
Religious Studies

RE Dept

Unit 10
Roman Catholic Christianity

Please do not remove from the RE office without checking with Emy

Stephen Darlington

A PEARSON COMPANY

Published by Pearson Education Limited, a company incorporated in England and Wales, having its registered office at Edinburgh Gate, Harlow, Essex, CM20 2JE. Registered company number: 872828

www.pearsonschoolsandfecolleges.co.uk

Edexcel is a registered trademark of Edexcel Limited

Text © Pearson Education Ltd 2009

First published 2009

12 11 10 09 1
10 9 8 7 6 5 4 3 2 1

British Library Cataloguing in Publication Data
A catalogue record for this book is available from the British Library.
ISBN 978 1 846904 25 7

Edited by Florence Production Ltd, Stoodleigh, Devon
Typeset and illustrated by HL Studios, Long Hanborough, Oxford
Original illustrations © Pearson Education Ltd, 2009
Cover design by Pearson Education
Picture research by Zooid
Cover photo/illustration © South West Images Scotland/Alamy
Printed in Italy by Rotolito

Acknowledgements
The author and publisher would like to thank the following individuals and organisations for permission to reproduce copyright material:

67photo/Alamy, p. 92; Alessandra Benedetti/Corbis UK Ltd, p. 82; andrew parker/Alamy, p. 75; ArkReligion.com/Alamy, pp. 64, 68; Arte & Immagini Srl/ Corbis UK Ltd, p. 80; Brooklyn Museum/Corbis UK Ltd, p. 12; Chris Clark/Alamy, p. 50; Claudia Kunin/Corbis UK Ltd, p. 12; CoverSpot/Alamy, p. 83; David Barnet/Illustration Works/Corbis UK Ltd, p. 100; David Hartley/Rex Features, p. 96; David Hoffman Photo Library/Alamy, p. 111; David Karp/Associated Press/PA Photos, p. 92; Elizabeth Dalziel/Associated Press/PA Photos, p. 40; Francis G. Mayer/Corbis UK Ltd, p. 46; Franco Origlia/Getty Images, p. 44; frans lemmens/Alamy, p. 62; The Gallery Collection/Corbis UK Ltd, p. 8; Greenshoots Communications/Alamy, p. 75; imagebroker/Alamy, p. 74; Imagno/Getty Images, p. 46; Jackie Schear/Associated Press/PA Photos, p. 52; James Schutte/Alamy, p. 75; Jamie Grill/Corbis UK Ltd, p. 34; Janine Wiedel Photolibrary/Alamy, p. 38; Jennie Woodcock; Joern Sackermann/Alamy, p. 75; John Birdsall MR/PA Photos, pp. 89, 99, 104; JUPITERIMAGES/BananaStock/ Alamy, p. 6; Kevin Carter/Megan Patricia Carter Trust/Sygma/Corbis UK Ltd, p. 110; Kristian Dowling/Getty Images, p. 70; Lebrecht Music and Arts Photo Library/Alamy, p. 20; The London Art Archive/Alamy, pp. 16, 36; Magdalena Kucova/Shutterstock, p. 72; Mary Evans Picture Library/Alamy, pp. 70, 77; Matt Glover/KidzMatter Ministries Inc., p. 90; Michael Dwyer/Alamy, pp. 60–61; Mike Abrahams/Alamy, p. 89; Mike Hayward/photoshropshire.com/ Alamy, p. 89; Moodboard/Corbis UK Ltd, p. 18; Paul J. Richards/AFP/Getty Images, p. 102; Philippe Lissac/Godong/Corbis UK Ltd, p. 89; Photo Scala, Florence, pp. 10, 15; Pietro Baguzzi/akg-images, p. 42; Plinio Lepri/Associated Press/PA Photos, p. 94; Reflections Photolibrary/Corbis UK Ltd, p. 76; Reuters/Corbis UK Ltd, p. 61; Robert F. Bukaty/Associated Press/PA Photos, p. 26; Roger Coulam/Alamy, p. 74; Ron Giling/Still Pictures, p. 89; Science Photo Library/Science Photo Library, p. 8; Sean Gallup/Getty Images, p. 66; Stan Kujawa/Alamy, p. 108; TOPICMedia/ H. Heine/Alamy, p. 75; Wojtek Radwanski/AFP/Getty Images, p. 54; www.CartoonStock.com, p. 78.

Every effort has been made to contact copyright holders of material reproduced in this book. Any omissions will be rectified in subsequent printings if notice is given to the publishers.

Websites
There are links to relevant websites in this book. In order to ensure that the links are up to date, that the links work, and that the sites are not inadvertently linked to sites that could be considered offensive, we have made the links available on the Heinemann website at www.heinemann. co.uk/hotlinks. When you access the site, the express code is 4257P.

Disclaimer
This material has been published on behalf of Edexcel and offers high-quality support for the delivery of Edexcel qualifications.

This does not mean that the material is essential to achieve any Edexcel qualification, nor does it mean that it is the only suitable material available to support any Edexcel qualification. Edexcel material will not be used verbatim in setting any Edexcel examination or assessment. Any resource lists produced by Edexcel shall include this and other appropriate resources.

Copies of official specifications for all Edexcel qualifications may be found on the Edexcel website: www.edexcel.com

Contents

RE Dept.

Welcome to this Edexcel GCSE in Religious Studies Resource

These resources have been written to support fully Edexcel's new specification for GCSE Religious Studies. Each student book covers one unit of the specification which makes up a Short Course qualification. Any two units from separate modules of the specification make up a Full Course qualification. Written by experienced examiners and packed with exam tips and activities, these books include lots of engaging features to enthuse students and provide the range of support needed to make teaching and learning a success for all ability levels.

Features in this book

In each section you will find the following features:

- **An introductory spread** which introduces the topics and gives the Edexcel key terms and learning outcomes for the whole section.

- **Topic spreads** containing the following features:

- **Learning outcomes** for the topic

- edexcel ⠿ key terms

> **Specification key terms** – are emboldened and defined for easy reference

- **Sacred text references** include any references which are used in the topic or would be useful for students to look at. Students must have a thorough understanding of those which are emboldened, as these are the references that appear in the specification

- **Activities** and **For discussion** panels provide stimulating tasks for the classroom and homework

- A topic **Summary** captures the main learning points.

How to use this book

This book has been written to support you through your Edexcel Religious Studies GCSE paper Module C Unit 10 Roman Catholic Christianity.

Throughout the series the version of the Bible is the New International edition.

The book is split into the four sections of the specification. In the book you will find the following:

A dedicated suite of revision resources for complete exam success. We've broken down the six stages of revision to ensure that you are prepared every step of the way.

How to get into the perfect 'zone' for your revision.

Tips and advice on how to effectively plan your revision.

Revision activities and exam-style practice at the end of every section plus additional exam practice at the end of the book.

Last-minute advice for just before the exam.

An overview of what you will have to do in the exam, plus a chance to see what a real exam paper will look like.

What do you do after your exam? This section contains information on how to get your results and answers to frequently asked questions on what to do next.

ResultsPlus

These features are based on how students have performed in past exams. They are combined with expert advice and guidance from examiners to show you how to achieve better results.

There are four different types of ResultsPlus features throughout this book:

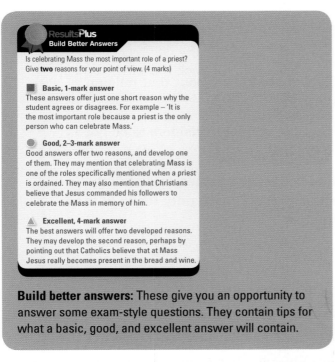

Build better answers: These give you an opportunity to answer some exam-style questions. They contain tips for what a basic, good, and excellent answer will contain.

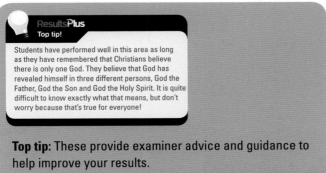

Top tip: These provide examiner advice and guidance to help improve your results.

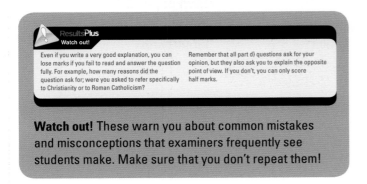

Watch out! These warn you about common mistakes and misconceptions that examiners frequently see students make. Make sure that you don't repeat them!

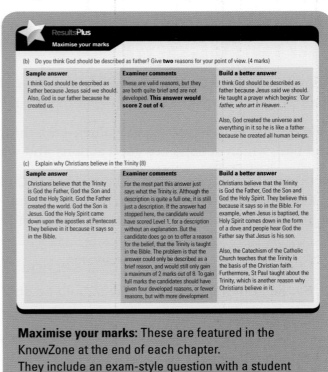

Maximise your marks: These are featured in the KnowZone at the end of each chapter.
They include an exam-style question with a student answer, examiner comments and an improved answer so that you can see how to build a better response.

Beliefs and values

Introduction

All religions have certain key beliefs and if we really want to know about that religion then we must start by knowing what those beliefs are.

Side by side with beliefs come values – the things that the religion considers to be good and bad, which actions are good actions and which are bad.

In this section we are going to be looking at Christian beliefs and values, and at Catholic beliefs and values in particular. Because Catholicism is part of Christianity many of those beliefs and values are the same, but not all of them are.

> ### Learning outcomes for this section
>
> By the end of this section you should be able to understand:
>
> - what Christians mean when they say God is Unity and Trinity
> - what Christians believe about God as creator and why they call God their father
> - what Christians believe when they say Jesus is the Son of God born of a Virgin Birth, and how he was resurrected
> - what role the Holy Spirit has in the lives of Christians
> - what Christians believe about sin and salvation
> - how Christians believe people can show their love for God and each other.

edexcel ▦ key terms

atonement	creeds	monotheism	Trinity
catechism	faith	repentance	Unity
compassion	incarnation	salvation	Virgin Birth

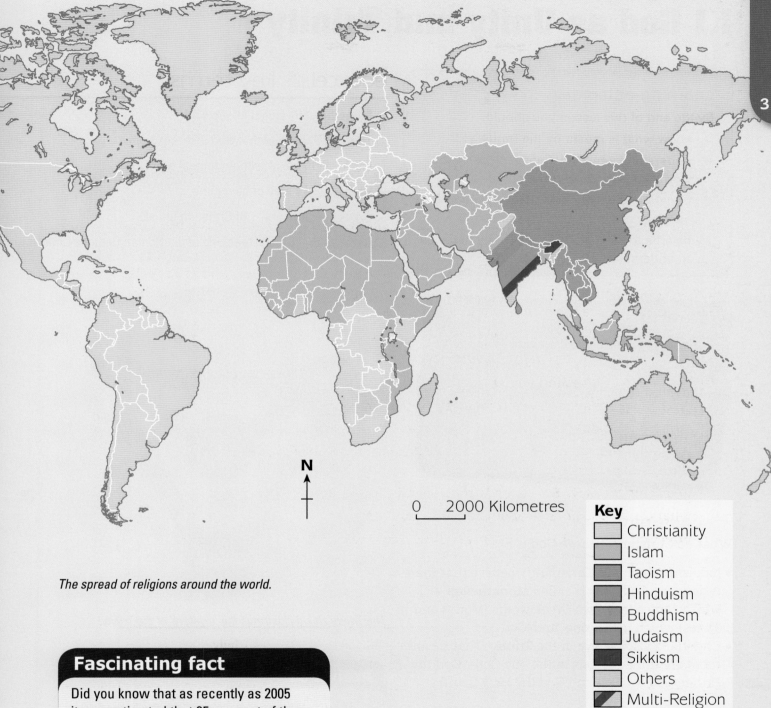

The spread of religions around the world.

Key
- Christianity
- Islam
- Taoism
- Hinduism
- Buddhism
- Judaism
- Sikkism
- Others
- Multi-Religion

Fascinating fact

Did you know that as recently as 2005 it was estimated that 85 per cent of the world's population say they believe in God? That's over five billion people. Of those five billion, about two billion are Christians, and of those Christians, over one billion are Catholics. (The remaining three billion either do not have a religious faith or live in countries in which religion is outlawed.)

The map and fascinating fact show that there are a lots of Christians in the world and about half of all Christians are Roman Catholics. In small groups, draw ideas maps of everything that you already know about what Catholics believe. You could come back to this at the end of the section and update your ideas map with all you have learned.

1.1 God as Unity and Trinity

Learning outcomes

By the end of this lesson you should:

- know what is meant by the Trinity
- understand why Christians believe in one God who is made of three persons
- understand why both God as unity and God as Trinity are important for Christians
- be able to evaluate how the Trinity helps us to understand the nature of God.

edexcel ⠿ key terms

Monotheism – Belief in one God.

Trinity – The belief that God is three in one.

Faith – Firm belief without logical proof.

Unity – God's way of being one.

Creeds – Statements of Christian belief.

Catechism – Official teaching of the Roman Catholic Church.

Sacred texts

Jesus says the Father will send the Holy Spirit
John 14:16–17

The Father sends the Holy Spirit upon his Son
Matthew 3:16–17

St Paul invokes the Trinity
2 Corinthians 13:14

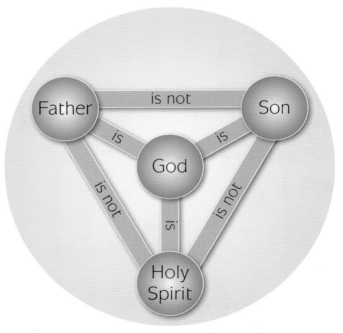

The Trinity shield illustrates the 'mystery' of the Trinity.

Three-in-one

What do Christians believe God is like?

- Judaism, Islam and Christianity believe that there is only one God. This is called **Monotheism** – which comes from two Greek words (Monos and Theos) which mean 'one' and 'God'.
- Christians also believe in the **Trinity**. That means there are three persons in the one God – God the Father, God the Son and God the Holy Spirit.

If you find this confusing, don't worry! For 2000 years some of the wisest Christians have tried to explain the idea of the Trinity and have only partly succeeded. Even today it is called the 'mystery' of the Trinity for that reason! It is something Christians believe as a matter of **faith**.

Activities

1 Draw a shamrock and write 'God the Father', 'God the Son' and 'God the Holy Spirit' onto each of the three petals. Does the shamrock have one leaf or three? This is how St Patrick, the patron saint of Ireland, tried to explain the mystery of the Trinity.

Meaning and importance of God as unity

Unity means 'being one'. For Christians, God is unity which means that there is only one God and everything comes from him. Christians believe this because the Bible and the Christian Churches teach it. The first of the Ten Commandments tells people to only worship the one God and not to worship idols.

The unity of God is important for Christians because:

- it means the God worshipped by the Jews, and later by Christians and Muslims, is the only true God
- this one God is more important than anything else
- if he is the only God, then all people on earth should be united, as brothers and sisters, in worshipping him and in obeying him.

Activities

2 What 'idols' might some people 'worship' today? Jot down some ideas and then discuss how you think Christians would respond to this.

The meaning and importance of God as Trinity

Christians believe in God as three separate persons, each having separate roles:

- Christians believe that God is the creator, and therefore the father of everything that exists.
- Jesus, who came down to earth and died on the cross to save people from sin, is the Son of God.
- The Holy Spirit is the presence of God on Earth.

Many Christians believe that the Trinity is basically a way of describing what God is like and the different roles and powers he has. If you take away one of the three then that characteristic cannot be explained by the other two and some essential part of God would be missing. For example, without 'the Son' Christians would have no means of being forgiven by God, without the Holy Spirit Christians would not be able to feel God's presence today, and so on. The Trinity is therefore important for Christians because it is at the heart of their beliefs about God's different roles and powers.

Why do Christians believe in the Trinity?

Christians believe the Trinity is the basis of the Christian faith because:

- There is evidence of the Trinity at work in the Old Testament.
- When Jesus was baptised, God the Father and the Holy Spirit were present.
- When Jesus commissioned the disciples he referred to the Trinity, he told them to go and baptise in the name of the Father, Son and Holy Spirit.
- The Trinity is a key teaching of the Christian Churches. All the **creeds** and the **Catechism** speak of one God seen in three persons.

Activities

3 On the shamrock that you drew in Activity 1, write details of the characteristics of each part of God – Father, Son and Holy Spirit.

4 Work in pairs. One of you should explain to the other why the Unity of God is important for Christians, then the other should explain why the Trinity is important for Christians.

 Results**Plus**
Top tip!

Students have performed well in this area as long as they have remembered that Christians believe there is only one God. They believe that God has revealed himself in three different persons, God the Father, God the Son and God the Holy Spirit. It is quite difficult to know exactly what that means, but don't worry because that's true for everyone!

Summary

- Christians believe in one God who is made up of three different persons – the Father, the Son and the Holy Spirit.
- The creeds and the Catechism make it clear that belief in the Trinity is an essential part of the Christian faith.

1.2 God the Father

Learning outcomes

By the end of this lesson you should:

- know what Christians mean when they call God their father
- understand why the belief that God is their father is important for Christians
- understand what qualities Christians believe God displays as a father
- be able to evaluate whether the idea that God is a father helps Christians understand the nature of God.

Sacred texts

Our Father (The Lord's Prayer)
Matthew 6:9–13

Father's Love
John 14:23–25

Children of God
Romans 8:14–17

Our father

When Jesus' apostles asked him to teach them to pray he told them to use these words, 'Our Father, who art in Heaven…'. It is clear that Jesus wanted his followers to see God as their father, as someone who will always look after them. If God is a father to all people, then all people are brothers and sisters, and members of one family.

Activities

1 Make a list of words you think would best describe what a father should be like. Try to put them in order, starting with the word which you think to be the most important.

2 What five most important words describe how brothers and sisters should treat each other?

Our Father who art in Heaven
Hallowed be thy name
Thy kingdom come
Thy will be done on earth

Give us this day our daily bread
Forgive us our trespasses
Deliver us from evil

Jesus said we should think of God as being like a father.

God as a father

Jesus often used the word 'father' when talking about his own relationship with God. Before Jesus said that God was like a father, many religions viewed God more as a king or a judge.

- Jesus refers to God as 'Abba', an affectionate name used by children, perhaps best translated as 'dad'. Jesus wanted his followers to look upon God with the same respect and affection as they looked upon their own fathers.

- For Christians, God the Father is a loving and caring God, someone who will give his children their 'daily bread' and will forgive them when they do something wrong. To look upon God in this way is something special to Christianity.
- If God is a father to all people, then all people are brothers and sisters.
- The Apostles Creed, which is one of the earliest statements of Christian belief, starts with the words: 'I believe in God, the Father almighty'.

Fathers also make rules

In a sense God is like a biological father, because he created all human beings. But as we have seen, the Christian idea of God as a father is much more complex.

- It also includes something of the Old Testament idea of God as ruler and law-maker. Just as a father often needs to direct and guide his children, so God is seen by Christians as a guide to what is right and wrong.
- Earthly fathers have to set rules for their children, to protect them, and may even have to punish them if they break the rules. In the same way, God the heavenly father gives his children the Commandments and Jesus' teaching.
- The Catechism says that God provides authority for his children in the same way as a father.

Activities

3 Read the prayer 'Our Father' (The Lord's Prayer). Think carefully what each of the phrases mean (such as 'hallowed be thy name'; 'forgive us our trespasses'). Then write each phrase out again in your own words so that you can understand its meaning better. You might need a dictionary!

For discussion

Do we treat **all** other human beings as our brothers and sisters?

Activities

4 Does it make God into less of a caring father if he is also seen as someone who makes rules, and punishes people who break those rules?

ResultsPlus
Build better answers

Should God be described as father?
Give **two** reasons for your point of view. (4 marks)

■ **Basic, 1-mark answer**
One brief reason with no development. For example, 'We should call God father because Jesus said we should'.

● **Good, 2–3-mark answer**
- Develop the reason, by mentioning that Jesus said we should pray to God using the prayer 'Our Father'. (2 marks)
- Add another reason such as 'God should be called father because he created us'. (3 marks)

▲ **Excellent, 4-mark answer**
Also develop the second reason, for example point out how that is similar to the way we refer to our earthly fathers, who were also involved in our creation.

Summary

- Jesus said we should pray to God as 'Our Father'.
- Christians see God as their father because he created everyone.
- Christians also call God their father because he treats people the way a father treats his children: caring, forgiving, but also setting rules to guide us.
- Because they consider God to be their father, Christians believe that we are all brothers and sisters and members of God's family.

1.3 God the Creator

8

Learning outcomes

By the end of this lesson you should:

- know what Christians believe about the origins of the universe
- understand why Christians believe that God created everything that exists
- be able to explain why the belief in God as Creator is important for Christians
- be able to evaluate the importance of the belief in God as Creator for Christians.

Sacred texts

The Creation
Genesis, Chapter 1

The Creation speaks of God
Psalm 19:1

John proclaims God as creator
John 1:3

Was the world created in six days, or over billions of years?

How did the world come to exist?

The question of how the universe came to exist is one of the most important questions of all.

Christians, like believers from most religions, say that God created the world and everything in it. The story of Creation can be found in Genesis, the first book of the Bible. 'Genesis' means 'beginning'.

According to Genesis, God created human beings as the final part of Creation. He created them in his own image.

On the other hand, some scientists, who do not believe that God exists, continue to look for a totally scientific explanation of how the universe began, which does not rely on a belief in God.

Chapter 1 of Genesis also teaches us that God's creation was 'good' (Genesis 1:31). This means that anything wrong with our world is the result of what human beings have done. God gave men and women free will and at times they have used that free will to act in a harmful way.

But they still insist that God is the creator, who created the universe by setting off the 'big bang'. Most Catholics also accept the scientific evidence that human beings evolved from simpler life forms.

The Catechism teaches that scientific discoveries about the origins of the world should increase our admiration for the greatness of God the Creator.

Activities

1 Read the story of Creation in Genesis. Draw six boxes, and in each box write down what the story says God created on each of the six days.

2 Create two lists:
- A list of those things in the world which you consider to be good (such as the beauty of lakes and mountains)
- A list of those things which you think are bad (such as war and disease).

How fair is it to say that God's creation is 'good'? Can humans be blamed for all the bad things?

Did God create the world?

There are some very famous arguments which try to prove that the universe must have been created by God. Two of the most famous are about cause and effect, and design:

- The cause and effect argument says that everything that exists has been caused by something else. So there must be a first cause outside of the universe that caused the universe itself to come into existence. That first cause is said to be God.
- The design argument says that because the world is so well designed and so beautiful, it must have been designed by someone with great intelligence. That someone must be God.

Scientists often talk about a 'big bang' millions of years ago as the cause of the universe. Some Christians disagree with this. Creationists, for example, think that the story of Creation in the Bible is literally true, and that the world was created in six days less than 10,000 years ago.

Most Catholics accept that the universe came into existence about ten billion years ago, and many think that it came about as a result of a 'big bang'.

Why God as Creator is important for Christians

- The creation story shows that God is all-powerful (omnipotent) as he created everything.
- God created everything, including people for a purpose. This means that Christians should trust in God.
- As God created the world it shows that it is important to Him. He created people to look after and be 'stewards' of the Earth. Therefore Christians believe that they should care for God's creation.
- Because God created all life, it is sacred and should be respected.
- Since God created humans in his own image they are a particularly important part of creation.
- It is a key teaching of the Christian Churches as the Apostle's Creed states that God is the creator of Heaven and Earth.

Activities

3 Prepare a PowerPoint® presentation which explains why believing in God as Creator is important for Christians.

Summary

- Christians believe that God created the whole universe and also human beings.
- Some Christians believe this happened in six days, as it says in the Book of Genesis.
- Catholics and many other Christians believe in the 'big bang' and in evolution.
- It is essential for Christians that God is the origin of everything and that, because God is good, his creation is also good.

1.4 Jesus, the Son of God

10

Learning outcomes

By the end of this lesson you should:

● understand what is meant by saying that Jesus is both God and man

● understand why it is important for Christians that Jesus is the Son of God

● be able to evaluate how Christianity would change if Jesus was not the Son of God.

edexcel ::: key terms

Incarnation – The belief that God took human form in Jesus.

Virgin Birth – The belief that Jesus was not conceived through sex.

Sacred texts

Jesus is 'God-with-us'
Matthew 1:23

The Transfiguration
Matthew 17:1–9

Peter's profession of faith
Matthew 16:15–16

Who was Jesus?

Many people who aren't Christians have great respect for Jesus. Some say he was a great teacher, others that he was a prophet sent by God. But for Christians, Jesus is even more important than that.

In the picture we see a moment in Jesus' life called the Transfiguration. Jesus climbed a mountain with some of his apostles. He began to shine, like a bright light. The apostles heard the voice of God say 'This is my Son, listen to him'.

It is important for us to understand what God meant when he said that Jesus was his son. The word 'son' is used in different ways to mean different things. There are biological sons,

'They heard a voice say, "This is my Son, the Beloved".'

adopted sons, stepsons and foster sons. Sometimes priests use the expression 'my son' when speaking to a member of their parish. In American slang an older man might use the term 'son' when addressing someone younger.

Activities

1 Write down as many different types and uses of the word 'son' as you can think of. In just a sentence or two for each, explain what the word 'son' means in each case.

Jesus – God and man

Jesus would have been known as Jesus Bar Joseph (which means 'son of Joseph'). But the Gospels tell us that Joseph was Jesus' foster father. Christians believe in what is called the **Virgin Birth** – that Mary gave birth to Jesus without having had sexual intercourse. Jesus was therefore conceived through a miraculous act of God. It is God, not Joseph, who is the father of Jesus.

When God called Jesus his son, he didn't mean his biological son. He wanted us to know that Jesus is God. As you and I are human because our parents are human, so Jesus is God because his father is God. At the same time, Jesus is also human because his mother, Mary, was human, and she gave birth to Jesus in a normal physical sense. This event is known as the **Incarnation**. Rather like the Trinity, this idea is not at all easy to understand – another mystery!

For discussion

Catholics believe that Mary was a virgin when Jesus was born. They also believe that Mary and Joseph had no children and so Jesus had no brothers or sisters. Discuss why both these things are thought by Catholics to be so important.

Son of God

Jesus was a wise teacher, and what he taught is held in great respect even 2000 years later. So, is it really important whether or not Jesus was the Son of God? For Christians it is essential because:

- It meant that when Jesus told people that their sins were forgiven (for example in Matthew 9:1–8), he had the authority to do that.
- It meant that Jesus' teachings about how to live a good life were not just wise, but also they came directly from God.
- It gives meaning to Jesus' death and resurrection. He had the power to come back from the dead. This proved that he was God, confirmed that he has saved everyone from their sins, and promised life after death for everyone.
- It means that Jesus didn't just live 2000 years ago in Israel, but he is 'the alpha and the omega, the beginning and the end'. In other words he has always existed, he lives now, and he will live for all eternity.

Activities

2 Read the account of the Transfiguration. There are other times in the Gospels where Jesus is called the Son of God. Explain why this occasion might be seen as particularly important.

3 Draw a spider diagram of all the reasons why it is important to Christians that Jesus is the Son of God. What do you think is the most important reason for Christians to believe that Jesus is God? Why did you choose that reason?

4 What difference would it make to Christianity if it could be proved that Jesus wasn't God? You could discuss this in class.

Summary

- Christians believe Jesus is the Son of God.
- Christians worship Jesus as God.
- Because Jesus is God, everything he said and did – his teachings, his miracles and, most of all, his death and resurrection – are all given special meaning and importance for Christians.

1.5 Jesus, the Son of God (2)

12

Learning outcomes

By the end of this lesson you should:

- know what the Gospels tell us about the life of Jesus
- understand the importance to Christians of Jesus' death and resurrection
- be able to evaluate whether the Christian faith depends on the truth of the death and resurrection of Jesus.

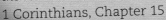

Sacred texts

The death and resurrection of Jesus
Matthew, Chapters 27 and 28

St Peter proclaims the death and resurrection
Acts 2:22–24

St Paul states the importance of belief in the resurrection
1 Corinthians, Chapter 15

Christians believe that Jesus died on the cross, but rose again after three days.

What do we know of Jesus' life?

Most of the evidence about the life of Jesus comes from the accounts in the Gospels, but references to Jesus can also be found in the writings of Jewish and Roman historians who lived at around the same time. From the Gospels we learn that:

- Before Jesus' birth an angel told Mary that her child would be the Son of God. Jesus was born to Mary in Bethlehem in Judea (now part of Israel). Choirs of angels announced his birth to shepherds, and Wise Men from the East visited him.
- When Jesus was in his late twenties he began to teach and perform miracles. He gathered around him a large number of followers, called disciples.

- His teaching upset the Jewish leaders and they called for his execution, saying that he had offended against the Jewish religion and was also a threat to the authority of the Roman Empire. The Roman Governor Pontius Pilate ordered his execution by crucifixion.
- His disciples said that three days after his death Jesus rose again, and appeared to them on various occasions. Eventually they saw him ascend from the earth and return to Heaven.

Activities

1 Jesus died by crucifixion. Find out all you can about this Roman death penalty. How did those who were crucified die? What sorts of people were crucified?

Jesus' death and resurrection

St Paul wrote that if Jesus did not rise from the dead, then the whole of the Christian faith was pointless. Why is this belief of such importance to Christians?

- By allowing his own son to die, God showed his love for the world.
- Because Jesus died to save everyone from sin, his death means that all people have been given salvation.
- God alone has the power to rise from the dead, so Jesus' resurrection proves that he is the Son of God.
- Because Jesus proved himself to be the Son of God, everything that he taught has divine authority.
- Because Jesus rose from the dead, Christians believe that everyone has the hope of life after death.
- Jesus is no longer limited by space and time, and so is alive in the world today. He is present in the bread and wine when Christians celebrate the Eucharist.

Most Christians believe in what is known as the 'empty tomb' – that on Easter Sunday the body of Jesus rose from the dead and the tomb in which he had been placed was empty. However, some Christians believe that the body of Jesus did not rise from the dead, but only that his spirit lived on, and this gave courage and hope to the apostles.

Activities

2 Do you think that the story of the life of Jesus told by the apostles is accurate? Which details are easier to believe and which are more difficult? Why? Discuss this with your teacher.

3 'If Christ has not been raised your faith is pointless and you have not been released from your sins.' So says St Paul in his first letter to the Corinthians. Do you agree with him? Write a short article which looks at both sides of the argument.

The Ascension

Forty days after Jesus' resurrection, he took his apostles up onto a mountain and they watched him ascend into Heaven. It is part of Christian belief that Jesus now sits at God's right hand and that at the end of time he will come again to judge the living and the dead. At first the apostles were frightened that Jesus was no longer with them. But before he left them he promised that he would send the Holy Spirit to them to give them courage and guidance.

Summary

- Christians believe that Jesus died on the cross and then rose again from the dead.
- Jesus' death means that everyone has been saved from sin and his resurrection gives hope that there is life after death.
- Jesus' resurrection proves that Jesus was God and that his teachings have come directly from God.
- Many Christians believe that their entire faith depends on the truth of the death and resurrection of Jesus.

1.6 The Holy Spirit

Learning outcomes

By the end of this lesson you should:

- understand why Christians believe that the Holy Spirit is part of God
- understand the role of the Holy Spirit at Pentecost
- understand how Christians believe the Holy Spirit works in the world today.

Sacred texts

The Holy Spirit present at the Creation
Genesis 1:2

The Holy Spirit gives life to dry bones
Ezekiel 37:1–14

The Descent of the Holy Spirit upon the Apostles
Acts 2:1–13

God the Holy Spirit

- Christians talk a lot about God the Father and Jesus, God the Son, but not so much about the Holy Spirit. This is not because they believe the third person of the Trinity to be less important, but because the Holy Spirit works in ways that are less obvious.
- In fact in the Old Testament God is never called the Holy Spirit by name, but we are aware of what God does as the Holy Spirit. In the Bible, each time the Holy Spirit performs an action he brings new life or new hope.
- To help describe the work of the Holy Spirit, it is sometimes said to be like water, sometimes like fire, and sometimes like the air (in the wind or in breath).

'The Holy Spirit is like a burning fire.'

Activities

1 Think about water, fire and air. Think about the good things that come from each of them, for example, water can help things to grow and fire can make you feel warm. How many can you think of?

Pentecost

The most famous act of the Holy Spirit was when he came down upon the apostles at Pentecost, after the ascension of Jesus. The apostles were afraid because they no longer had Jesus physically present among them, and they hid themselves away in a locked room. But the Holy Spirit came upon them and gave them courage. He inspired them to leave the room and preach about Jesus, even though it meant risking their lives.

Activities

2 Look at the following passages from Luke's Gospel, and create a spider diagram with the Holy Spirit at the centre. Write down briefly what the role of the Holy Spirit is in each of these passages.

Luke 1:15, 1:35, 1:41, 1:67, 2:26, 3:22, 4:1, 4:14, 4:18

The Holy Spirit gave the apostles courage and hope to go and preach what Jesus had taught them.

Why is the Holy Spirit important to Christians?

- Christians believe the Holy Spirit is God acting in the world today.
- They believe the Holy Spirit is working to make us better people. The qualities we develop are called Fruits of the Spirit, such as love, kindness and faithfulness.
- Christians also believe that they can call upon the Holy Spirit for guidance when they face difficult moral decisions and for courage when they try to live up to life's challenges.
- Catholics believe that the Holy Spirit guides the leaders of the Church, so they can look to the Church when they want to know what God wants them to do.

There are many examples of Christians who claimed that the Holy Spirit has inspired their work, such as Mother Theresa, or acts of courage, such as Maximilian Kolbe and Oscar Romero.

Activities

3 Get into pairs, then, one at a time, give reasons why the Holy Spirit is important to Christians.

4 Find out about the life of one of the Christian martyrs of the 20th century. What kinds of qualities do you think a person needs to be a martyr? Prepare a short talk for the rest of the class.

Summary

- The Holy Spirit is God, the third person of the Trinity.
- Christians believe the Holy Spirit has been active throughout history, giving people new life and courage in times of trial.
- Christians believe the Holy Spirit gives wisdom to individuals and to the Church, so they can understand better what God wants them to do.
- In the courageous lives of modern martyrs we see that the Holy Spirit is still active today.

1.7 Salvation from sin

Learning outcomes

By the end of this lesson you should:

- understand what Christians mean by 'sin' and 'salvation'
- be able to explain how Christians believe they have been saved by Jesus' crucifixion
- understand the importance for Christians of repentance and the commitment to leading a good moral life.

edexcel ⠿ key terms

Atonement – Reconciliation between God and humanity.

Repentance – The act of being sorry for wrongdoing and deciding not to do it again.

Salvation – The act of deliverance from sin, or being saved from evil.

Those who live a good life go to Heaven.

Sin

'Sin' is a very short word but in many ways it is one of the most important of all the words we will come across in this course. A sin is an action which is against God's rules. Catholics believe that if we die without our sins being forgiven, we may go to Purgatory or even to Hell rather than to Heaven.

- Purgatory is a temporary place of purification to which people with unforgiven sins are believed to go after death.
- Hell is a place of eternal punishment reserved for those who die having committed serious sins for which they have not shown **repentance**.

Some Christians believe that throughout our lives our main task is to try to avoid doing sinful things, and that's not easy. It sometimes seems as though our lives are full of things that are considered sinful.

Activities

1   Think of as many things as possible that might be thought of as sins. Write them up on the board, or in your books. It may be quite a long list! Then separate them into two lists – the ones you think are serious and those that are less serious. What is the difference?

2   Discuss what you think Heaven and Hell might be like. Some Christians say that Hell doesn't really exist. If it didn't, would that make a difference to the way people behave?

Christian beliefs about sin

According to the Bible, people started sinning as soon as they were created, and have carried on sinning throughout history. Christians believe that God is without sin. However, original sin is the sin inherited from when Adam and Eve disobeyed God. Some Christians believe that all humans are born with original sin. This is different from sins which an individual commits – personally disobeying God.

Christians also believe that, without God's help, people would just carry on sinning, and do a lot of damage to the world and to their fellow human beings.

Activities

3 Why do people sin? Go back through the list of sins that you created in Activity 1 and try to explain the motives for why people behave in this way. Do they have something in common?

What is salvation?

When we do things wrong we often have to suffer the consequences. But God doesn't want to punish people, he prefers to offer them **salvation**. Salvation means being saved from sin. That's one of the reasons why God sent his Son. All of Jesus' teachings, and the example of his own life, show us how to live a selfless, sin-free life.

This priest is waiting to hear people's confessions. Catholics believe that the sacrament of confession is an important part of achieving salvation.

When Jesus, the Son of God, died on the cross, he was not being punished for his own sins (he was sinless) but for other people's sins. This is often called the act of **Atonement**.

This doesn't mean that people can behave however they want to because Jesus has saved us! What it means is that Jesus has brought the possibility of salvation to humankind. If people are truly sorry for the bad things they have done, try to put things right and ask God to forgive them, this leads to their own reconciliation with God. For Catholics, sins can be forgiven through the act of confession – confessing your sins to a priest.

Salvation is of central importance to all Christians because:

- If a Christian is saved from sin it means they will have eternal life in Heaven.
- Jesus' life, death and resurrection were about bringing salvation to all people; so it must be what God wants for the world.
- The belief in salvation encourages Christians to live good lives and behave towards others in a loving way.

Activities

4 Write a short story in which someone has done something wrong, but another person takes the blame and the punishment. Explain the possible reasons why they are willing to do this.

5 Explain what is meant by 'salvation' and why it is important for Christians.

Summary

- Christians believe that if they live a sinful life they risk eternal punishment.
- God doesn't want to punish us and so he sent his Son to die on the cross to take away our sins. That is what is meant by salvation.
- God still expects people to live sinless lives, or at least be genuinely sorry when they do wrong.

1.8 The importance of loving God

By the end of this lesson you should:

- understand what Christians mean when they say they love God
- understand why Christians believe that loving God is so important
- understand the ways in which Christians try to show their love for God and how this affects their lives.

Loving God

Jesus said that his followers should love God as they would love their father. This sounds simple, but 'love' is not an easy word to understand and can mean many different things. Loving someone is to do with how we feel and behave towards them, but it can be a lot more than that.

Activities

1 Here are a few of the feelings and actions through which we might show love for our fathers or mothers:
   - spending time with them
   - helping them with their work
   - listening to their advice
   - looking after them when they are sick.

   What else would you add to the list and why?

Sacred texts

Love the Lord your God
Deuteronomy 6:4–9

If we don't love, we don't know God
1 John 4:8

We love because God loves us
1 John 4:19

For Christians, God is like a loving father.

The importance of loving God for Christians

People often wonder about the meaning of life. What is the point of our existence? For Christians the answer is clear – we exist in order to love God.

Some years ago Catholic children were taught religion using a little book of questions and answers, often called the Penny Catechism. The first question was, 'Who made you?' Answer: 'God made me'. The second question was, 'Why did God make you?' Answer: 'God made me to know him, love him and serve him.' Christians believe that God created people as an act of love, and the point and meaning of our existence is that we can love God in return.

The reasons why loving God is so important for Christians are:

- All Christian Churches teach that love of God is fundamental to the Christian faith - from this everything else comes.
- Jesus taught that loving God was the most important of God's commandments.
- It is through loving God that Christians can hope for eternal life with him.
- It is through the love of God that Christians find the inspiration and strength to show their love of others through their deeds and actions – helping to make the world a better place.

The idea that God wants to have a personal relationship with every human being is one of the most important ideas within the Christian faith. Christians see God as a father. He is not seen simply as a law-maker or a remote ruler. Christians believe that God knows us, talks and listens to us, as individuals. He loves each person as his own child.

For discussion

Look again at your list of the ways we can love our parents. Can we show our love for God in the same ways? How? Are there different ways that we can show our love for God in our everyday lives? Think of some examples. This could be discussed in groups or with the whole class.

Loving the God we cannot see

So how do Christians 'love' God?

- Through talking to him regularly through prayer.
- Through learning more about him by reading the Bible and going to Church.
- Through following the teachings of the Bible and the Church.
- Through living their lives as God wants them to.

St John acknowledged that it can be quite a challenge to love God when we can't see him. On the other hand, we can see the world and the people God created. St John says we can show our love for God by loving our fellow human beings. This is why Jesus spoke of the love of God and the love of others as though they went hand in hand.

Activities

2 St Augustine once said, 'Love and do what you will'. Do you agree that any action is acceptable, provided it is motivated by love? Is it possible to lie or even to kill someone out of love?

3 Write an article for a church magazine entitled 'Why loving God is so important for Christians'.

Summary

- Christians believe that God created human beings to love, and also so that they could love God in return.
- For Christians, God is someone with whom we can have a personal relationship.
- That means that loving God is the most important act of a Christian, and that love must be the reason for everything we do.
- Because God can seem far away, we have to look for special ways of showing God how much we love him.

1.9 Christian teaching on loving others

Learning outcomes

By the end of this lesson you should:

- know the 'greatest commandment' and the parables of The Good Samaritan and The Sheep and the Goats
- understand the meaning and importance to Christians of loving their neighbour
- be able to evaluate the importance of loving others to Christians.

edexcel :::: key terms

Compassion – A feeling of pity which makes one want to help the sufferer.

Sacred texts

The Good Samaritan
Luke 10:25–37

The greatest commandment
Mark 12:29–31

The Parable of the Sheep and the Goats
Matthew 25:31–46

Loving your brother
1 John 4:20–21

You cannot love God and hate your brother

'Anyone who says "I love God" but hates his brother is a liar, since no one who fails to love the brother whom he can see can love God whom he has not seen.' Those are strong words, written by John, one of Jesus' apostles. The message is simple – the best way to show love for God is to love our fellow human beings, to 'love your neighbour'.

The Good Samaritan

The 'Greatest Commandment'

Jesus taught that to love your neighbour is the second most important commandment of God. The commandment to love God and to love others is often called 'The Greatest Commandment'. Religions often seem to have lots of laws and rules. The Jewish religion in Jesus' time was no exception. But Jesus taught that every rule and action must demonstrate our love for God and love and **compassion** for our neighbour. Any action that comes from hatred rather than love is wrong.

Jesus told parables that help Christians to understand what love of others means. Two of the best known are The Good Samaritan and The Sheep and the Goats.

The Good Samaritan

Who particularly needs our love? Jesus taught that everyone is your neighbour, even people from far away, even people you think of as your enemies. If everyone is a child of God, then everyone is equally important to God. Christians must therefore love everyone as their brother or sister. The parable of The Good Samaritan tells us how important it is to love people in need. Loving is not just a feeling – it must lead to action. You can't say you love someone and then ignore their suffering. For Jesus and for Christians, loving means helping.

Circles of concern – Who should we love?

(diagram labels: Self; Family and friends; People in the local community; People in the rest of the country and the whole world)

Those who show love of others in this way will be rewarded by gaining a place in Heaven.

Serving others is important in the Christian faith. Some modern-day Christians, such as Mother Teresa (see page 24), dedicate their whole lives to caring for those in need.

Activities

3 Prepare a presentation or a storyboard that tells the Parable of the Sheep and the Goats and explains what it means.

4 Draw an ideas map of why it is important for Christians to show love of others. Which of these do you think is the most important? Explain why.

Activities

1 Read the parable of The Good Samaritan. Try to find out why the Jews and the Samaritans were such enemies. Your teacher will help. Rewrite the story but set it in modern times and using modern enemies instead of Jews and Samaritans.

2 Look at the diagram of the 'circles of concern' above. Recreate the circles in your exercise books, but leave enough space to write in them.

   In each circle write down three examples of people who might be suffering and in need of help.

   Discuss in class how we might be able to help them.

The parable of The Sheep and the Goats

In this parable Jesus makes it clear that when we help others, by giving them food or by visiting them when they are sick for example, we are helping God himself, but when we fail to help others, then we are failing to help God, too.

Summary

- Christians put loving others alongside loving God as the greatest of all the commandments.

- Jesus taught what 'loving others' means using examples such as the parables of The Good Samaritan and The Sheep and Goats.

- Jesus demanded that his followers live a life of service or practical action, always thinking about the needs of others and always trying to help them.

- Christians who show love for others through their actions will be rewarded by going to Heaven.

- Loving others is one of the most important ways in which we show we love God.

1.10 How religious communities express their love of God

Learning outcomes

By the end of this lesson you should be able to:

● give your own opinion, with a reason, about how the love of God is expressed at Taizé

● explain how the love of God is expressed at Taizé

● evaluate the importance of love of God as expressed through a religious community such as Taizé.

Look carefully at this poster and list all the activities you think take place at Taizé.

The Taizé community

Taizé is a village in central France that is home to a community of monks. The monks are drawn from the Roman Catholic and Protestant traditions and from many countries across the world. Each year tens of thousands of young people, aged 17–30, visit the community to share in its way of life. Time for worship, prayer and reflection are at the heart of the Taizé experience.

How Taizé began

The community was started by Brother Roger in 1940. During and after the Second World War he helped many refugees. Many were Jews escaping from Germany. In 1949 Brother Roger founded a religious community. The rules for the community included:

● celibacy (see page 52)
● the sharing of material goods
● obedience
● silence at meals.

Today the community is self-supporting. Welcoming others to help them explore their Christian faith is an essential part of Taizé life.

DAILY LIFE AT TAIZÉ

Monday to Friday

8.15am   Morning Prayer, then breakfast

10.00am   Introduction to the day and quiet reflection or small group discussion

12.20pm   Midday prayer, then lunch

2.00pm   Optional song practice

During the afternoon international small groups or work to support the community

5.15pm   Tea

5.45pm   Theme workshops

7.00pm   Supper

8.30pm   Evening prayer, with songs in the church. Followed by night silence.

For discussion

How do you think the love of God is expressed at Taizé?

Activities

1 Imagine you are a young Christian visiting Taizé for the first time. Write a letter home describing what you do and your thoughts and feelings about your stay.

Thoughts about Taizé

> The luxuries in life are stripped away allowing you to just think about God.

> Time at Taizé allowed me to think about my future and what direction God wanted me to go in.

> Learning from others, prayer, and bringing people together in the love of God is what Taizé is about.

> After my stay at Taizé I now feel ready to energise my local church.

How can a visit to Taizé help a Christian today?

Worship at Taizé

Taizé has developed its own distinctive style of singing used in worship. Short songs, repeated again and again help people to focus on the meaning of the words. It can become almost a form of meditation.

Prayer follows the monastic tradition and the community gathers for prayers three times a day. The services at Taizé are often candlelit and include hymns, psalms, scripture readings and prayers.

How the Love of God is shown through the life at Taizé

The monks have dedicated their lives to God and to serving others by helping them to explore and strengthen their faith.

Many young Christians make a pilgrimage each year to spend time in prayer and study to show their love of God. A simple lifestyle is adopted by all; prayer and communion with God are central to the daily routine.

The music and style of worship used expresses the love of God and has helped many Christians who haven't been to Taizé to share in this.

For more information about the life of the monks at Taizé go to www.heinemann.co.uk/hotlinks (express code 4257P) and click on the appropriate link.

For discussion

'Love of God is best expressed through good deeds, not through prayer.

Activities

Challenge

2 When Pope John Paul II visited Taizé he said; *'Like you ... the pope is only passing through. But one passes through Taizé as one passes close to a spring of water. The traveller stops, quenches his thirst and continues on his way.'*
What do you think he meant by this?

3 **Role play** In pairs imagine one of you has just been to Taizé and the other thinks that the money spent on the trip would have been better used by giving it to a charity. Write down what you say in your conversation.

4 Explain how the love of God is shown through a religious community.

Summary

- Many young Christians spend time at Taizé to express their love of God.
- Through worship, prayer, study, and in their daily life, the monks and visitors to Taizé express their love of God.

1.11 How religious communities express their love of others

Learning outcomes

By the end of this lesson you should be able to:

- give your own opinion, with a reason, about the work of the Missionaries of Charity
- explain how the love of others is expressed through the work of the Missionaries of Charity
- evaluate the importance of love of others as expressed through a religious community.

'No, I can't afford to buy you those trainers or any chocolate today!'

Cheapo Budget Brand

Cheapo Budget Brand

Is this child poor? What does it mean to be poor today?

The Missionaries of Charity

The Missionaries of Charity are a religious community founded by Mother Teresa in 1950 in Kolkata (Calcutta) in India. The aim of the community was to care for those too poor to care for themselves. The Missionaries of Charity have expanded today to consist of over 4500 nuns who work in over 100 countries.

The nuns follow the vows of celibacy, poverty and obedience and a fourth vow to give 'Wholehearted and free service to the poorest of the poor'.

The Missionaries of Charity serving the community

The Missionaries of Charity help sick and abandoned children, the old and dying, lepers and AIDS victims and the homeless. The sisters work in many different communities from Kolkata to New York and in towns around the UK. How they help will depend on the needs of the community.

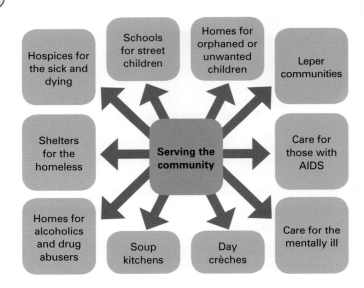

Hospices for the sick and dying

Schools for street children

Homes for orphaned or unwanted children

Leper communities

Shelters for the homeless

Serving the community

Care for those with AIDS

Homes for alcoholics and drug abusers

Soup kitchens

Day crèches

Care for the mentally ill

For discussion

Is it important for a religious community to show love of others?

Activities

1 Explain how the Missionaries of Charity show love of others.

How love of others is expressed through the work of the Missionaries of Charity

- The sisters follow the Christian teaching to love your neighbour, as they are willing to help all those that are in need, whatever their religion or background.
- Real love of others is shown by the sisters, as they are often required 'to love the unlovable' – those in the community who others have rejected.
- They are an active community showing their love of God through serving the poorest of the poor. They are acting like the sheep in the parable of The Sheep and the Goats.
- Love of others is often seen in the small things that are done for other people. For those who are dying, the important thing is to show that in their last hours of life someone cares for them.

Activities

2 Imagine you are a journalist doing a story about the work of the Missionaries of Charity. Write a short article to go with the picture above.

3 Find out the work of the Missionaries of Charity in the UK.

For discussion

'Loving the unlovable' is the only way to show true Christian love of others. Do you agree?

Activities

4 In groups, research and prepare a presentation for the rest of the class on another religious community that shows love of others through its life and work.

5 Explain how love of others is expressed through the life of a religious community.

Challenge

6 This is a prayer Mother Teresa said and shared with others. Why would the Missionaries of Charity continue to find this of help to them?

Lord, make me an instrument of your peace:
where there is hatred let me sow love;
where there is injury, pardon;
where there is doubt, faith;
where there is despair, light;
where there is sadness, joy.
Lord, may I not so much seek to be consoled, as to console;
to be understood, as to understand;
to be loved, as to love.
Because it is in giving that we receive,
in pardoning that we are pardoned.

Amen.

Summary

- The Missionaries of Charity express their love of others by helping the poorest of the poor in many communities throughout the world today.
- The Missionaries of Charity put the Christian teaching to love your neighbour into practice by helping many different groups of people, many of whom are ignored or rejected by the rest of society.

1.12 How a church shows love for God and others in the local area

26

Activities

1 Create a spider diagram with 'The needs of the local community' in the centre. Add the Corporal Works of Mercy to the diagram. Are there people with needs like these in your local community?

The parish is the heart of the Christian community.

Loving God

Worship is the most obvious way that Christians express their love of God and the church is the centre of worship for Christians. Catholics attend Mass in their local parish at least every Sunday, and they may also receive communion and go to confession regularly. They will also try to call into church when they can, to be quiet, alone with God and to pray to him.

The church is also central in marking key moments in people's lives – baptism, weddings and funerals all take place in church, where Christians again show their love of God.

Corporal Works of Mercy

The Catholic Church has created a list of Corporal Works of Mercy – ways in which people should help each other, based upon the teaching of Jesus in the Gospel.

- Feed the hungry and give drink to the thirsty.
- Shelter the homeless.
- Clothe the naked.
- Care for the sick.
- Help the imprisoned.
- Bury the dead.

Christians show their love of God by trying to find out more about him. Many churches have study and discussion groups which help people to do this. Catholic churches are run by a priest who has taken holy orders and spent many years studying their faith in depth. They help their parishioners learn more about God and also offer advice and support on moral issues.

Loving others

At the end of Mass in a Catholic church the priest encourages the people to 'Go in peace, to love and serve the Lord'. It is a weekly reminder that God wants us to show our love for him through the love and care for those around us.

- On an individual level, some people find out about the older people who live in the area, and spend time with them or offer to help with shopping.
- When someone is sick, perhaps in hospital, they will visit them.
- Some volunteer to be special ministers, and they take communion each week to those who can't get to church for Mass.
- If someone local dies, they show their love and support for the family by attending the funeral.

The church itself is the centre for many social activities for the local community – youth groups, cubs and brownies, lunch clubs or coffee mornings, holding events to raise money for charities – all these are examples of how the church helps people show love for others.

In many Catholic parishes there are groups that are dedicated to helping those in need in the local area. They take their inspiration from the Gospel. One such organisation is the St Vincent de Paul Society or the SVP, which has branches in parishes and schools. You can find out more about the SVP on pages 108–109. There is also the Legion of Mary which was founded about 70 years ago and whose members visit the sick of the parish, for example, and sometimes also go into prisons to talk to prisoners. In this way they respond to the teaching of Jesus in the parable of The Sheep and the Goats.

Activities

2 Find out about all the activities that take place in a church in your local area. You could perhaps visit the church, interview a member of the church or carry out some research using the Internet (many churches will have their own websites or newsletters). Then decide if and how you think each of the activities show love of God, love of others or both.

For more information about the work done by the Legion of Mary in Catholic parishes go to www.heinemann.co.uk/hotlinks (express code 4257P) and click on the appropriate link.

The Spiritual Works of Mercy

Apart from providing 'corporal' or physical help, the Catholic Church also believes that we can show our love for others by offering spiritual help. It provides a list of Spiritual Works of Mercy. They include giving advice to those who need it, being patient with others, forgiving those who hurt you and giving correction where needed. The final spiritual work of mercy asks us to comfort the suffering and pray for the living and the dead.

Activities

3 In what ways might this 'spiritual' help be just as important as helping people physically?

Summary

- A local church shows the love of God through being the focal point for worship and study of the Christian faith.
- The members of a church show their love of others through concern for those in their local community and in the wider world.
- The Church teaches the 'works of mercy' which are ways in which we can help each other both physically and spiritually.

examzone

KnowZone
Beliefs and values

Quick quiz

1 What is meant by the 'Virgin Birth'?

2 What is meant by 'repentance'?

3 Why do Christians believe Jesus is the Son of God?

4 Suggest two ways in which a Christian could show their love for God.

5 Do Christians believe in one God or three gods?

6 Suggest two ways in which Christians show their love for others.

7 Can Christians believe that the universe was created by a 'big bang'?

8 Name two ways in which the SVP serve the local community.

9 Name two ways in which the Holy Spirit guides people on Earth.

10 Do Christians believe that those who aren't Christians can get into Heaven?

Plenary activity

1 Imagine that a young person you know is thinking of becoming a Catholic. They know you have studied about Catholicism and have come to ask your advice.

They want to know the most important things that Catholics believe. Based on what you have studied in this section, select ten beliefs that you think are most important for Catholics, and explain briefly what each belief involves.

They then go on to ask if you think that living a Catholic life would be difficult. What would you tell them, and why?

Student tips

Some of the key words are quite hard to understand. But I noticed in the sample exams that part a) questions often ask for a definition of key terms, so it I think it is worth remembering them. Key terms are defined at the beginning of lessons: the glossary at the back of the book contains other definitions that are useful.

Student tips

I checked to see if the school had a copy of the Catechism of the Catholic Church. It is a really helpful book for this course so I suggested it should be kept in the reference section of the library.

Student tips

It is easy to get confused about belief in the Trinity. At first I thought that God the Father, God the Son and God the Holy Spirit were three different gods. But in fact Christians believe there is only one God.

Student tips

The parables of The Good Samaritan and The Sheep and the Goats seem to be really important for this section, so I learnt them. It wasn't too hard. I just read them through a couple of times, and then wrote down all the details I could remember.

Self-evaluation checklist

Read through the following list and evaluate how well you know and understand each of the topics.
How well have you understood the topics in this section? In the first column of the table below use the following code to rate your understanding:

Green – I understand this fully

Orange – I am confident I can answer most questions on this

Red – I need to do a lot more work on this topic.

In the second and third columns you need to think about:

● Whether you have an opinion on this topic and could give reasons for that opinion if asked

● Whether you can give the opinion of someone who disagrees with you and give reasons for this alternative opinion.

Content covered	My understanding is red/orange/green	Can I give my opinion?	Can I give an alternative opinion?
● What it means to say that God is both Unity and Trinity.			
● What it means when Christians call God their father.			
● What Christians believe about God the Creator.			
● What it means to say that Jesus is the Son of God.			
● What Christians believe about the Holy Spirit.			
● What is meant by salvation from sin for a Christian.			
● For each of the topics above why these beliefs are important for Christians.			
● How religious communities show their love of God.			
● How religious communities show their love of others.			
● How a Christian church expresses its love of God and others in the local area.			

Find out more

The Catechism of the Catholic Church is the best summary of Catholic belief. It has been compiled with the approval of the Pope and bishops. It has an index that is very easy to use.

There are a number of Christian and Catholic Encyclopaedias which may be available in your school library.

The Vatican has its own website which is available in a number of languages. Both CAFOD and the SVP also have very good websites. They will tell you more about their work, and also why they believe the work they do is so important.

If you are feeling really ambitious, have a look at the Documents of the Second Vatican Council. These are the official documents about Catholic teaching that were written in the 1960s, following a great gathering in Rome of all the Bishops for what is called an Ecumenical Council. Some of the language can be hard to understand, but it also has a good index. Look up terms like 'Trinity' and 'Virgin Birth'.

exam zone

KnowZone
Beliefs and values

Introduction

In the exam you will be given a choice of two questions on this section. Each question will include four tasks (a–d), which test your knowledge, understanding and evaluation of the material covered.

A 2-mark (a) question will ask you to define a term; a 4-mark (b) question will ask your opinion on a point of view; a 6-mark (d) question will ask for your opinion on a point of view and ask you to consider an alternative point of view; an 8-mark (c) question will ask you to explain a particular belief or idea.

You can give your own point of view, but be sure to give two reasons. If you don't have a point of view of your own, you can use reasons you have learned in class.

Mini exam paper

(a) What is monotheism? (2 marks)

(b) Should God be described as Father? (4 marks)

Give **two** reasons for your point of view.

(c) Explain why Christians believe in the Trinity. (8 marks)

(d) 'God created the world in six days'.

In your answer you should refer to Roman Catholic Christianity.

(i) Do you agree? Give reasons for your opinion. (3 marks)

(ii) Give reasons why some people may disagree with you. (3 marks)

You need to give a short accurate definition – just a single sentence. This is a key term so the definition would score full marks.

When you are asked to 'explain' something you must give more than just examples. You can say what Christians believe about the Trinity, but you must also say why Christians believe this. This question is worth 8 marks so you must be prepared to spend some time answering it. You will also be assessed on your use of language in this question.

You only need to give one point of view at this stage but you must give reasons why you hold this point of view.

Now you have to give the opposite point of view, again, using material you have learned during your studies. You don't have to say what you think about these alternative points of view, but you do need to give reasons why people might hold them.

Support activity

1   Look at these two part (d) questions.

- God created the world in six days.

- Only Christians can go to Heaven.

Each question will ask you to give reasons for your opinion and to give reasons who some people would disagree with you. Practise using these two questions. Write a list of reasons for agreeing and add reasons for disagreeing.

ResultsPlus
Watch out!

Even if you write a very good explanation, you can lose marks if you fail to read and answer the question fully. For example, how many reasons did the question ask for; were you asked to refer specifically to Christianity or to Roman Catholicism?

Remember that all part d) questions ask for your opinion, but they also ask you to explain the opposite point of view. If you don't, you can only score half marks.

ResultsPlus
Maximise your marks

(b) Do you think God should be described as father? Give **two** reasons for your point of view. (4 marks)

Sample answer	Examiner comments	Build a better answer
I think God should be described as Father because Jesus said we should. Also, God is our father because he created us.	These are valid reasons, but they are both quite brief and are not developed. **This answer would score 2 out of 4**.	I think God should be described as Father because Jesus said we should. He taught a prayer which begins: *'Our father, who art in Heaven…'* Also, God created the universe and everything in it so he is like a father because he created all human beings.

(c) Explain why Christians believe in the Trinity. (8 marks)

Sample answer	Examiner comments	Build a better answer
Christians believe that the Trinity is God the Father, God the Son and God the Holy Spirit. God the Father created the world. God the Son is Jesus. God the Holy Spirit came down upon the apostles at Pentecost. They believe in it because it says so in the Bible.	For the most part this answer just says what the Trinity is. Although the description is quite a full one, it is still just a description. If the answer had stopped here, the candidate would have scored Level 1, for a description without an explanation. But the candidate does go on to offer a reason for the belief, that the Trinity is taught in the Bible. The problem is that the answer could only be described as a brief reason, and would still only gain a maximum of 2 marks out of 8. To gain full marks the candidates should have given four developed reasons, or fewer reasons, but with more development.	Christians believe that the Trinity is God the Father, God the Son and God the Holy Spirit. They believe this because it says so in the Bible. For example, when Jesus is baptised, the Holy Spirit comes down in the form of a dove and people hear God the Father say that Jesus is his son. Also, the Catechism of the Catholic Church teaches that the Trinity is the basis of the Christian faith. Furthermore, St Paul taught about the Trinity, which is another reason why Christians believe in it.

Community and tradition

Introduction

When people speak about the Christian religion they will often refer to 'the Church'. Of course when they hear the word 'church' most people will think of church buildings, thousands of which have been built around the world. But the word Church, sometimes written with a capital 'C', can also be about people, not buildings. The Church is the community of God's people wherever they are found, in a parish or a diocese, or even the entire people of God throughout the world.

The Church can also refer to the way groups of Christians are organised and structured, usually with a particular set of beliefs and rules, with particular ways of worshipping God, and with Church leaders, such as the Pope, and other priests and ministers.

Learning outcomes for this section

By the end of this section you should:

- understand what is meant by the word 'Church' and the role of the Church in helping to lead people through faith to God and salvation
- know about the Bible, what it is, and what authority it has to guide the lives of Catholics
- understand the organisation of the Catholic Church and the role of the Magisterium, the Pope, and bishops and priests
- understand why Protestants do not share Catholic beliefs about the authority of the Church
- understand why Christians disagree about whether priests and bishops should be allowed to marry
- understand why the Virgin Mary is so important to Roman Catholics.

edexcel ⠿ key terms

Anglican Churches	**catholic**	**laity**	**ordination**
apostolic	**celibacy**	**Magisterium**	**Orthodox Churches**
bishops	**holy**	**Nonconformist Churches**	**papacy**

Fascinating fact

Before John Paul II (who was Polish) and Benedict XVI (German) all popes had been Italian since 1523. The last, and only, English pope was Pope Adrian IV. His real name was Nicholas Breakspear and he came from Hertfordshire. He ruled as pope from 1154 until 1159.

1 What do you think a pope does? Discuss in pairs or small groups and come up with a list of as many things as you can think of. When this section is finished have a look at that list again, and see how much of it was right, and what needs to be added.

2.1 Faith and salvation

Learning outcomes

By the end of this lesson you should:

● understand what is meant by 'faith' and 'salvation'

● understand why Catholics believe that the Church can strengthen their faith

● understand why Catholics believe that the Church helps them get to Heaven

● be able to evaluate whether only Christians can get to Heaven.

edexcel ⠿ key terms

Catholic – Universal or worldwide.

Sacred texts

Jesus gives Peter the keys to Heaven
Matthew 16:19

Jesus passes his authority to the Apostles
Matthew 28:18–20

A child has faith that their father will keep them safe.

Faith is about trust

If we have faith in someone, this usually means that we trust them. Many children would have faith that their father would save them from dangerous situations. That is because they have come to know him and to trust him.

The Church and faith

Although faith can be defined as believing in something without having proof, faith in God is rather like the child's trust in a moment of danger. Christians believe that God has planted in our hearts the desire to love him as a father. We do not understand everything about God, or about the meaning and purpose of life, but we trust that God knows what is best for us, and that he will lead us to Heaven.

'**Catholic**' means 'universal'. It can also mean 'all-embracing'. This means that everyone is invited to join the Church. It is a fellowship open to everyone of any race or nationality, provided they are committed to sharing in its beliefs and its mission.

Catholics see their Church as the means to faith because:

- Catholic Christians believe that the Church keeps alive the true faith that was handed down to the disciples from Jesus and passed on to the bishops. This is known as the Apostolic succession (see pages 42–43). The Church is the guardian of the true faith and interprets it for Christians today. Therefore the Church is the one source of faith, as it preserves the Christian message as taught by Jesus.
- It is part of Catholic belief that the Church has been given to us by God to help us on that journey to Heaven. The Church isn't just a Christian club, which people may choose to join or not. If the Church was given to us by God then he must have thought we would need it.
- The Church is a human society because its members are human, but it is divine because it is being guided all the time by the Holy Spirit.

Catholics believe that only the Pope and the bishops (see pages 48–49) can interpret the Bible and the tradition of the Church, as they are guided by God. Therefore they are the ones who have authority to pass on the Christian faith.

Activities

1 Can you think of other times when we put our faith and trust in someone we know? Take a little while to think about it and then write down some examples to share with the rest of the class.

2 List some different ways in which the Catholic Church can lead people to faith in God.

The Catholic Church and salvation

Like all Christians, Catholics believe that salvation has been made possible through the resurrection of Jesus and that people need to follow the teachings and example of Jesus in order to be saved. However, Catholics do have specific teachings about how people can be saved through the Church and the sacraments:

- As the Church is the guardian of the 'one true faith' (see above) Catholics believe that in the Church, and only in the Church, can someone find the absolute truth about God and about how they can be saved.
- It is through receiving the body and blood of Christ during the Mass that Jesus comes into people's daily lives, making salvation possible (see pages 70–71).
- The sacraments of baptism and confirmation (see pages 62–65) bring people into the Church and therefore help enable people to achieve salvation.
- Catholics also believe that confessing their sins to a priest (the sacrament of confession) is an important part of achieving salvation.
- Through the centuries the Catholic Church has taught that everyone must be a member of the Catholic Church, if they want to be sure of salvation. 'Extra ecclesiam non salus est' is a Latin expression which means, 'Outside the (Christian) Church there is no salvation'.

However, today the Church teaches that it is possible for non-Catholics to achieve salvation if they have lived their life in accordance with the spirit of Jesus' teaching.

Activities

3 Write a leaflet or magazine article for non-Catholics, which explains the importance of the Catholic Church as the means to faith and salvation.

For discussion

Should Christians believe that only those who follow Jesus can be saved?

Summary

- Catholics believe that the Church is God's gift to help us have faith in him and to achieve salvation.
- Some Christians think that all people can be saved simply by living a good life, according to Jesus' teaching.
- Some Christians say that unless you are a Christian you cannot go to Heaven.

2.2 The Church as the Body of Christ

Learning outcomes

By the end of this lesson you should:

- understand what it means to compare the Church with parts of a body
- understand why Christians call the Church the Body of Christ
- be able to evaluate the significance of disunity within the Christian Church.

Sacred texts

All are united in the Body of Christ
1 Corinthians 12:12, 27

Christ is the head of the body
Ephesians 4:15

The body is made of many parts
1 Corinthians 12:17

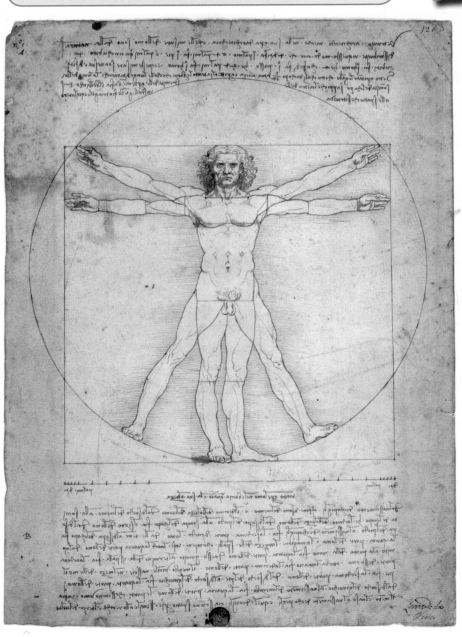

A body is made up of many parts.

The Human Body

Think about how a human body works. The body is made up of many different limbs and organs, such as eyes and legs, all with a different but important role, and all work together for the benefit of the whole body.

The Body of Christ

When Jesus was on Earth as a man he was able to walk around Israel to meet people and talk to them about God. He was able to stretch out his hand to help those in need, sometimes to heal them. He could also listen when people asked him questions or told him their concerns.

Once Jesus had ascended to Heaven, he relied on his followers, first his apostles and then all Christians throughout history up to the present day, to do this work for him. That is why the Christian Church, the people of God, is called the Body of Christ. Some people travel to remote parts of the Earth to teach people about Jesus and to respond to their physical suffering. They use their tongues, eyes, arms and legs to preach about Jesus, to see the people who are in great need, and to help them.

Activities

1 Draw a human body. It can be a simple outline or you could trace the one on this page.

   Think about the important parts of the body – arms and legs, tongue, eyes and ears, heart and brain. Take each of them, and give examples of ways in which Christ's followers today can act like these parts of his body and so continue his work.

St Paul teaches that the Church is the Body of Christ

St Paul, in his many letters to the first Christians, often uses this image of Christ's body when referring to the Church.

- He uses the image to point out that all members of Christ's body, with Jesus as the head, are united to form a single community of believers.
- He says that Christ did not want his followers to act in his name as individuals – he wanted them to form a community of believers, a Church, so that everyone can cooperate to continue his work.
- Paul taught that the various parts of the body have their own special function. They are all needed to make the body work. It is like this in the Church: some are teachers, some are leaders, some marry and raise families, some remain unmarried, some are great speakers, and some are great listeners.
- It is this diversity that makes the Church strong, just like the human body.

Activities

2 Read Chapter 12 of Paul's first letter to the Corinthians. Explain in your own words what you think Paul is trying to tell the early Christians.

The importance to Catholics of the Church as the Body of Christ

The idea that the Church is the Body of Christ is something that many Christians believe, but it is a teaching of special importance to Catholics. It shows how Catholics believe that the Church and Jesus himself are intimately united. It also explains why Catholics believe that all Christians should be united together in the Catholic Church, so that everyone can see that Christians are one in Christ.

Activities

Challenge

3 The Church was established to unite and strengthen all Christians and to make the message of Christianity more convincing and effective. In what ways do you think the work of Christ may be damaged by the divisions that exist within the Christian community?

4 Prepare a short presentation on what is meant by the Church as the Body of Christ. Include an explanation of its importance for Catholics.

ResultsPlus
Top tip!

Remember that when the church is spelt with a small 'c' it refers to the building, but when it is spelt with a capital 'C' it refers to all the people who follow Christ, or to a particular group of Christians, such as the Catholic Church.

Summary

- Christians believe that the Church functions as Jesus' body, continuing to do the work he did while on Earth.
- As a human body has many parts, the Church is made up of different people playing different roles.
- Christians believe that each person performs an equally important role as part of Christ's body.
- Christianity teaches that Christ himself acts as the head of the Church, directing it as the human brain directs a human body.

2.3 The Church as the communion of saints

Learning outcomes

By the end of this lesson you should:

- understand what it means to call someone a 'saint'
- understand what is meant by calling the Church the 'communion of saints'
- be able to evaluate the Christian practice of praying to the saints.

edexcel ::: key terms

Holy – Of, or relating to, God, sacred.

Sacred texts

God's chosen race
Colossians 3:12–17

Everyone is called to be a saint.

The call to holiness

Most people understand 'saints' as very good and **holy** people who have died, like Mother Teresa or St Francis. In that case not many people see themselves as becoming saints. In fact, Christians believe that every person is called to be a saint. Every time someone does the work of Jesus they are behaving as a saint would behave. That might just mean listening to someone who is upset, or speaking up for someone who is being treated unfairly.

Activities

1   You will know many saints – you may even act like one yourself sometimes! Pick someone you know (not yourself!) – someone at school or among your family or friends – who sometimes acts like a saint. Write a brief account of what they do, and why you think it is saintly. Your teacher may invite some of you to read out what you have written for the rest of the class.

What is a saint?

There is no doubt that in the course of Christian history there have been many very holy men and women:

- The apostles Peter and Paul, who were both executed by the Romans because they would not stop preaching about Jesus.
- St Francis of Assisi, a rich young man who gave away everything he owned to live a life of great simplicity, poverty and hardship.
- In modern times a follower of St Francis, St Maximilian Kolbe, who in a Nazi concentration camp offered his life in exchange for a man with a family who was about to be executed.

What many saints have in common is that they dedicated their entire lives to doing Jesus' work, often at great personal risk. They didn't always live faultless lives. Some have written that they had to fight the temptation to sin, and didn't always succeed. When someone lives an heroic and holy life sometimes the Catholic Church honours them by publicly naming them as Saints. This is a process called canonisation, and the Church says that those who are canonised are certainly in Heaven with God.

The communion of saints

We must now think about the word 'communion' in the 'communion of saints'.

The word 'communion' is just like the word 'community'. Being a community means being united, like a family. We could just as easily talk about the 'family of saints'. That unity exists between all followers of Christ who are still alive on Earth, those who have died but may not yet be with God in Heaven, and the saints who are with God.

That is why the Catholic Church teaches that people can and should pray to God for those who have died. By praying for them we continue to keep them in our hearts and minds. We also ask God to take them into Heaven, something we want very much for someone we have loved.

The Catholic Church also teaches that those who have already died and have gone to Heaven can intercede for us – that means they can hear our prayers and can bring our needs before God. This is why Catholics often pray to the saints, and why there are often statues of saints in Catholic churches and schools. We can also ask family members and friends who have died to intercede for us.

Activities

Your school or local library may have a dictionary of saints, which contains information about the lives of some of the more famous saints.

2   Find out about one particular saint of your choice and write a brief life story. What special things did they do to mark them out as particularly holy?

3   Christians honour the saints, but they do not worship them. What is the difference between honouring and worshipping? By praying in front of statues of saints, do Catholics risk idolatry (worshipping saints as though they were gods)?

Summary

- Every follower of Christ is called to be a saint, and many people perform some saintly acts during their lives.
- Some people, who have lived particularly heroic or selfless lives, are publically acknowledged as saints by the Catholic Church by being canonised.
- All Christians, living and dead, form a community called the 'communion of saints'.
- Catholic Christians pray for those who have died, and ask the saints in Heaven to intercede with God on their behalf.

2.4 Why the Bible has authority and importance for Roman Catholics

40

Learning outcomes

By the end of this lesson you should:

● understand what Catholics believe about the Bible

● understand why the Bible is so important for Catholics

● be able to evaluate the relevance of the Bible today.

Activities

1   Discover how much your class knows about the Bible. Can you name some books of the Old and New Testaments, or recount some of the most famous stories?

Sacred texts

Luke tells why he has written about Jesus and the Apostles
Acts 1

John confirms the accuracy of his Gospel
John 21:24–25

Christians consider the Bible to be the Word of God.

Why is the Bible important to Catholics?

Not all Christians believe exactly the same things about the Bible but all believe it has authority and is important. Catholics believe:

- The Bible was inspired by God the Holy Spirit and is therefore the Word of God.
- The Bible tells us about God, and how he wants us to live our lives on Earth. It also contains accounts of what Jesus said and did while he was on Earth. It teaches that Jesus is the Son of God.
- Not everything in the Bible is literally true, but everything in the Bible tells us something that is true. For example, most Catholics believe that the account of Creation in the book of Genesis is a story which tells us that God *did* create the world, but not *how*.
- God has given the Pope and bishops the authority to interpret the meaning of the Bible for all Christians. This happens, for example, when the Pope writes an encyclical, which is an official letter addressed to all God's people.
- It is important that the Word of God is proclaimed regularly to all people, and that it is read and explained to Christians when they gather to worship. If we listen to and read the Bible regularly then it can bring us closer to God and inspire us to change the way we live our lives.
- At the Second Vatican Council the Church taught that 'ignorance of the scriptures is ignorance of Christ' and said that Catholics should read the Bible frequently so that they can become closer to God.

Activities

2 What is the difference between something being true and being literally true? Read Chapter 3 of Genesis, about Adam and Eve. Do you think that story can be literally true? If you think it is symbolic, what messages do you think the writer wanted to convey?

3 Draw an ideas map of all the reasons you can think of why the Bible is important for Catholics and why they believe it has authority. Do you agree with all, some or none of these reasons? Explain your own view on the authority and importance of the Bible.

How relevant is the Bible today?

Some people believe that the Bible is an old book and no longer as relevant today as it used to be. Times have changed and the Bible has nothing to say about modern issues like global warming or nuclear weapons, for example.

But Catholics believe the Bible is the Word of God and cannot go out of date. Because it is inspired by the Holy Spirit, what it tells us about God, and about how we should live, will always be true. Catholics also believe that the Church can interpret the Bible to answer today's moral problems (see the Magisterium, on pages 44–45).

For discussion

What are the big moral problems facing the world today? Do you think the Bible can help us to deal with them?

Summary

- Catholics believe that the Bible has authority because it was inspired by the Holy Spirit.
- The Bible is important for Catholics because it tells us about God and how we should live. It also reveals that Jesus is the Son of God.
- Catholics believe that the Catholic Church has the authority to interpret what the Bible teaches about the modern world.

2.5 Apostolic tradition and succession

Learning outcomes

By the end of the lesson you should:

● understand what is meant by apostolic tradition and apostolic succession

● be able to evaluate the importance of both apostolic tradition and succession for Catholics.

edexcel ▦ key terms

Apostolic – The belief that the Church can only be understood in the light of the apostles.

Bishops – Priests specially chosen by the Pope who are responsible for all the churches in a diocese.

Magisterium – The Pope and the bishops interpreting the Bible and tradition for Roman Catholics today.

Sacred texts

Keys to the Kingdom of Heaven given to Peter
Matthew 16:18–19

Jesus sends the Apostles into the world to teach
Matthew 28:16–20

The Holy Spirit guarantees true teaching
John 16:13–15

How can we know what Jesus taught?

It is difficult to be sure exactly what he taught. Only a small part of it was ever written down and much of it was passed down from the apostles by word of mouth.

Activities

1 How much can you remember about someone else in your class?

In just two minutes find out as much as you can about a person sitting near to you. Try to remember all you can, because you may be asked to share what you have learned with everyone else. In class, discuss how much more difficult it might be for us to know who Jesus was and what he taught.

The apostles passed on to their followers what Jesus had taught.

Apostolic tradition

How much do we know about Jesus? The most important record of what Jesus said is the four Gospels of Matthew, Mark, Luke and John. These books are not very long and, if they were all the information we had about Jesus, there would be huge gaps in our knowledge.

- It is thought that at some time there existed a collection of the sayings of Jesus, written down by some of the apostles. Also, Jesus must have spoken to the apostles alone on many occasions, explaining who he was, and what he was trying to teach.
- There are many passages in the Gospels which indicate that the apostles and their successors will be guided by the Holy Spirit. This would ensure that the teaching of the Church would always be faithful to what Jesus taught.
- The Catholic Church believes that, from generation to generation, all the knowledge that the apostles possessed was handed on to the next generation right down to the present time. That is what is known as **apostolic** tradition. The word 'tradition' comes from a Latin word which means 'to hand on'.
- Because they are both guaranteed by the Holy Spirit, the Bible and this tradition form one single body of truth and can never be in conflict.

Activities

2   Is it better for there to be different Christian Churches, or just one Church with everyone recognising the authority of the Pope? How can we know how Jesus would want us to behave today?

Apostolic succession

Most schools used to have prefects, also a Head Boy or Head Girl. Perhaps yours still does. Each year a new generation of senior prefects takes over, and this important role of leadership and service is passed on from generation to generation.

Catholics believe it was similar in the early Church. Before they died, the apostles passed their authority to a new set of leaders (who became known as **bishops**) and that process has continued to today. Catholics believe the present Pope and bishops are the direct heirs of the authority of the apostles.

- This is what is known as apostolic succession.
- Together, the Pope and bishops form the **Magisterium** (see pages 44–45).
- Those Catholics who remain faithful to this line of succession can be certain that what they are taught comes from God.
- The Catholic Church teaches that accepting this apostolic leadership of the Pope and bishops is the only way in which the Christian Church can be united and wholly faithful to the teachings of Jesus.

Activities

3   Explain why apostolic tradition and succession are important for Catholics. (Hint: think about authority.)

Summary

- Catholics believe that the teaching of Jesus has been handed down from the apostles to each new generation of Christians.
- Catholics believe the teaching of Jesus is present in both the Bible and in tradition.
- Catholics also believe that the leadership of the Catholic Church has been passed on from the apostles to the Pope and bishops.
- This leadership is believed to be the only way in which the Christian faith can be united and faithful to the teaching of Jesus.

2.6 The Magisterium

Learning outcomes

By the end of this lesson you should:

- understand what is meant by the term 'Magisterium'
- know some of the important things taught by the Magisterium
- understand why the Magisterium is so important to Catholics
- be able to evaluate the teaching that the Magisterium is infallible.

Activities

1　In your life so far, what things have you learned all by yourself and what have you been taught by someone else? Make a list of each. Which is the longest list?

For Catholics, the Pope and bishops are their most important teachers.

Who needs teachers?

If we are being honest, we all do. From our parents who help us to walk and talk, to our children who teach us how to use a computer properly! We can learn that fire burns by putting our hands into one, but it is a lot safer to take our parents' word for it when we are children. In this lesson we are looking at something called the Magisterium. This word comes from the Latin word for teacher, 'Magister'. For Catholics, the Church is another one of our teachers, and a very important one.

The Magisterium

The Bible is one of the main sources of teaching for Christians, telling them about God and about how to live a good life. But Catholics believe the Bible doesn't contain everything that Jesus taught. Jesus' teachings do not, of course, say anything about the problems of the modern world such as stem cell research or pollution.

Therefore, the Pope leads the Council of Bishops in interpreting the Bible and apostolic tradition for Catholics today. Their interpretation is known as the Magisterium. It gives teachings on moral issues and defines the beliefs of the Catholic Church.

The teachings of the Magisterium are either found in the Catechism or 'encyclicals' – official letters from the Pope.

Because God wouldn't allow the Church to make mistakes on such vital issues, he guarantees that when the Pope and bishops agree on any matter of faith or morality they speak with infallible authority – which means that what they say is certainly true.

The Magisterium is important for Catholics because:

- it updates and interprets Catholic teachings in response to modern-day issues
- it makes sure that the key beliefs of the Church are not changed
- Catholics throughout the world follow its teachings, so ensuring unity amongst the Church worldwide
- it gives clear guidelines on how to live a good life so that salvation is possible.

For discussion

Is it important that the Pope and bishops are infallible? What problems would there be if they were able to teach things that were mistaken?

What has the Magisterium taught?

Here are some of the things the Pope and bishops have taught in recent years. Some of the teachings are widely accepted, but some are more controversial.

- In the 1960s the Magisterium taught that a 'just war' could not be fought with nuclear weapons.
- Pope Paul VI declared that artificial contraception is contrary to natural law (the law established by God to govern human relations).

- The Magisterium has taught repeatedly that life begins at conception and that abortion is murder.
- It has also taught that only God can decide when life should end, and that euthanasia is contrary to the law of God.
- It is Catholic teaching that everyone has the right to paid work.
- In 1950 the Church taught that when the Virgin Mary died she was taken straight to Heaven in special recognition of her status as the Mother of God.

Many non-Catholic Christians may agree with some of these teachings, but they do not accept that the Catholic Church has the authority to teach them as being unquestionably true. Even some Catholics do not accept that every one of these teachings is infallible and argue that the Pope and bishops speak infallibly only very rarely.

Activities

2 What do you think Jesus would feel about the great moral problems of today?

Choose an issue such as abortion, global warming or terrorism and explain what you think Jesus would have taught about this and why.

3 Prepare a presentation about the magisterium – you must explain what it is and how it works and why it is so important for Catholics. Finally, include your own views of the Magisterium – what do you think about it?

Summary

- Catholics believe that the Magisterium, the Pope and bishops, have God's authority to teach about faith and morality.
- The Magisterium applies the Bible and apostolic tradition to answer moral problems in the modern world.
- In certain circumstances, when the Pope and bishops speak about faith and morals they are believed to be infallible.

2.7 Protestant beliefs about the authority of the Church

46

What are Protestants?

The word 'Protestant' comes from the word 'protest'. The first Protestants were Christians in Europe who protested against some of the beliefs and practices of the Catholic Church, mainly in the 15th and 16th centuries.

• Many of them felt they could no longer be members of the Catholic Church and they broke away to form new Churches, in a movement known as the Reformation.

• Perhaps the most famous Protestant of all is Martin Luther, who was a German monk, and some Protestants are called Lutherans after him.

• In England, King Henry VIII disagreed with the Pope and Henry declared himself Head of the Church in England. He separated the English Church from the authority of the Pope. This Church is now known as the Church of England.

• Over time, many other Protestant Churches were formed, including Baptists and Methodists.

Activities

1 Write down in your own words what you understand a Protestant to be. You could use a spidergram to help you.

Henry VIII proclaimed himself Head of the Church in England. Thomas More (above) was executed because he disagreed, saying the Pope was Head of the Church in every country.

Who should be in charge of the Church?

Catholics believe that the Church is a hierarchy, rather like a business, with the Pope at the head, having supreme and absolute authority. Protestants do not accept that Jesus had any intention of creating a Church with one person having so much power.

One of the main causes of the Reformation was an argument about authority. Protestants believed there was evidence that leaders of the Church had gone astray, both in the example of how they lived their lives and in their interpretation of the Bible. They believed they saw no evidence that the Catholic Church was being guided by the Holy Spirit in any special way.

These groups of Protestants believed that the only authority upon which Christians could rely was the Bible, which every individual could interpret for themselves with the guidance of their faith in God. Protestants do not believe that the Pope is infallible when he teaches about the Christian faith and morality.

Although in recent times the various Christian Churches have been trying to resolve their differences, the problem of authority remains a major obstacle to unity between Christians.

Robert Bolt's play *A Man for All Seasons* is about the struggle between Sir Thomas More and Henry VIII to agree on who should be Head of the Church in England. It was made into a famous film, starring Paul Schofield as Thomas More.

Protestants in Britain

In the United Kingdom there are many Protestant Churches which have different structures of authority.

- **Anglican Churches** continue to ordain bishops and priests. The Church of England accepts that bishops carry on the work of the apostles and have a role of leadership over members of the Christian Church. But they do not accept that the Pope has the authority to preside over the Church in Britain.

- Most of the **Nonconformist Churches** do not have either priests or bishops. They have ministers who guide and advise the members of their Churches. They consider that the Church is an invisible association of believers. For them the organisation known as 'the Church' is man-made, without the authority to tell them what they ought to believe.

- For most Protestants, knowing God's will comes through reading the Bible and applying your own conscience to an understanding of the scripture.

- Most Protestant Churches in Britain allow women to be ordained as priests and ministers. This allows women to play a role in governing their Church.

Activities

2 Does the Christian Church need a centralised figure of authority? Is it possible for each individual Christian to interpret the Bible for themselves?

3 Find out more about one of the Protestant Churches, such as the Baptists or Methodists. How are they organised and how does this differ from the Catholic model of authority? What role can women play in leading this Church?

Summary

- The Christian Church in the West is divided between Catholics and Protestants.

- One of the main reasons why the Church is divided is because there are disagreements about authority and leadership.

- Christians believe that this lack of unity weakens the ability of the Christian Church to preach the Gospel.

- Protestants and Catholics have been trying to find ways to bring about greater unity between Christians.

2.8 The Pope and bishops

Learning outcomes

By the end of this lesson you should:

- understand the role the Pope plays in leading the worldwide Catholic Church
- understand how bishops care for the people in their dioceses
- be able to evaluate the importance of the Pope's position of leadership.

edexcel ::: key terms

Papacy – The office of the Pope.

Ordination – making someone a priest, bishop or deacon by the sacrament of holy orders.

Laity – All the people of the Church who are not chosen to be bishops, priests or deacons.

Key
% of the world's Catholics to be found in each part of the world

- Latin America 42%
- Europe 27%
- Africa 12%
- Asia 10%
- North America 7%
- Oceania 1%

Members of the Catholic Church can be found in every continent.

Sacred texts

St Paul recognises the role of bishops Philippians 1:1

A worldwide Church

The Catholic Church is a very large organisation. Throughout the world there are over one billion Catholics, around 400,000 priests and almost a million members of religious orders. To keep such a large number of people faithful to Catholic teaching, and to look after their spiritual needs, is a huge task. That responsibility lies with the Pope, who is the leader of the Catholic Church, and a large number of bishops who share in the Pope's role of leadership.

The role of the Pope and bishops

Perhaps the best way to appreciate the importance of the **papacy** and the role of bishops is to look at some of their titles and job descriptions. Remember that the Pope is also a bishop, the Bishop of Rome, so his jobs and titles are in both!

Activity

1 Draw up a flow chart showing how you believe your school is run, explaining who is in charge of which aspects of the school. Does the head teacher have to answer to anyone? How much more difficult would it be to look after a billion people and why?

VICAR OF CHRIST
The word 'vicar' means substitute, so the Pope plays the role of Jesus, as leader of the Church on Earth. In that role he also has to represent the Church to all the various figures of authority in the world, such as Monarchs and Presidents.

HEAD OF THE MAGISTERIUM
The Magisterium has the task of teaching the truth about God to all people, the truth being guaranteed by the inspiration of the Holy Spirit. The Pope leads that teaching office.

SUCCESSOR OF ST PETER
This is what is known as the apostolic succession (see page 43). Jesus gave the leadership of the Church to Peter, who passed it on to another leader before his death, and that line has continued for nearly 2000 years up to the present Pope.

HEAD OF THE COLLEGE OF BISHOPS
As we shall see, all Bishops have the particular task of leading and guiding the Church. Together the bishops form a College, and the Pope is the Head of that College. It is the Pope who decides who can be a bishop.

What does the Pope do?

PASTOR OF THE UNIVERSAL CHURCH
The word 'pastor' means to act like a shepherd. The Pope has the responsibility to guide and minister to Catholics all over the world.

SUCCESSOR OF THE APOSTLES
Bishops are seen as the successors of the apostles who, like St Peter, passed on their role of leading and teaching to others before they died. Once they have been appointed by the Pope they take part in a special **ordination** ceremony.

CHIEF SHEPHERD
Bishops are often likened to shepherds. The people in a diocese are in his special care. Although he can delegate others to teach his people, to minister to them and give them the sacrament of confirmation (see page 64), these tasks are his responsibility and he has to ensure that they are carried out properly.

What are bishops?

HEAD OF A DIOCESE
The main task of a bishop is to be leader and pastor of all aspects of the Church in an area called a diocese. In this role he not only cares for the **laity**, but also he looks after the priests, and decides where in his diocese the priests will work. Only bishops can ordain priests. Large dioceses can have as many as 500 priests taking care of many hundreds of parishes.

Activities

2 Try to find out about the work of your local bishop. Have a look at the website of your local diocese – you may be surprised by how much work the Church does locally. Make a list of the bishop's responsibilities. Be ready to explain what you have discovered to the rest of the class.

3 In what ways might the Church be more effective if it were organised more democratically? What problems might there be if there was not one overall leader?

Summary

- The Pope and bishops are the leaders of the Catholic Church.

- The Pope has supreme authority over the Church throughout the world, a role Catholics believe was given to him by Christ himself.

- Bishops look after the whole Church in an area called a diocese, which can contain hundreds of parishes.

2.9 The role of a priest in a local parish

Learning outcomes

By the end of this lesson you should:

- know what a parish priest does
- understand why priests are so important for Catholics
- understand why it is important to have priests to celebrate Mass
- be able to evaluate the importance of having priests to lead the local parish community.

What is the job of the local Catholic parish priest?

Those who are not involved in a parish may think that a parish priest's job is mainly just to celebrate Mass. That is certainly an important part of his work, but a parish priest does a lot more than that. In the photograph you can see a priest celebrating a marriage. Below are some of the other things a typical parish priest might do.

Celebrates Mass

Visits and takes communion to the sick

Chaplain to a school or a hospital

Preaches about the teachings of Jesus

Celebrates baptisms, marriages and funerals

School governor

Hears confessions

Being available to give spiritual advice

Looking after the church buildings and finances

The parish priest has many different roles.

Activities

1 Create a diamond nine diagram to show which of the jobs done by a priest you think are the most important. Explain why you selected the one you consider to be the most important.

The parish

Parish priests are appointed by the bishop. It isn't possible for the bishop to minister to everyone in his diocese personally, so he has the help of priests, many of whom look after their own area of the diocese called a parish. The size of a parish can vary. In some parts of the world a priest can have many thousands of parishioners, though in the United Kingdom most parishes are much smaller. It is estimated that in England and Wales up to 40 per cent of Catholics attend Sunday Mass on a regular basis, but the priest is not just responsible for those who go to Church. He also has the duty to help every member of his parish to live a life in accordance with the teaching of Jesus, to pray and to worship God.

The priest is encouraged by the Church to enlist the help of his parishioners, and often he will have someone to help him with the parish finances, with the upkeep of the church and many other tasks.

In many parishes there are now permanent deacons. These are ordained men, some of whom are married, who help the parish priest with the celebration of the sacraments. But only a priest can preside at Mass and only a priest can hear confessions.

Celebrating Mass

For most Catholics, the most important role of a priest is to celebrate Mass. When a priest is ordained, his hands are anointed with oil in recognition that, at his hands, the miracle of the Mass will take place each day.

Activities

2 Look again at the roles of a priest. Try to find out more about these jobs, and explain which you think must be done by a priest, and which could be done better by members of the laity. You could discuss this with your local priest or school chaplain.

For discussion

What might be the effect on the Christian faith if local parishes were closed due to the shortage of priests?

There are Christians who think that any believer can preside over the communion service, but the Catholic Church teaches that, because of the importance of this event, it is a role only for those chosen by God to be priests. In fact, the word 'priest' means someone who 'offers sacrifice'. This is a tradition inherited from the Jewish faith, when only priests were allowed to offer the sacrifices to God in the Temple in Jerusalem.

ResultsPlus
Build Better Answers

Is celebrating Mass the most important role of a priest? Give **two** reasons for your point of view. (4 marks)

■ **Basic, 1-mark answer**
These answers offer just one short reason why the student agrees or disagrees. For example – 'It is the most important role because a priest is the only person who can celebrate Mass.'

● **Good, 2–3-mark answer**
Good answers offer two reasons, and develop one of them. They may mention that celebrating Mass is one of the roles specifically mentioned when a priest is ordained. They may also mention that Christians believe that Jesus commanded his followers to celebrate the Mass in memory of him.

▲ **Excellent, 4-mark answer**
The best answers will offer two developed reasons. They may develop the second reason, perhaps by pointing out that Catholics believe that at Mass Jesus really becomes present in the bread and wine.

Summary

- The priest has the job of helping the bishop to care for the Christian community.
- He lives near the local church, celebrates the sacraments and leads the services that take place in the church.
- The priest may also be involved in the running of local schools and hospitals.
- For many Catholics, the most important role of the priest is to lead the celebration of Mass.

2.10 Attitudes to celibacy of the clergy

52

Learning outcomes

By the end of this lesson you should:

● know the different Christian attitudes towards celibacy of the clergy

● understand why some Christians do not believe priests and bishops should marry

● be able evaluate the importance of celibacy for the Christian Church.

edexcel ⠿ key terms

Celibacy – Living without engaging in any sexual activity.

Orthodox Churches – National Churches which are in union with the Patriarch of Constantinople (e.g. the Russian Orthodox Church).

Sacred texts

Being celibate for the sake of the Kingdom of Heaven
Matthew 19:12

St Paul favours celibacy
1 Corinthians 8:32–35

Different Churches have different rules

Catholics use the word **celibacy** in two different ways. Generally a person who is celibate lives without having sexual relations. When the term is used to describe a priest, it also means that the priest is unmarried. This is a deliberate choice that allows the priest to devote himself entirely to the service of the Church.

The rules about celibacy of the clergy (priests and bishops) in the Christian Churches are a little confusing.

● In the **Orthodox Churches** priests can marry, but a married priest cannot become a bishop.

● In the Protestant Churches (Church of England, Baptist, Methodist and so on) all the clergy are allowed to marry.

● In the Catholic Church the normal rule is that neither priests nor bishops may marry. However there are some parts of the Catholic Church in the East where priests may marry – in Ukraine for example. Married Anglican priests sometimes leave the Church of England to become Catholic priests and can therefore stay married. But there are no married bishops in the Catholic Church.

Should bishops and priests be allowed to marry?

Activities

1   Create spider diagrams for the Orthodox, Protestant and Catholic Churches. Complete them in your own words with their particular rules about celibacy.

Why are some priests celibate?

The men Jesus chose to be leaders of the Church were not celibate. The Gospels indicate that Jesus was never married but St Peter was (there is a reference to his sick mother-in-law). There was a time when the Catholic Church believed that sexual desire was sinful and could lead a person away from God, though this is not the belief of the Church today.

The belief that a bishop or a priest needed to be celibate to be fully committed to the work of preaching the Gospel and leading the Church developed gradually.

- First of all the work itself was very demanding and it was thought that if a member of the clergy was free from family ties he would have more time to devote to his work. St Paul makes this point very strongly in a letter to the Corinthians (1 Corinthians 8:32–33).
- At the same time, priests and bishops were seen as people who stood in the place of Christ, especially when they celebrated Mass, and it was thought they should live lives as close to Jesus' life as possible, and among other things that meant being unmarried.

For discussion

Try to think of as many advantages as you can for priests and bishops to be celibate. Then consider the benefits of a married clergy. Perhaps you can debate in class which side seems to have the more convincing arguments.

Is celibacy necessary?

Orthodox and Protestant Christians do not follow Catholic rules about celibacy. Some argue that the impulse to marry, have sexual relations and raise children is very strong and that it can be dangerous to interfere with that desire.

Others will say that a married priest or bishop brings to their ministry the benefit of the experiences that are part of the normal life of the people they serve.

There have been many calls within the Catholic Church for a change in the rules about celibacy. Many argue that celibacy is a human law, and not one that God has demanded. But the Pope and many Catholic bishops continue to teach that the celibate state is the best way of life for priests, and encourage priests to see it as a call from God and a gift that can help to deepen their relationship with God.

Activities

2   Fewer men today want to become Catholic priests. Could celibacy be a factor in this decline? Perhaps you could discuss this with a chaplain or your local parish priest.

Summary

- There are different traditions regarding celibacy between the Catholic, Orthodox and Protestant Churches.
- The Catholic Church believes that celibacy is a gift that can bring priests closer to God.
- There are married Catholic priests – priests who have converted from other Christian Churches and in some countries in the East.
- There is an active debate in the Church about whether Catholic priests should be allowed to marry.

2.11 The Virgin Mary

Learning outcomes

By the end of this lesson you should:

● know what is meant by the title 'Virgin Mary'

● understand why Mary is seen as a role model for all Christians

● be able to evaluate the importance of the Virgin Mary for Catholics.

Sacred texts

The role of Mary is foretold by Isaiah
Isaiah 7:14

The Archangel Gabriel appears to Mary
Luke 1:26–38

Mary gives birth to Jesus
Luke 2:1–19

Catholics have a special reverence for the Virgin Mary.

Mary, our mother

We have seen that all Christians look upon God as their father. The Catholic Church encourages us to look upon Mary, who was the mother of Jesus, as our mother, too. Of course Mary was a human being like us, she was not divine and Catholics do not worship her. But they welcome the thought that they have someone to care for them as a mother cares for her children.

Catholics often pray to Mary and ask for her help when they are in trouble. The Rosary, for example, is a very popular form of prayer among Catholics. While they pray, they think about the important moments in Mary's life, from the time the angel told her she would be the Mother of God, until the day she died and was taken to Heaven. Often Catholics refer to Mary as 'Our Lady'.

Mary – a role model for all Catholics

Christians often refer to Mary as the 'Virgin Mary'. This is because they believe that she did not have sexual relations with Joseph before Jesus was born. That way we can be sure that Jesus was God's son, and not Joseph's. But Mary was Jesus' mother and is called the Mother of God. Because God gave Mary this tremendous privilege she is revered by all Christians.

Catholics see Mary as the perfect model of how a Christian should behave.

- When she is asked by the angel to take on the responsibility of being the Mother of Jesus, something that will bring pain as well as joy, she quickly agrees (Luke 1:38).
- During her life she nurtures Jesus, not for her own sake, but so that she can give the gift of her son to all people (Luke 1:54).
- When Jesus is crucified she is one of the few people who did not run away, but she stood courageously at the foot of the cross (John 19:25).

So Mary is a role model – she is God's servant, she is seen as faithful, generous and courageous – and Catholics try to be like her.

The importance of Mary for Catholics

Although the Virgin Mary is important for all Christians, the Catholic Church has a very special devotion to her. Most Catholic Churches will have a statue of Mary, and the Church celebrates many special occasions in her honour and gives her important titles. Here are just three of the most important Catholic beliefs about Mary.

THE IMMACULATE CONCEPTION

This is the belief that when Mary (not Jesus) was conceived she had already been chosen to be the Mother of God, and so she was born without the stain of original sin (see page 63) so that she would be worthy to give birth to Jesus.

THE ASSUMPTION

When other human beings die, Christians believe they must wait in the grave until the day of judgement. But the Church teaches that, when she died, Mary was granted by God the special favour of being assumed (carried up) to Heaven, body and soul.

MARY AS MOTHER OF THE CHURCH

Catholics believe Jesus intended that Mary should continue to have a special role of caring for the people of God, the Church. This is based upon a moment in St John's Gospel (John 19:26–27). When he is dying, Jesus says to Mary 'Woman, this is your son' and indicates the beloved disciple John. John is therefore thought to represent all Christians.

Summary

- Christians believe that Mary was specially chosen to be the mother of God and that she was a virgin when she gave birth to Jesus.
- Mary is thought to be a role model for all Christians.
- Catholics often look upon Mary as their mother and pray to her when they are in trouble.
- Catholics celebrate the life of the Virgin Mary with many special celebrations.

KnowZone
Community and tradition

Quick quiz

1 What is meant by 'apostolic'?

2 What is the 'papacy'?

3 Why do Catholics believe the Church is the 'Body of Christ'?

4 Give two roles played by the priest in the local parish.

5 Describe two of the roles of a bishop.

6 Give two reasons why the Bible might be thought to be out of date.

7 Do Protestants believe the Pope is infallible?

8 Are there any married Catholic priests?

9 Give one reason why the Pope is important for Catholics.

10 What is the difference between the Virgin Birth and the Immaculate Conception?

Student tips

In this section there is a lot of material about the Pope and the Church. There are difficult ideas about faith and apostolic tradition. I didn't find this easy and sometimes it was helpful to ask my teacher for a simple explanation of some of the important ideas – just to make sure I understood them correctly.

I found it useful to talk to a priest about his role in the Church. I was able to make an appointment with the local parish priest, and the chaplain was also very helpful in giving me useful information.

Plenary activity

There are many similarities in the beliefs of the main Christian Churches, but also quite a number of differences.

Your teacher will divide the board into 'Similarities' and 'Differences' and invite members of the class to come forward and write one belief the Christian Churches have in common, or one way in which they disagree.

At the end your teacher will tell you how many you have remembered correctly. Be sure to copy down the accurate list!

Find out more

You will find a very useful summary of Catholic beliefs in The Catechism of the Catholic Church. It has been compiled with the approval of the Pope and bishops. It has an index that is very easy to use.

You may find Christian and Catholic Encyclopaedias available in your school library.

In the front of many Anglican prayer books you will find the 'Thirty-nine Articles'. This is a summary of the beliefs of the Church of England.

Butler's *Lives of the Saints* gives an account of the lives of almost all those who have been declared saints by the Catholic Church.

The Vatican has its own website which is available in a number of languages.

If you are feeling really ambitious, have a look at the Documents of the Second Vatican Council. These are the official documents about Catholic teaching that were written in the 1960s. They were written following a great gathering in Rome of all the Bishops for what is called an Ecumenical Council. In the index you could look for references to 'celibacy' or the 'Magisterium'. But remember that the language will sometimes be quite difficult to understand.

Self-evaluation checklist

Read through the following list and evaluate how well you know and understand each of the topics.
How well have you understood the topics in this section? In the first column of the table below use the following code to rate your understanding:

Green – I understand this fully
Orange – I am confident I can answer most questions on this
Red – I need to do a lot more work on this topic.

In the second and third columns you need to think about:

- Whether you have an opinion on this topic and could give reasons for that opinion if asked
- Whether you can give the opinion of someone who disagrees with you and give reasons for this alternative opinion.

Content covered	My understanding is red/orange/green	Can I give my opinion?	Can I give an alternative opinion?
In what ways Catholics believe the Church can help strengthen their faith and help them attain salvation.			
Why this is important for Catholics.			
What it means to talk about the Church as the 'Body of Christ'.			
Why this is important for Catholics.			
What it means to talk about the Church as the 'communion of saints'.			
Why this is important for Catholics.			
What authority Catholics believe the Bible has in guiding their lives.			
The meaning of the terms apostolic tradition and apostolic succession.			
Why this is important for Catholics.			
What the Magisterium is and what role it plays in the Catholic Church.			
Why this is important for Catholics.			
How and why Protestants have a different view of the authority of the Pope and bishops from that of Catholics.			
The roles played in the Catholic Church by the Pope and bishops.			
Why the Pope and bishops are important for Catholics.			
What is meant by the term 'parish priest' and what a parish priest does.			
Why priests are important for Catholics.			
What is meant by celibacy of the clergy and different opinions about it.			
What Catholics believe about the Virgin Mary.			
Why the Virgin Mary is important for Catholics.			

examzone
KnowZone
Community and tradition

Introduction

In the exam you will be given a choice of two questions on this section. Each question will include four tasks (a–d) which test your knowledge, understanding and evaluation of the material covered; a 2-mark (a) question will ask you to define a term; a 4-mark (b) question will ask your opinion on a point of view; a 6-mark (d) question will ask for your opinion on a point of view and ask you to consider an alternative point of view; an 8-mark (c) question will ask you to explain a particular belief or idea.

You need to give a short accurate definition – just a single sentence. This is a key term so the definition would score full marks.

When you are asked to 'explain' something you must give more than just examples. You can describe what a priest does, but you must go on to say why these roles are important for Catholics. This question is worth 8 marks so you must give up to four simple reasons or fewer reasons with some of them developed. You will also be assessed on your use of language in this question.

Mini exam paper

(a) What is celibacy? (2 marks)

(b) Does the Pope have any role to play in the world today? (4 marks)

Give two reasons for your point of view.

(c) Explain why priests are important to Catholics. (8 marks)

(d) 'The Bible is out of date'.

In your answer you should refer to Roman Catholic Christianity.

(i) Do you agree? Give reasons for your opinion. (3 marks)

(ii) Give reasons why some people may disagree with you. (3 marks)

You can give your own point of view, but be sure to give two reasons. If you don't have a point of view of your own, you can use reasons you have learned in class.

Here again you can use reasons you have learned in class. You only need to give one point of view at this stage but you must give reasons why you hold this point of view.

Now you have to give the opposite point of view, again using material you have learned during your studies. You don't have to say what you think about these alternative points of view, but you do need to show you understand why they are just as important to consider as your own opinion.

This section talks about Anglican Churches, Nonconformist Churches and Orthodox Churches, as well as the Catholic Church. It is important that you know the main differences between these Churches. Look back through the material in this section and make brief notes about each of them.

Watch out!

- Many students get confused between the Virgin Birth and the Immaculate Conception. The first refers to the birth of Jesus – that he was born without Mary having had sex with anyone. The second refers to the moment of Mary's own conception – that she was conceived without the stain of original sin.

- The 'communion of saints' is not just about the holy men and women who have been canonised – named as saints by the Church – but all followers of Christ living and dead. That's because Christians believe everyone is called to holiness.

- With some of the part d) questions, you may feel strongly in favour of one point of view and be tempted just to say that the opposite argument was worthless! But that would only earn you half marks for the question, so make sure you properly consider all points of view.

ResultsPlus

Maximise your marks

(c)   Explain why Priests are important for Catholics. (8 marks)

Student answer	Examiner comments	Improved student answer
Priests are important for Catholics because they celebrate Mass on Sundays. Catholics believe that at Mass Jesus becomes really present and only priests can bring this about.	This is a correct reason for why priests are important for Catholics. Also the reason has been developed, pointing out a key Catholic belief about what happens at Mass. However, the mark scheme will only allow a maximum of 4 marks to be awarded for one developed reason. The candidate needs to add some more reasons, or at least one more that is also developed.	Priests are important for Catholics because they celebrate Mass on Sundays. Catholics believe that at Mass Jesus becomes really present and only priests can bring this about. Priests baptise people and welcome them into God's family. Catholics believe that it is only as a result of baptism that the stain of original sin is washed away. So, in baptising someone, the priest also washes away their sins.

Worship and celebration

Introduction

Like believers from other religions, Christians like to celebrate their faith. They celebrate the joy they feel because they are the children of God, and because God is looking after them.

Some celebrations are acts of worship, where Christians make God aware of their love and respect for him. Other celebrations mark important moments in the life of a Christian, such as their birth and reaching adulthood.

Then there are also the important celebrations that take place throughout the year to commemorate the most important events in Jesus' life.

Christians also enjoy the non-religious aspects of these celebrations.

In this section of the course we will look at some of the most important celebrations in the Christian year.

Learning outcomes for this section

By the end of this section you should:

- understand what is meant by the sacraments of initiation and their importance in the lives of Christians
- know the structure of a Catholic Mass and understand its importance to Catholics
- understand why not all Christians celebrate the Eucharist in the same way
- understand the practice, meaning and significance of the sacraments of healing
- know the features of a Catholic church and to understand their purposes
- understand what happens during the most important Christian events and why these celebrations are so important.

edexcel ⁞ key terms

absolution	contrition	Liturgy of the Word	rite of communion
chrism	Holy Week	penance	sacrament
commemoration	Liturgy of the Eucharist	penitential rite	transubstantiation

Think of as many non-religious events as you can that are marked with a party or some other form of celebration. This should include family celebrations such as birthdays, and national occasions such as Royal events. What kinds of activities, such as ceremonies, food and music are involved? Now do the same for religious festivals.

What do national and religious celebrations have in common?

Fascinating fact

Although Christians celebrate Christmas on 25 December, no one has any idea at what time of the year Jesus was actually born. The Gospels don't even tell us whether it was winter or summer. Some people say it must have been summer because the Romans wouldn't have called a census in the coldest season of the year.

December 25 was chosen as the date for Christmas to replace a pagan festival which marked the winter solstice which, following the shortest day, marked the return of the light.

3.1 Baptism

62

Sacrament of welcome

Most religions have special ceremonies which welcome people into that religion. These are sometimes called Rites (or ceremonies) of Initiation. In the Christian Church this ceremony is called baptism. In the Catholic Church it is traditional to welcome people into membership of the Church as babies because the Church is seen as like a family.

The main part of the ceremony of baptism involves the priest pouring water over the baby's head as a sign of washing away sins and giving new life.

Activities

1 In small groups, discuss the many ways in which water is important to human beings. Appoint a spokesperson who will feed back your ideas to the rest of the class.

Sacred texts

Baptism of Jesus
Mark 1:9–11

Jesus tells the apostles to baptise
Mark 16:15–17

The early Christians are baptised
Acts 3:37–41

edexcel ⣿ key terms

Sacrament – An outward sign through which invisible grace is given to a person by Jesus.

Chrism – The oil used in baptism, confirmation and ordination.

Key parts of the baptism ceremony

The priest or deacon welcomes the family

Parents and godparents renew their baptismal vows – these vows make clear that they accept Christian teachings about God, the presence of evil in the world and the role of the Church

The child is clothed in a white garment

The child is baptised 'in the name of the Father, and of the Son and of the Holy Spirit' by the pouring of water

The child is anointed with **chrism**

The ceremony of baptism

The parents and godparents are given a lighted baptismal candle

More about signs and symbols

The word '**sacrament**' means sign or symbol. Whenever a sacrament is celebrated, certain symbols are used and these symbols represent gifts from God (Catholics often use the word 'grace' instead of gift). In baptism, for example, the pouring of water symbolises the washing away of sin. The use of such symbols is not limited to religion. A national flag is the symbol of a country, and certain coloured kit immediately make you think about a particular football team.

Other baptismal symbols

Apart from water, other symbols of baptism are also very important. The oil of chrism is used to make the sign of the cross on the baby's forehead. Oil is a sign of the strength that comes from the Holy Spirit. The garment symbolises 'putting on Christ' and it is white to symbolise the child's purity, having had their sins washed away by being baptised. The lighted baptismal candle is a sign that the baptised person has received the light of Christ.

For discussion

Sometimes teenagers are asked to be godparents to a young child. What helpful advice and guidance do you think that a teenager could give to a young Catholic as they are growing up?

Why infant baptism is important to Catholics

For most Catholics, the baptism of babies is important because:

- Parents want their children to be members of God's family and join the Christian community.
- The parents and godparents promise before God to provide a Christian upbringing for the child.
- Parents want their children baptised straightaway to cleanse them from original sin (see below).

Some Christians believe it is important that, before someone is baptised, they are able to fully understand what being a Christian means. Therefore they practise what is known as 'adult baptism'.

Original sin

Christians believe that humanity's relationship with God was damaged when Adam and Eve (or the first men and women) disobeyed God for the first time. That act is called original sin. Baptism is seen as the way in which human beings have that sin washed away and are reunited with God.

Activities

Most churches have special short pamphlets about preparing for baptism. Your teacher or chaplain may be able to provide some copies to share around the class.

2 Should Christians be baptised as babies or as adults? Prepare two boxes side by side. On one side write down the reasons why it may be best to baptise babies, and on the other side write down why it may be best to baptise adults.

3 Prepare a presentation or storyboard on what happens during Catholic baptism and explain the symbolism involved.

4 Write a short paragraph explaining why baptism is important for Catholics and what your own opinions of baptism are.

Summary

- Baptism is the first sacrament of initiation, or 'welcome' into the Christian Church.
- The sacrament of baptism uses many symbols, such as water and a lighted candle.
- Christians believe that baptism washes away original sin.
- There is a debate within Christianity about whether it is better to baptise babies or adults.

3.2 Confirmation

64

Learning outcomes

By the end of this lesson you should:

● know what happens during a confirmation ceremony

● understand the meaning of the symbols used at confirmation

● understand why many Christians choose to be confirmed

● be able to evaluate the importance of confirmation.

Sacred texts

Jesus promises to send the Holy Spirit
John 16:4–15

Pentecost
Acts 2:1–13

Choosing for oneself

Baptism is often called a sacrament of initiation, or of welcome, into the Christian faith. But the welcome doesn't end at baptism. When Catholics are older, and more able to make choices for themselves, they are invited to receive the sacrament of confirmation in which they make their own commitment to being disciples of Jesus Christ.

At confirmation a person makes their own choice to be a follower of Christ.

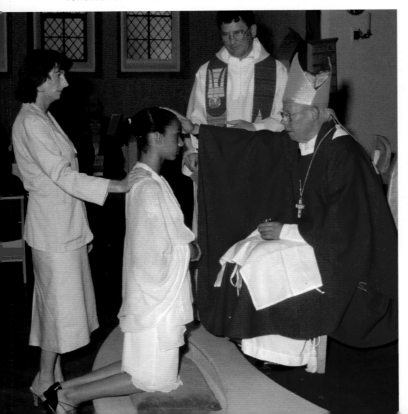

Key parts of the confirmation ceremony

The ceremony takes place during Mass, after the Gospel and Homily.

● The candidate indicates their willingness to be confirmed.
● The candidate renews the baptismal vows.
● The laying on of hands takes place – with his hands stretched out over the candidates the priest or bishop says a prayer asking for the gifts of the Holy Spirit.
● Each candidate goes forward with their 'sponsor', who is a confirmed Catholic. The sponsor places their hand on the candidate's shoulder during the anointing.
● The bishop (or another priest) anoints each candidate individually with the oil of chrism and says 'Be sealed with the gift of the Holy Spirit'.
● With a sign of peace, the bishop or priest welcomes the candidate as a full member of the Catholic Church.

The symbols of confirmation

RENEWAL OF BAPTISMAL VOWS
At confirmation the candidate makes these vows for himself, which symbolises their personal commitment to Christ.

LAYING ON OF HANDS
This symbolises the coming down of the Holy Spirit, as happened at Pentecost. The Holy Spirit is believed to bring the gifts a Christian needs to live a good life.

ANOINTING WITH CHRISM
This symbolises that the person being confirmed belongs to Christ. Chrism is also a symbol of strength. In fact the term 'Christian' literally means 'anointed'.

CONFIRMATION NAME
Sometimes those being confirmed choose a new saint's name, someone whose life they admire, to symbolise their commitment to live a holy life.

Why be confirmed?

- After Jesus' death the Holy Spirit came down upon the apostles to make their faith stronger and give them courage. They then went out and preached about Jesus. The Church wants those who are confirmed to become like apostles – witnesses to their Christian faith in what they say and do.

- Sometimes confirmation is called a rite of passage, a ceremony which marks an important moment in a person's life – the passage from childhood to becoming a young adult.

- In the sacrament people confirm their own vows as Christians, the vows that were made by their parents and godparents on their behalf when they were baptised.

- They are also expected to take responsibility for their own Christian faith, to pray and receive the sacraments and to respect God's laws without being prompted by their parents.

Activities

1. Make a list of all the things that teenagers can do for themselves which their parents had to do for them when they were babies.

2. There are said to be seven gifts of the Holy Spirit. Find out what they are. Your teacher will help. Then choose the three you think are the most important, and explain why a young Catholic might need those gifts in the world today. Write a short essay about this.

3. Prepare a presentation or storyboard on what happens during confirmation and explain the symbolism involved.

For discussion

Confirmation is more important than baptism. Do you agree?

Summary

- The sacrament of confirmation completes baptism.
- At confirmation young people make their own choice to be Christians.
- Confirmation uses symbols such as the laying on of hands and anointing with chrism.
- Christians believe that at confirmation they receive the gifts of the Holy Spirit.

3.3 Reconciliation

Learning outcomes

By the end of this lesson you should:

- know what happens in the sacrament of reconciliation
- understand why the sacrament is so important to Catholics
- be able to evaluate the importance of confessing sins to a priest.

edexcel ⠿ key terms

Absolution – Through the act of the priest, God grants pardon and peace.

Contrition – Feeling sorrow for the sin committed and deciding not to sin again.

Penance – An action to show your contrition.

A sacrament of healing

The sacrament of reconciliation is a ceremony to heal someone. This means that, by receiving the sacrament, Catholics can mend their relationship with God, which has been damaged because of the sins they have committed. They do this by admitting what they have done wrong and by asking God to forgive them.

Key parts of the sacrament of reconciliation

REPENTANCE   CONFESSION   FORGIVENESS

PENANCE   RECONCILIATION

Catholics are encouraged to receive the sacrament of reconciliation regularly.

Repentance – first of all, a person has to repent – to be truly sorry for their sins – before they can receive the sacrament. This sometimes also called **contrition**.

Confession – then the person tells, or confesses, their sins to a priest. The priest offers help and advice to the penitent.

Penance – usually the person is asked to do something to make up for the sins they have committed, such as say some extra payers for someone they have hurt, or return something they have stolen.

Forgiveness – through the **absolution** then given by the priest, God forgives the sins of anyone who is truly sorry.

Reconciliation – through this sacrament, people are reconciled with God, and also with other people whom they may have hurt because of their sins.

Activities

1 Make a spider chart, showing all the various names given to the sacrament of reconciliation. Write 'Reconciliation' in the centre of your diagram and write the different names around it. In your own words, say what that name tells us about the sacrament.

The seal of confession

What a person tells the priest in confession is private, between the priest, the penitent (the person making the confession) and God. It is protected by what is known as the Seal of Confession. The priest can tell no one what he has heard. That is important because people are more likely to want to say what they have done, even very serious or embarrassing things, if they know it won't go any further.

The Seal of Confession is considered so important that some priests have been prepared to die rather than betray what they have heard.

Does confession permit Catholics to go on sinning?

Some people think that if they can be forgiven even very serious sins, they can just sin as much as they like provided they go to go to confession afterwards. But God only grants forgiveness if there is true contrition:

- The person has to be truly sorry for what they have done. This is known as 'repentance'.
- They must genuinely want to try not to do it again.

ResultsPlus
Build better answers

Do Christians have to go to confession to have their sins forgiven?
Give **two** reasons for your point of view (4 marks).

 Basic, 1-mark answer
A brief undeveloped reason. 'No because God is all good and will always forgive us if we are sorry.'

 Good, 2–3-mark answer
Add a development – 'Jesus said we could ask God's forgiveness simply by saying the 'Our Father'.' Also add another reason – 'Confession is a Catholic practice, Protestants don't have to go to confession'.

 Excellent, 4-mark answer
Develop the second reason – 'Protestant Churches teach that Christians do not need a priest to intercede for them.'

Activities

2 Some Christians do not believe there is a need for a sacrament of reconciliation. Organise a class debate. The motion: 'Going to confession helps sinners make a fresh start.' What would you want to say? Remember, you may be asked to speak either for or against the motion.

Why do Catholics go to confession?

The Catholic Church teaches that sin is not something personal. When we sin we do a lot of damage – we may have hurt someone close to us or hurt the community in which we live.

To put all of that right we really need to say sorry in a public way, even if what we have actually done is kept secret. By doing this we can feel we have been reconciled with everyone we have hurt.

The Catholic Church teaches that this authority to forgive sins was handed down by the apostles to their successors, to bishops and to priests who are their co-workers. Although that means a priest can forgive sins, in fact he does so in God's name.

For discussion

Do you think priests should ever tell someone else what they heard in confession? If so, under what circumstances?

Summary

- The sacrament of reconciliation is the means by which Catholics express sorrow for their sins and receive forgiveness.
- Catholics believe it is important to receive the sacrament of reconciliation, rather than just say sorry to God privately.

3.4 Anointing the sick

Learning outcomes

By the end of this lesson you should:

- know what happens during the sacrament of anointing
- understand why the sacrament of anointing is so important for Catholics
- be able to evaluate the importance of faith for those who are sick or dying.

Sacred texts

Jesus' Apostles anoint the sick
Mark 6:13

St James tells Christians to anoint their sick
James 5:14–15

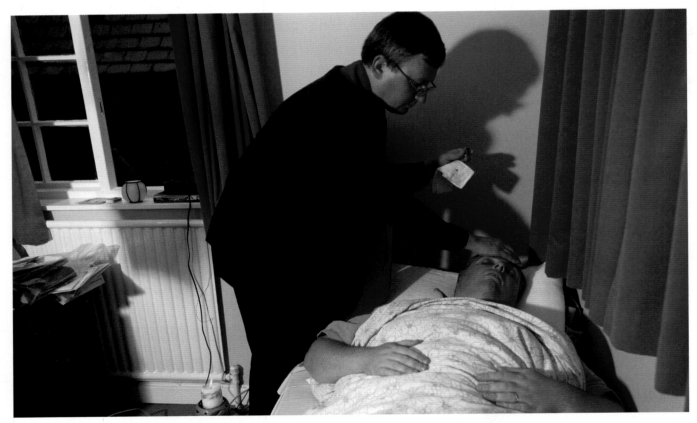

The sacrament of anointing strengthens the faith of the sick and dying.

Coping with illness

Sickness can cause all kinds of physical symptoms, such as pain or a high temperature. It can also make people feel bad in other ways. It can make them feel anxious because they are missing work, or worried about how serious their illness is. They may also feel lonely because they are stuck in their rooms while everyone else is going about their daily business.

Activities

1 How do you feel when you are sick? Write a list of all the ways people feel when they are ill – remember to include both physical and emotional symptoms. Now select the feelings you think are the worst, and briefly explain why you have chosen them.

What happens during the Sacrament of Anointing?

Sacraments are signs that God is with us to help us through important or difficult times. This is very clear when we look at the sacrament of anointing. When a person is very sick they will need help in many ways, more than just medicine. Catholics are encouraged to ask a priest to visit a person who is seriously ill, or dying, in their homes or in hospital, and to give them the sacrament of anointing.

- The sick person confesses their sins to remove any anxiety they may have about dying without having told God they are sorry for their sins.
- A special prayer of healing is said, asking God to give the person the strength to fight against the illness, or at least to be free from fear.
- Special oil is used to anoint the sick person as a symbol of the strength and the courage God gives them to face their suffering, or even their death. Even those who believe in God and Heaven can be frightened when they are about to die, and this sacrament tries to help them feel at peace and to face death without fear.
- They may also receive communion – the bread and wine which Catholics believe is the body and blood of Jesus, to help them feel that Christ is with them in this difficult time. Receiving anointing and communion in this way when a person is close to death is called 'Viaticum', a Latin word which signifies the journey from life through death to eternal life.
- When they receive this sacrament they will have the priest and often their family and friends around them, and this helps them not to feel alone, but supported by the Christian community.

Activities

2 What happens at the sacrament of anointing? Use the information above to write a short story about someone who is ill, describing what happens when the priest comes to administer the sacrament.

Activities

3 Consider what it must be like for someone when they are close to death.

What kinds of things would be important to them?

Why is it important to Catholics?

Christians believe that prayer and strong faith can help sick people get better. There are Christians who believe this so firmly that they will not seek medical help when they are sick, but rely on the power of prayer. Most Catholics do not take such an extreme view. They would always be encouraged to follow medical advice, but at the same time to have faith that God helps people deal with sickness.

This sacrament reminds us of the Christian belief that death is not the final end. Christians look forward to eternal life with God, and they see their life on Earth as a period of preparation, sometimes a period of suffering and testing for which they need God's help. Eternal life with God is called Heaven.

For discussion

Is it possible for Christians to have so much faith in God that they believe that prayer, not medicine, will make them better?

Summary

- The sacrament of anointing is a sacrament especially for the sick and those who are close to death.
- The ceremony may include both confession and receiving communion, as well as anointing with holy oil.
- Anointing strengthens a Christian's faith in God and their confidence that God can bring healing.
- Anointing comforts those believers who are dying and prepares them for their journey from this life to eternal life.

3.5 The nature and importance of Catholic Mass

Learning outcomes

By the end of this lesson you should:

- understand why the Mass is said to be like the Last Supper
- understand what is meant by the term 'the Real Presence'
- understand why Catholics say that the Mass is a 'sacrifice'
- be able to evaluate the importance to Catholics of celebrating the Mass.

edexcel ⠿ key terms

Penitential rite – The confession and absolution at the beginning of Mass.

Liturgy of the Word – The Bible readings in the second part of the Mass.

Liturgy of the Eucharist – The re-enactment of the Last Supper during which the bread and wine are transubstantiated.

Rite of communion – Receiving the body and blood of Jesus.

Transubstantiation – The belief that the bread and wine become the body and blood of Jesus.

The Last Supper

Just before he died Jesus shared a final meal with his disciples. This meal is usually called the Last Supper. Jesus told his disciples to re-enact the Last Supper regularly in memory of him. For 2000 years Christians have been doing just that. Catholics usually call that celebration the Mass, while other Christians call it either the Eucharist or Holy Communion.

The Church says that Catholics must attend Mass every Sunday and on other special holy days such as Christmas Day. Those who do no not go to Mass on Sundays, except for a good reason, are believed to have sinned against God.

Sacred texts

Last Supper
Matt 26:26–29

St Paul teaches about celebrating the Eucharist
1 Corinthians 11:17–34

Activities

1 Read what St Paul says about the Last Supper in 1 Corinthians 11:17–34. Try to express in your own words what he says happened at the Last Supper and his concerns about the way the Christians in Corinth are celebrating the Eucharist.

The Mass re-enacts the Last Supper.

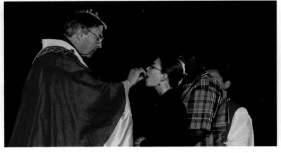

What happens in the Mass?

Introductory and penitential rites
- The priest and people gather, and welcome each other
- They confess their sins, and ask God's forgiveness so that they can celebrate the Mass worthily
- Sometimes a hymn called the Gloria is sung, and there in an opening prayer called a collect

Liturgy of the Word
- The congregation listens to passages from the Bible culminating in a reading from the Gospels
- In his sermon the priest tries to help them apply the teachings of the Bible to their everyday lives
- At some Masses the people recite the creed and offer prayers for the needs of the local community and the wider world

Liturgy of the Eucharist
- This is the heart of the celebration, where the priest repeats what Jesus did at the Last Supper
- He takes the bread and wine and says a prayer of blessing and thanksgiving. He asks that the bread and wine should become the body and blood of Christ
- After saying the 'Our Father' and sharing a sign of peace, the people then receive the body and blood of Christ in the **rite of communion**

Concluding rites
- At the end of Mass there is a final prayer
- The priest asks God to bless everyone who has taken part
- The priest tells the congregation to 'go in peace, to love and serve the Lord'

Activities

2 Draw an ideas map of reasons why the Mass is so important for Catholics. Which do you think Catholics would say is the most important reason? Do you agree with them?

Why is the Mass so important for Catholics?

For Catholics, the Mass is much more than just a meal in memory of Jesus. There are two teachings which help us to understand why the Mass is so important to Catholics.

- Catholics believe that Jesus meant his words 'this is my body' and 'this is my blood' to be taken literally. Although the bread and wine continued to look and taste like bread and wine, in fact they were transformed into his body and blood. This is called **transubstantiation**. Jesus wanted his followers to experience his real physical presence every time they re-enacted the Last Supper and received communion. That is why Catholics believe in what is known as the Real Presence. They believe that the bread and wine really do become the body and blood of Christ. They are not just symbols.
- 'Sacrifice' means giving up something important as a penalty for some fault or mistake. Catholics understand that Jesus' death on the cross was a sacrifice – Jesus was the victim who, like a sacrificial lamb, was put to death for the sins of the world. At Mass Catholics believe that the priest re-enacts the sacrifice of Jesus on the cross.

It is also important because when Catholics receive Christ at Mass (which is called 'receiving Holy Communion') they believe that it can have many beneficial effects in their lives. For example:

- It builds up their relationship with Jesus and with God the Father.
- As members of the Church gather to receive communion they are united together.
- Receiving communion gives members of the Church new strength to live according to God's will.

Summary

- Jesus told his followers to celebrate the Mass in memory of him and Catholics are obliged to attend Mass every Sunday and on other special occasions.
- Catholics believe that Jesus is really present at Mass, in the form of the bread and wine, and that the mass re-enacts the sacrifice of Jesus on the cross.

3.6 Eucharist in other Christian traditions

Learning outcomes

By the end of this lesson you should:

- understand the different Christian beliefs about the Eucharist
- understand the problems created for Christianity by these different beliefs
- be able to evaluate the need for Christians to celebrate the Eucharist together.

Sacred texts

See The Catholic Mass, page 70

Christians are divided over the meaning of the Eucharist.

edexcel key terms

Commemoration – The belief that the Eucharist is simply a remembrance of the Last Supper.

One bread, one body?

Over the centuries there have been splits in the Christian Church. Some of these disagreements were about who should be in charge of the Church, others were about what Christians should believe.

One effect of these splits is that, although nearly all Christian Churches celebrate the Mass or Eucharist, they don't agree about what happens. There are also some differences in the way they celebrate.

Activities

1 Read the account of the Last Supper in St Matthew's Gospel. Describe what happened, and what Jesus said, in your own words.

In fact, some Christians will not share communion with each other. Jesus intended that the Mass should be a way of keeping his followers united (one bread, one body) and all Christians believe that this lack of unity among Christ's followers is a very serious problem.

Disunity between Christians

Some Christians, such as the Salvation Army and the Society of Friends (Quakers) do not celebrate the Eucharist at all. They emphasise that God's grace comes to us in all aspects of our lives and therefore sacraments, such as the Eucharist are not necessary to achieve salvation.

In most Protestant Christian Churches, the Eucharist is celebrated as a response to the wish expressed by Jesus at the Last Supper, that it should be celebrated to help keep his memory alive. These Christians believe that when Jesus said 'This is my Body' he didn't intend this to be taken literally. For example, he could have meant it symbolically – that when Christians attend the Eucharist, the bread and wine remind them of Jesus and that the Eucharist is simply a **commemoration**.

Therefore, unlike the Catholic and Orthodox Churches, most Protestants do not believe in transubstantiation, the Real Presence or that the Eucharist is a re-enactment of Jesus' sacrifice on the cross (see pages 70–71).

For Protestant Christians, the Eucharist is usually only held every few weeks and the celebrations tend to be quite simple. Let's have a look at an example.

The Eucharist in the Baptist Church

The Baptist service is less formal than Catholic Mass, has no set order and can vary from church to church. It is called The Lord's Supper, and is usually held once or twice a month. The service starts with the minister calling the people to take the bread and wine in memory of the Last Supper and the death of Jesus. An account of the Last Supper is read over the bread and wine. Ordinary bread and grape juice are usually used. They are seen only as symbols of Jesus' presence. The people remain in their seats as the bread and the wine or grape juice is given to them in small cups, taken to them by the elders of the church. They all drink at the same time to show a sense of unity; all one in Jesus. For Baptists the Eucharist is important because it helps them remember Jesus and what he did.

A Commission of Catholics and Anglicans looked into the problem of Christian disagreements about the Eucharist. You can find out more by going to www.heinemann.co.uk/hotlinks (express code 4257P) and clicking on the appropriate link. Or look for any information or articles about 'ARCIC' (Anglican Roman Catholic International Commission).

The Eucharist – a way of uniting Christians?

The Catholic and Orthodox Churches teach that receiving communion is a sign of unity among Christians. Because the Christian Church has these divisions, those in the Catholic and Orthodox Churches do not normally share the Eucharist with members of other Churches. Most Protestant Churches look upon sharing communion as a way in which the divided Church may become more united, and many will share communion with other Christians. Nearly all Christians will agree that this lack of unity about something as important as the Eucharist is not good for the Church.

For discussion

Does it matter if Christians do not celebrate the Eucharist together?

Activities

2 Imagine that a pen-pal who is not a Christian has asked you to explain what you have learnt in RS this week. Write a letter back to them explaining why you think all Christians do not celebrate the Eucharist together.

Summary

- Nearly all Christians celebrate the Eucharist but they do not all believe the same things about what happens.
- Catholics emphasise that the Eucharist is a sacrifice, whereas Protestants place greater emphasis on the Eucharist as a memorial meal.
- These disagreements about the Eucharist are a source of division and disunity between Christians.

3.7 Features of Catholic churches

74

The shape of a church

This ground plan of a Catholic church is in the traditional shape – a cross, to symbolise the crucifixion of Jesus. In the past the priest used to celebrate Mass at one end of the church while most of the congregation prayed quietly at the other end. Many modern Catholic churches have a different shape. Some of them are half circles, or even circular. Now that everyone takes an active part in the celebration of Mass, this allows all those present to feel close to the altar.

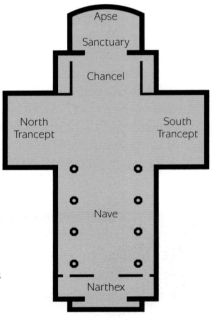

Apse

Sanctuary

Chancel

North Trancept

South Trancept

Nave

Narthex

A traditional Catholic church

Activities

1 Draw the ground plan of the Catholic church. The one above is in the traditional shape (like a cross). Make it quite large because later you will be asked to show where certain features can be found.

Perhaps your teacher will take you to visit a local Catholic church. If so, be sure to make your own sketch of where everything is.

Features of Catholic churches

Although Catholic churches are not all the same size and shape you will find the same things in most of them. Here are the main features, with an explanation of what they are for, and where they might be found.

STATUES
Images of Jesus (such as crucifixes) and of Mary and the saints. They are usually placed around the inside of the church, against the walls. Some churches have a special chapel for the statue of Mary, called the Lady Chapel.

FEATURES OF CATHOLIC CHURCHES

LECTERN
Where readings from the Bible are proclaimed. This is also where the priest preaches his sermon. It is in front of the altar to one side of the church. This shows that the Bible and teachings of the Church are important but that the Eucharist is the focus, symbolised by the positioning of the altar.

THE TABERNACLE

This is an ornate container, where the Body of Christ is kept after Mass is over. It is sometimes found just behind the altar, though some churches place it in a special chapel called the Blessed Sacrament Chapel.

THE ALTAR

This is where the bread and wine are blessed. It is at the east end (front) of the church, in the centre, in a special area called the sanctuary (which means the holy place). The altar is focus point of Catholic churches because worship is centred on the celebration of the Eucharist.

STATIONS OF THE CROSS

A series of 14 images depicting Jesus' suffering and death. These are placed on the walls around the inside of the church. Catholics use the stations to remind them of Jesus' passion.

THE BAPTISMAL FONT

This is where people are baptised. It is usually at the back of church, near the doors where people enter the church. Some modern churches place it near the altar, symbolising its importance at the first sacrament.

BISHOP'S THRONE

These are not found in every church but only in Cathedrals, which is a church for use by the bishop. His throne is a grand seat in the sanctuary, to the side but facing the altar. This symbolises the importance of the bishop but his focus is again on the Eucharist.

Activities

2 Use the description of each of the features to try to place them in the right position in your plan of a traditional Catholic church.

Summary

- Traditional Christian churches are in the shape of a cross, but modern churches allow everyone to feel close to what is going on.
- The church has many features which form part of the celebration of Mass or the other sacraments, or help people to pray.
- The features of Protestant churches are not the same as Catholic churches because of their different beliefs.

3.8 Christmas

76

Learning outcomes

By the end of this lesson you should:

- know what happened when Jesus was born
- understand why Christmas is so important to Christians
- evaluate the meaning of Christmas today.

Sacred texts

The Prophets foretell Jesus' birth
Isaiah 11:1–9, Micah 5: 2

The birth of Jesus
Luke 2:1–20,
Matthew 2:1–12

Activities

1 This is a scene from a traditional Christmas nativity play. How many people from the story can you identify? Use the picture to write the story of Jesus' birth in your own words.

Children re-enact the Christmas story

What happened when Jesus was born?

Christmas is the day when Christians celebrate the birth of Jesus. According to tradition Jesus was born in a stable in Bethlehem to where Mary and Joseph had travelled to take part in the Roman census. Because all the inns were full, Mary and Joseph had to sleep in a stable, and it was there that Jesus was born. The Gospels tell us that angels proclaimed his birth and that shepherds came to the stable to give homage. St Luke also tells the story of wise men (Magi) who, guided by a star, came from the East to find Jesus and to bring him gifts of gold, frankincense and myrrh. The visit of the Magi is celebrated 12 days after Christmas, on the 6 January. It is called the Epiphany.

A family celebration

Christians celebrate Christmas as a family in memory of the Holy Family – Jesus, Mary and Joseph.

- They go to Christmas Mass together, often at midnight.
- They also have a traditional meal together.
- The tradition of giving presents recalls the gifts that the wise men gave to Jesus.

But many Christians believe that Christmas has become too commercial, with too much emphasis on eating and drinking and spending. In giving presents it is the act of thoughtfulness and generosity that is important to Christians, not the size or value of the gifts. Christians remember the many people around the world who do not receive presents and don't even have enough food to eat.

Activities

2 Make two lists. In one, write down all the things that people do to celebrate Christmas which have no religious meaning. In the other list write down all the religious things that Christians do to celebrate Christmas. Do any activities appear in both lists? What does this tell you about the nature of the celebration of Christmas?

ResultsPlus
Top tip!

If you are asked to explain how Christians celebrate Christmas, it is all right to mention the exchange of presents. However, you **must** explain the religious significance of giving presents – that they symbolise the gifts brought to Jesus by the Magi or wise men. You could mention that in some countries the exchange of gifts takes place on the feast of the Magi (Epiphany), on 6 January.

Why is Christmas important to Christians?

- Christians believe that Jesus is the Son of God and that his birth – which is often called the incarnation – is therefore one of the most important events in history.

- They believe that many of the prophets of the Old Testament, especially the prophet Isaiah, foretold the birth of Jesus many hundreds of years before the event.

- The Christian Church teaches that although Mary was Jesus' mother, Jesus is God's son. Jesus was conceived without Mary having any sexual relationship. This is known as the Virgin Birth. Joseph is honoured by Christians because of his willingness to accept Jesus as his foster son.

- Without Jesus' birth the Christian faith would not have begun. Jesus would not have given his life for us, and so we would not have been saved from our sins.

- The wise men were not Jews. Christians believe that Jesus did not come just to the Jews but that he came to save all people.

Activities

3 Produce a poster to be displayed outside a Catholic church at Christmas. On it write just six of the most important things you think Catholics should remember at Christmas time.

For discussion

At Christmas 1914, during the First World War, there was a short truce. The British took on the Germans at football in 'no man's land', while German soldiers sang Christmas carols. For a short time no gunshots were heard. Why do you think this brief truce took place?

Summary

- Christmas is celebrated to mark the birth of Jesus whom Christians believe was their saviour.

- The feast is particularly special because of the Christian belief in the incarnation – that Jesus is God in human form.

- Christmas is a time when families get together for a special meal, and go to Mass together, sometimes at midnight on Christmas Eve.

3.9 The meaning and importance of Lent

78

Sacred texts

Jesus fasts in the desert
Matthew 4:1–11

Isaiah speaks about fasting
Isaiah 58:1–12

What is Lent?

Lent is the name given by Christians to the 40 days leading up to Easter and is a period of preparation and prayer.

Lent begins on Ash Wednesday. It ends with the celebration of Jesus' resurrection on Easter Sunday (see page 82). It is 40 days because Jesus fasted and prayed in the desert for 40 days before he started his public ministry.

There is a tradition of asking people to give something up for Lent, something they really like. Many Catholic children say they will not eat sweets, but not all of them last the whole 40 days!

AND WHAT ARE YOU GIVING UP FOR LENT, REVEREND ?

RELIGION

Activities

1 Look at the Lent cartoon. What kinds of activities are Christians supposed to practise? In the cartoon how are they failing to observe Lent properly?

Activities

2 Have a survey in class. Have any of you given up something for Lent? What did you give up and what was it like? What kinds of things do you think it would be a good idea to give up and why?

How and why do Christians observe Lent?

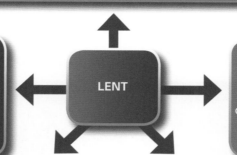

Ashes
On Ash Wednesday Christians go to Church. During the religious service, the priest makes the sign of the cross with ashes on everyone's forehead. Ashes are a sign of repentance and Christians wear them on Ash Wednesday to symbolise the beginning of this period of repentance.

Prayer
During Lent many Christians spend more time in prayer. This helps them to put God and spiritual things into the forefront of their minds.

LENT

Repentance
Throughout Lent Christians spend time thinking about things they have done wrong and will repent for them. They can then approach Easter in a less sinful condition.

Fasting
On Ash Wednesday and Good Friday adult Catholics eat less food than normal (fasting) and do not eat any meat (abstinence). This is done as a reminder that Jesus spent 40 days fasting in the desert. It also helps Christians to remember that many people in the world do not have enough food to eat, and that it is the duty of a Christian to keep them in mind and try to help them.

Good works
Because Lent focuses on Jesus' suffering, Christians are encouraged to be more aware of the suffering of others. Some people save money by fasting, and then donate what they have saved to a charity; others might visit elderly neighbours who may be lonely, or do similar good works.

For discussion

What other events in life do we prepare for, and how do we prepare? Why is preparation for some events so important? How does Lent make Christians better prepared to celebrate Easter?

Activities

3 Study the spider diagram carefully then write a paragraph explaining why lent is important to Christians.

Summary

- Lent is the 40 days from Ash Wednesday leading up to Easter.
- The period of Lent recalls the 40 days that Jesus spent in the desert.
- These 40 days are a time when Christians prepare for Easter by fasting, praying and doing good works.
- Both Christians and Muslims have a season of fasting, though in modern times the Muslim fast is stricter.

3.10 Holy Week

80

edexcel key terms

Holy Week – The week before Easter Sunday.

What is Holy Week?

Holy Week is the name given to the last week of Jesus' human life, the week leading up to his crucifixion and resurrection. In the Christian calendar it is the holiest week of the year, and certain days that week (Palm Sunday, Maundy Thursday and Good Friday) are remembered and celebrated in a very special way.

Sacred texts

Palm Sunday
Luke 19:28–38

The Passion
Matthew:26 and 27

Dying for others
John 15:13

Jesus is proclaimed the Messiah by the crowd

Jesus enters Jerusalem on a donkey

The crowd demand Jesus' crucifixion

The trial before the Sanhedrin

Jesus is betrayed by Judas

Jesus washes his disciples' feet

Jesus celebrates the Last Supper

The trial before Pilate

Peter denies Jesus

Jesus dies on the cross

Jesus is taken from the cross and laid in a tomb

Activities

1 Look at all the events of Holy Week surrounding the picture. Try to write the events down correctly in the right order on the right day. If you need help you can read the account given by St Matthew.

2 Try to find out how unpleasant a death crucifixion was. What would have been the cause of death?

Why is Holy Week so important?

PALM SUNDAY

On this day Jesus arrived in Jerusalem with his disciples, riding on a donkey. So great was his reputation as a religious teacher and a miracle worker that great crowds came out to greet him. They waved palm branches and called Jesus the Son of David and the King of Israel. On this day many of the crowds recognised Jesus as their Messiah or saviour.

MAUNDY THURSDAY

On this day, Christians remember how Jesus celebrated the Jewish feast of Passover with his disciples. We are told that he washed his disciples' feet and in this way taught them that being a Christian is about showing service to others.

At the Last Supper Jesus celebrated the Mass (or the Eucharist) for the first time. Before he gave bread and wine to his disciples he said that they were his body and blood. He also told his followers they should celebrate the Mass regularly in memory of him. For 2000 years the Mass has been the central Christian act of worship.

Later that same evening Jesus went to the garden of Gethsemane to pray. While he was there he was betrayed by Judas, one of his apostles, and handed over to the guard of the Jewish Temple.

GOOD FRIDAY

On this day, Jesus was put on trial, in front of the Jewish religious council and in front of Pontius Pilate, the Roman governor of the region. He was taken to a place called Golgotha and there he was executed. After his death, his body was taken down and laid inside a tomb, and the tomb sealed with a stone.

Christians believe that Jesus' death was a sacrifice. He willingly suffered, even though he was innocent, so that others would not need to suffer for their sins. This is also sometimes called the 'Sacrifice of Calvary' – Calvary was the name of the hill where Jesus was killed.

For discussion

Read the account of Jesus' Trials (*Matthew 26: 57–66* and *Matthew 27: 11–26*).

Did Jesus get a fair trial? What else could the authorities have done to ensure that Jesus' trial was fair according to our standards today?

Did Jesus have to die?

Christians give many answers to this question.

- By dying he gave his followers an example of love. Jesus himself said 'No one shows greater love than when he lays down his life for his friends' (John 15: 13).
- By dying he willingly accepted the punishment for everyone's sins and therefore he is mankind's saviour. His death was an act of Atonement (see pages 16–17).
- He needed to die so that he could rise again, prove he was the Son of God and open the possibility of eternal life to his followers.

Activities

3 Find out all you can about what the term 'scapegoat' means.

   In what way can Jesus be described as a kind of scapegoat?

For discussion

Jesus was accused of blasphemy and rebellion. Was he innocent or guilty?

Summary

- Holy Week commemorates the final week of Jesus' life, and the events leading up to his death.
- On Maundy Thursday Jesus celebrated the Eucharist for the first time, at the Last Supper.
- On Good Friday Jesus was crucified.
- Christians believe that Jesus' death was an act of atonement.

3.11 Easter

Learning outcomes

By the end of this lesson you should:

- know the accounts of Jesus' resurrection and his appearances to the disciples
- understand why the celebration of Easter is so important for Christians
- understand how Christians celebrate Easter
- be able to evaluate the significance of the resurrection for Jesus' followers.

Sacred texts

Jesus is Risen
Matthew 28:1–8, Mark 16:1–8,
Luke 24:1–12 John 20:1–10

Apostles preach the risen Christ
Acts 2:29–36

St Paul proclaims the Resurrection
1 Corinthians 15:1–19

Did Jesus rise from the dead?

Christianity is founded on the belief that after Jesus died, he rose again three days later.

All four Gospel writers say that this happened, and their accounts of it, although different, tell the same story. In the Acts of the apostles we see that the resurrection of Jesus was the first thing the apostles preached after the Holy Spirit came down upon them at Pentecost. St Paul confirms that it is the most important of all Christian beliefs.

Clearly the apostles were in no doubt that Jesus had risen from the dead.

The Gospels give two different kinds of evidence to support this belief.

- The first is that some of the disciples of Jesus went to the place where he had been buried and found that the tomb was empty.
- Then, Jesus appeared alive to a number of his followers on several different occasions.

Belief in the resurrection is the basis of the Christian faith.

Activities

1 Read the whole Mark Chapter 16 and Luke Chapter 24.

   Make a list of:

   (a) those who visited Jesus tomb and

   (b) those to whom he appeared.

2 If you have time, do the same for the accounts given by Matthew and John.

   Do the Gospel writers agree about what happened at the resurrection?

How do Christians celebrate Easter?

- Easter Sunday is one of the most joyful of Christian celebrations. Many Christian families attend a special Vigil Mass on the Saturday night.
- This Vigil begins with the lighting of a fire, which symbolises the Light of Christ that has come into the world because of Jesus' resurrection.
- From this fire is lit a special candle known as the Paschal (or Easter) candle. The candle has special markings, including the Greek letters Alpha and Omega, which represent the beginning and the end – the belief that Christ has always existed and will always exist.
- The candle is carried into the dark church and as the candle lightens the church, the priest proclaims 'Christ our Light'.

Christians also renew their baptismal vows (see page 62) and re-commit themselves to fighting evil and doing good works.

The Paschal candle represents the Christian belief in the victory of Jesus' resurrection.

For discussion

St Paul said 'If Christ has not been raised, then our preaching has been in vain and your faith has been in vain'. Do you agree? How much less important would Jesus' life be without the resurrection?

The importance of the resurrection

When Jesus died on the cross his followers must have thought that everything they had believed about him has been a mistake. When he rose again three days later their faith was renewed. These are some of the things that Christians believe because of the resurrection:

- Jesus is the Son of God. The fact that Jesus was able to come back to life proves that he was the Son of God, because only God would have such power.
- Death is not the end. By rising from the dead Jesus conquered death. This means that God can grant eternal life to all his people. Christians believe death is not the end of existence, but only a transition from this world to Heaven.
- Jesus' teachings are confirmed. Because Jesus has proven that he is God, then we can also have confidence in all the other things that he has taught.
- Jesus lives. Jesus only had to conquer death once, he would never die again. Christians believe that now he 'lives and reigns for ever and ever'.

Activities

3 Find out more about the Paschal candle. What symbols are inscribed into the candle and what do they mean? Prepare a short report for the rest of the class.

To find out more about the Paschal candle go to www.heinemann.co.uk/hotlinks (express code 4257P) and click on the appropriate link.

Summary

- Jesus' resurrection is the central belief of the Christian faith.
- The resurrection confirmed the faith of the apostles that Jesus was God, and that his teachings and his promises of life after death are true.
- Christians celebrate Easter with a special Vigil Mass. They light the Easter candle and renew their baptismal vows.

exam zone

KnowZone
Worship and celebration

Quick quiz

1 What is meant by 'absolution'?

2 What is 'Holy Week'?

3 Describe two of the symbols used at baptism.

4 What happens during the Liturgy of the Word at Mass?

5 Describe two of the ways in which Christians observe Lent.

6 Give two reasons why Catholics go to Mass.

7 Do Protestants believe in transubstantiation?

8 What is a lectern used for?

9 Explain briefly why Jesus' death is important to Christians.

10 Give two reasons why Christians believe that Jesus rose from the dead.

Plenary activity

1 The sacraments you have studied are full of symbols such as water and chrism. Take each of the four sacraments of baptism, reconciliation, confirmation and the anointing of the sick and make a list of the symbols used in each. Then write a short description for each symbol, saying what the symbol represents.

Find out more

The Catechism of the Catholic Church is the best summary of Catholic belief. It has been compiled with the approval of the Pope and bishops. It has an index that is very easy to use.

There are a number of Christian and Catholic Encyclopaedias which may be available in your school library.

During the course of a year many Catholic churches will have celebrations of baptism and confirmation. Perhaps you could get permission to attend one of these.

Redemptorist Publications produces many simple guides to the Sacraments. Perhaps there are copies in your school library or local church.

Most churches produce weekly newsletters. At Christmas, Lent, Holy Week and Easter these will usually include a short article about the particular feast being celebrated.

Many churches are open most of the day and allow you to walk around to look at the various features. You might need to explain that you are doing it as part of your school work.

The Vatican has its own website which is available in a number of languages.

The Documents of the Second Vatican Council also consider such matters as worship and celebration. These are official documents about Catholic teaching that were written in the 1960s. They were written following a great gathering in Rome of all the Bishops for what is called an Ecumenical Council. In the index you could look for references to 'Eucharist' or the 'resurrection'.

Self-evaluation checklist

Read through the following list and evaluate how well you know and understand each of the topics.

How well have you understood the topics in this section? In the first column of the table below use the following code to rate your understanding:

Green – I understand this fully

Orange – I am confident I can answer most questions on this

Red – I need to do a lot more work on this topic.

In the second and third columns you need to think about:

- Whether you have an opinion on this topic and could give reasons for that opinion if asked
- Whether you can give the opinion of someone who disagrees with you and give reasons for this alternative opinion.

Content covered	My understanding is red/orange/ green	Can I give my opinion?	Can I give an alternative opinion?
● The meaning for Catholics of the sacrament of baptism.			
● Why this is important for Catholics.			
● The meaning for Catholics of the sacrament of confirmation.			
● Why this is important for Catholics.			
● The meaning for Catholics of the sacrament of reconciliation.			
● Why this is important for Catholics.			
● The meaning for Catholics of the sacrament of anointing the sick.			
● Why this is important for Catholics.			
● The meaning of the symbols used in the celebration of these sacraments.			
● What happens during the celebration of the Mass.			
● Why Mass is important for Catholics.			
● The meaning of the Eucharist for Protestant and Orthodox Christians.			
● What are the main features of Catholic churches and why.			
● The meaning of Christmas and why Christmas is important to Catholics.			
● The meaning of Lent and why Lent is important to Catholics.			
● The meaning of Holy Week and why Holy Week is important to Catholics.			
● The meaning of Easter and why Easter is important to Catholics.			

Student tips

There is a lot to learn for this section – what happens during the celebrations of the sacraments, how Christians celebrate the major festivals, etc. I found it quite useful to create lists and then try to remember things by heart.

BUT – many of the questions ask for explanations, not just descriptions, so it is really important to know both what Christians do and why they do it!

There are a lot of Protestant churches near my home, and my parents helped put me in contact with a local minister. She was very helpful in explaining the differences between Catholics and Protestants.

Introduction

In the exam you will be given a choice of two questions on this section. Each question will include four tasks (a-d), which test your knowledge, understanding and evaluation of the material covered. A 2-mark (a) question will ask you to define a term; a 4-mark (b) question will ask your opinion on a point of view; an 8-mark (c) question will ask you to explain a particular belief or idea; a 6-mark (d) question will ask for your opinion on a point of view and ask you to consider an alternative point of view.

You need to give a short accurate definition – just a single sentence. This is a key term so the definition would score full marks.

When you are asked to 'explain' something you must give more than just examples. Imagine that each of your answers should begin, 'Christians celebrate Christmas because…' For example, 'Christians celebrate Christmas because it was the day Jesus was born.' This question is worth 8 marks so you must give up to 4 simple reasons or fewer reasons with some of them developed. You will also be assessed on your use of language in this question.

Mini exam paper

(a) What is chrism? (2 marks)

(b) Is baptism more important than confirmation? (4 marks)
Give two reasons for your point of view.

(c) Explain why Christians celebrate Christmas. (8 marks)

(d) 'All Christians should celebrate the Eucharist together'
In your answer you should refer to Christianity.
   (i) Do you agree? Give reasons for your opinion. (3 marks)
   (ii) Give reasons why some people may disagree with you. (3 marks)

You can give your own point of view, but be sure to give TWO reasons. If you don't have a point of view of your own, you can use reasons you have learned in class.

You only need to give one point of view at this stage but you must give reasons why you hold this point of view.

Now you have to give the opposite point of view, again using material you have learned during your studies. You don't have to say what you think about these alternative points of view, but you do need to give reasons why people hold them.

ResultsPlus

Watch out!

The sacrament of reconciliation is sometimes given different names. Most commonly, Catholics talk about 'going to confession'. This means the same as 'going to receive the sacrament of reconciliation'. It just places the emphasis on the act of confessing sins.

Sometimes Christians talk about 'the Eucharist' and 'Holy Communion'. Catholics are more likely to talk about 'the Mass'. Whatever the term used, Christians are referring to the act of worship where the priest blesses the bread and wine, just as Jesus did at the Last Supper.

Support activity

1   It is important to know what happens during the celebration of the sacraments, so it would be a good idea to learn the various parts of the ceremony. Read the summary of what happens in the sacrament of baptism (pages 63–64) and then try to remember the detail without looking at the text book. Now do the same for the sacraments of reconciliation, confirmation and the anointing of the sick.

ResultsPlus

Maximise your marks

(c)   Explain why Christians celebrate Christmas. (8 marks)

Student answer	Examiner comments	Improved student answer
Christians celebrate Christmas because it is the day that Jesus was born. They also give presents and go to Midnight Mass.	'Because it is the day Jesus was born' is a correct reason for why Christians celebrate Christmas. It is also the answer that most candidates know well. But it is a very brief reason and would reach only Level 1 (1 or 2 marks). The facts that Christians give presents, and go to Midnight Mass, are just descriptions. You couldn't say 'Christians celebrate Christmas because they go to midnight Mass' for example! So they would not add any marks.	Christians celebrate Christmas because it is the day that Jesus was born and they believe that Jesus was the Son of God. Another reason is the Christian belief that the birth of Jesus is known as the incarnation – when God took on human form and lived on Earth.

Living the Christian life

Introduction

There are many different ways to live the Christian life. Catholics believe that God calls some people to serve him through their work in the world and in married life, while others are called to become priests, or monks and nuns. This section will help us to learn more about these different vocations.

Learning outcomes for this section

By the end of this section you should be able to:

- understand what is meant by vocation and describe the different types of vocation that Christians follow
- explain how and why Christians show vocation in their daily lives
- explain how and why some Christians show vocation by taking holy orders
- understand how Christians work for social cohesion and explain why it is important
- understand how and why Christians follow the Ten Commandments as a guide for living
- describe what Jesus taught about the reinterpretation of the Law of Moses and explain how and why Christians use this as a guide for living
- understand how and why Christians use Jesus' teachings on displaying religion, money and Judgement and the Golden Rule as a guide for living
- describe the work of the SVP and explain why the SVP is committed to helping to relieve poverty and suffering in the UK.

edexcel ⠿ key terms

active life	**displaying religion**	**holy orders**	**vocation**
charity	**the evangelical counsels**	**the monastic life**	**hypocrite**
contemplative life	**the Sermon on the Mount**	**religious community**	**the Law of Moses**

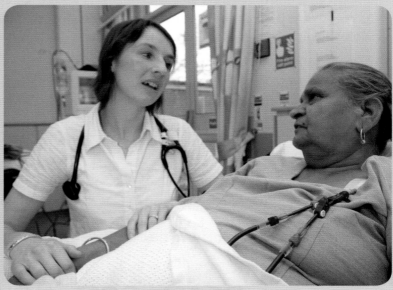

Fascinating fact

Once there were over 6000 Monasteries and Convents just in England and Wales. Even today there are over 60 Religious orders for men and over 200 for women, amounting to over 1000 religious communities.

Look at the photographs. They all show Christians involved in different ways of life. Write down all the things they tell you about the different ways in which people try to live a Christian life. Then share these ideas in a class discussion.

There are many different kinds of vocation.

4.1 Vocation

Learning outcomes

By the end of this lesson you should:

- know what is meant by the term 'vocation'
- understand how Christians believe God calls them to serve him
- be able to evaluate the difficulties and the rewards that come from serving others.

An invitation

There are all kinds of reasons why we behave as we do. Sometimes we do just what we want. Sometimes we do what we are told, even if we don't always want to. Sometimes we are forced to do something; we have no choice at all.

But every now and then we are *invited* to do something. Someone may recognise we are good at something and ask us to use our ability to help in some way. We may be good listeners and be asked for advice, for example. We may be asked to act in the school play, or play in a school team. We also receive invitations to joyful events, such as birthday parties.

Perhaps the things we do because someone has asked us to be involved are the actions that give us most satisfaction because they recognise that we have something special to offer.

edexcel ⠿ key terms

Active life – The life lived by religious orders who work in society as well as praying.

Contemplative life – The life of prayer and meditation lived by some religious orders.

The evangelical counsels – The vows of poverty, chastity and obedience.

Vocation – A call from God to lead the Christian life.

Activities

1   Think of any invitations you have received in the past year. Write down as many as you can. Don't just include invitations to parties, but also whenever someone has asked you to do something or to become involved. For example, to play in a school team or take part in a performance of some kind. Why do you think you were asked?

DEAR GOD, HOW COME I CAN NEVER HEAR YOUR VOICE?

Would you be able to hear if God was calling you?

Sacred texts

Call of Samuel
1 Samuel 3:1–11

Jesus calls the Apostles
Matthew 4:18–22

Conversion of St Paul
Acts 9:3–9

Activities

2 Is it hard to be a Christian? What do you think might
be the main obstacles to being a good Christian in the
modern world?

What talents do you think a person would need to work
with the elderly? Would they need different talents to work
with the young?

3 'A life spent serving others is happier and more rewarding
than one spent doing what we want.' Explain why you
might agree or disagree with this.

For discussion

What, in the modern world, might make it
harder to hear God calling?

What is a vocation?

The word '**vocation**' means a calling or
an invitation. Christians use the term to
mean their belief that God invites all of us
individually to become followers of Christ.
Every person is called to be a Christian,
and to live their life in accordance with
the example and teaching of Jesus.

Some Catholics use the expression 'having
a vocation' to refer specifically to those
called to the priesthood and religious
life. But each person is unique, and every
Christian receives their own special call
from God. Most people are called to get
married and have a family, for example,
and to raise that family in accordance
with God's will. Christians will also want
to find employment which can be used to
serve God and other people.

Some are called to remain celibate,
others to become priests, monks or nuns
(following either the **contemplative life** or
active life). Those who become monks or
nuns commit themselves to following
the evangelical counsels throughout
their lives.

How does God call us?

How does God make this call known? Some people believe
that God has called them directly, the way he called the boy
Samuel in the Old Testament, and told them exactly what
he wanted them to do. That is also what happened to St
Paul on the road to Damascus. But most Christians try to
discover God's will for themselves.

- First, many Christians believe that the work they do
should reflect their commitment to Christ and should
imitate what he did. They see from the Gospel that Jesus
was a teacher and a healer, and that he encouraged people
to visit prisoners and care for the sick.

- It is also a matter of using our skills, which God must have
given us for a reason. If we are good communicators, for
example, we may feel that God wants us to teach. If we get
on well with older people maybe God wants us to work in
the care of the elderly. We can find our vocation by being
aware of what we are good at, and then think of ways we
can use our talents to serve others.

Summary

- A vocation is not just how we choose to live our lives, but
an invitation from God to live and work in imitation of Christ.

- Christians believe that because each person has unique
gifts to offer, everyone receives their own special vocation.

- We can find our vocation by understanding the teaching
of Jesus.

- Christians also look for ways in which they can use their
talents in the service of others.

4.2 Vocation in daily life and work

Learning outcomes

By the end of this lesson you should:

- understand how Christians try to respond to God's call in the workplace
- understand what is meant by the 'role of the laity'
- be able to evaluate what kinds of jobs God calls people to do.

edexcel ::: key terms

The monastic life – Living as a monk or nun in a religious community.

Religious community – A religious order who live together as a group, e.g. the Benedictines.

Charity – Voluntary giving to those in need.

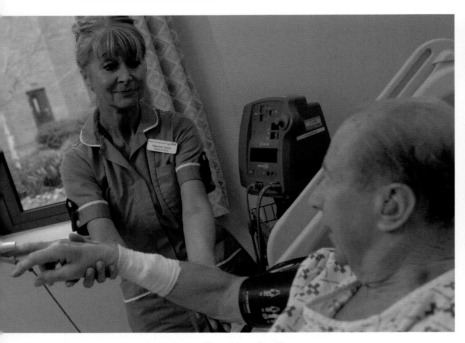

Are all types of work a calling from God?

Sacred texts

Parable of the Talents
Matthew 25:14–30

Variety of gifts
1 Corinthians 12:4–11

God and Money
Matthew 6:24

Called to serve God

We have seen that the word vocation means 'a calling'. Christians believe that God calls every person to live every aspect of their lives in accordance with the teachings of Jesus. That will affect the way they conduct their friendships, the way they speak to others, how well they live side by side with other members of their family.

In particular this means that every Christian must ensure that the job they do is something that reflects God's will for the world.

Some people choose to dedicate their lives to working with the poor, sometimes in developing countries. But not all jobs serve others other so directly. For example, could a Christian dealing in weapons believe that their work is a calling from God?

Activities

1. What kinds of jobs best reflect God's wish that we serve others? Are there any jobs that could never be acceptable to God? In groups, draw up two lists. Then see if the other groups have come up with similar lists.

Vocation in daily life and work

Most Christians do not feel called to be priests or to live **the monastic life** as part of a **religious community**. Instead they live family lives and go out to work each day to earn a living. Nevertheless, Christians believe that God wants them to consider how they can serve him in their daily lives. The Catholic Church makes clear what role the laity have in responding to God's call.

- Most Christians are called to marry and to raise children. Parents should ensure that their family lives reflect the teachings of Jesus and that children are brought up in the Christian faith.

- In whatever work they do they should be honest and just in their dealings with others, always reflecting the teachings of Jesus.

- They should pray and attend Mass regularly and receive the sacraments.

- The laity is also called to assist the priest as readers at Mass, as ministers of communion and as catechists (preparing children for confirmation for example).

- Like all Christians, they should work against immorality in society, by speaking out against sinful situations and by serving those who suffer.

Some jobs and professions are very well paid. Successful lawyers and those who work in the financial sector, football players and pop stars, for example, can earn a great deal of money. But there are Christians who believe that sometimes really well-paid jobs can distract people from serving God. Some people choose to do a job simply because they can earn a lot of money – it is the money not the job which is important. Other Christians would argue that earning lots of money is fine because good things can be achieved with that money. Many well-paid people are dedicated to serving others in their spare time. They can give money to **charity** and do voluntary work.

But a 'vocation' often refers to employment which may not be well paid, but which shows a special commitment to caring for other people. Some people may say that they have a vocation to be a nurse, for example, or even a teacher! They choose the job not for the financial rewards but because they want to dedicate their lives to answering God's call to serve others.

Activities

2   Try to think of as many jobs as possible that involve caring for others. How many of them are well paid? Select one caring job that is not well paid and think about why someone would choose to do that work.

   Does God call people to very well-paid jobs?

3   Soldiers are often called upon to fight and even kill, yet many are committed Christians. Why might a soldier believe that they are doing God's work?

ResultsPlus
Top tip!

If you are asked how Christians display their vocation in their everyday lives you should **not** write about the monastic life.

By using the term 'everyday lives' the examiner is asking about the Christian vocation of the 'laity' – those who do not belong to a religious order.

Summary

- The word 'vocation' can mean what you choose to do for a living.
- The laity are called upon to witness to their Christian faith in all aspects of their lives.
- Some Christians believe they are called to be priests or to spend their lives in a religious order.
- Many Christians believe that they are called by God to work in relatively low-paid jobs, if this involves greater service to others.
- Some Christians argue that certain kinds of work can be un-Christian.

4.3 Holy orders

94

Bishops and priests

Catholics believe that some men are called to serve God as ordained ministers. That means they have been asked by God to dedicate their entire lives to leading people in the worship of God and to making themselves available at all times to help people when they are in need of comfort and support.

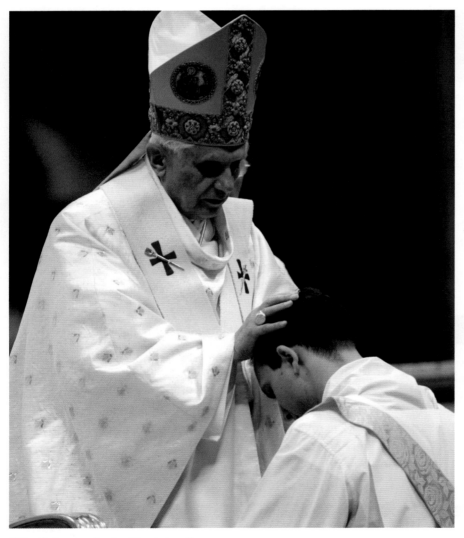

What is happening in this picture?

edexcel ::: key terms

Holy orders – The status of a bishop, priest or deacon.

Sacred texts

Laying on of hands in the Old Testament
Numbers 27:18–23

Laying on of hands in the early Church
Acts 12:2–3

Only men who are worthy may be elders
1 Timothy 5:22

● These men are called bishops and priests. So that they can concentrate on their jobs better, most priests and all bishops do not marry or have a family.

● Priests and bishops don't receive a proper salary, though they are given what they need.

● This is not just a choice made by the men themselves, but a very special calling from God which is given to just a few people.

Because the work can sometimes be hard and lonely, they receive a special sacrament called **holy orders** which asks the Holy Spirit to give them the strength to live up to their commitment. The sacrament is also sometimes known as 'ordination'.

Activities

1 Why might the work of a priest sometimes be hard and lonely? Discuss some possible reasons with your teacher. You may have an opportunity to meet a priest and find out more about his life and work.

Permanent deacons

The training to be a priest takes six years and towards the end of that time they receive the first of the Holy Orders called the diaconate – they become deacons. This role allows them to gain experience of preaching in church and celebrating some of the sacraments.

Deacons are allowed to baptise and to witness the vows of those who are getting married, for example. Usually they remain deacons for about one year. Some men believe they are called to be permanent deacons. This means that they will remain deacons all their lives and assist their local parish priest. Often these men are a little older and already have full-time jobs. They may also be married and have a family.

Ordained ministers in the modern world

In some ways it is much more difficult being an ordained bishop, priest or deacon in the modern world. Not so many people go to church, and the number of men who want to train to be priests is much smaller than it was fifty years ago.

In a world in which religion seems to be in decline, the priest perhaps has an even more important job to do. Ordained ministers need to be even more like the apostles. They have to go out and preach about Jesus and try to bring people back to a life of faith and the worship of God. Many priests find this an exciting and rewarding challenge.

Women priests

According to Catholic teaching, it is against the will of God for women to be ordained. Priests are supposed to represent Jesus and, because Jesus was a man, priests also need to be men. Also, Jesus only chose men as his apostles.

The Catholic Church and the Orthodox Church have both maintained this tradition of male priests throughout their history. The Church of England and other Protestant Churches have allowed the ordination of women for some years. These Churches argue that Jesus only chose men as apostles because no one would have accepted the idea of women travelling around preaching and teaching in his time. They also think that God would want women to have the same rights as men.

Activities

2 Why might someone want to be ordained? What special skills do you think a priest or a bishop might need?

3 Prepare for a debate on the motion 'Women should be allowed to become Catholic priests'. Depending on which side you are asked to take, you may need to do some more research on the various arguments.

Summary

- Catholics believe that some men are called to become ordained ministers and to dedicate their lives to preaching the Gospel and caring for the Catholic community.
- Bishops and most priests are required to remain celibate.
- They receive a special sacrament to give them the strength they need to be faithful to their work throughout their lives.
- It is the tradition in the Catholic Church that women may not receive Holy Orders.

4.4 Social cohesion

Sacred texts

Jesus mixes with tax-collectors and sinners
Mark 2:15–17

Jesus proclaims freedom for the oppressed
Luke 4:18–19

Jesus taught that those not against us are for us
Mark 9:40

Community cohesion means a common vision and shared sense of belonging for all groups in society. Many Christians believe that community cohesion is important and want to work towards:

- Equality of opportunities for all.
- Valuing different peoples' backgrounds.
- Fostering a sense of belonging.

This means challenging any form of prejudice and discrimination and looking for ways of bringing people together to foster good relationships, as a way of avoiding hatred and the harm it can cause.

Why do Christians work for social cohesion?

All Christians believe that they should follow the teachings and example of Jesus. There are many accounts in the Bible of Jesus trying to bring harmony to his own society. There are examples of Jesus treating all people equally no matter what their religion or race.

Sometimes AIDS victims may feel they are treated like modern-day lepers.

Activities

1 Who are today's outcasts? Discuss this in groups and come up with a list of those who are treated as outcasts in society today. Your teacher may ask for ideas to put on the board. Have a class discussion on how you feel about the way these people are treated.

We are told in the Gospels that Jesus used to get into trouble for mixing with 'outcasts and sinners'. In Jesus' time the Jewish people kept to themselves. They would not mix with Gentiles (those who aren't Jews) or with anyone who they thought was a sinner or in any way unclean. This group included tax collectors, lepers and Samaritans.

Jesus also refused to turn his back on those whom he did consider sinners, such as prostitutes. He made it clear that the duty of a Christian is to help sinners to change their lives.

The Jews believed that the Samaritans had turned away from the true religion, and were therefore enemies of the Jewish people. Jesus cured a Samaritan leper, and also told the parable of The Good Samaritan. He wanted people of different races and religions to show love and compassion to each other.

Social cohesion and the Catholic Church

Like other Christian Churches the Catholic Church believes that every person is made in the image and likeness of God. That means that everyone has the right to be treated fairly.

Pope John Paul II spoke of the need for social cohesion and was concerned that:

'*cities risk becoming societies of people who are rejected, marginalised, uprooted, and oppressed, instead of communities of people living together.*'

Over the past 100 years popes have written many encyclicals (letters to members of the Catholic Church) which teach that we should be open to other races and religions, and welcome cultural diversity.

The Catholic organisation Progessio works around the world to try to stop people being treated unfairly because of sickness, disability or poverty.

To find out more about 'Progressio' go to www.heinemann.co.uk/hotlinks (express code 4257P) and click on the appropriate link.

Activities

2   Write a speech or short presentation explaining why many Christians work for social and community cohesion.

3   Find out more about the work of the Catholic organisation Progressio. What do they do to support those who feel rejected?

Working for community cohesion in the UK

- Interfaith dialogue – Organisations have been set up for people from different religions to come together and share and celebrate their different faiths. The Inter Faith Network for the UK was founded 1987 to promote good relations between the faith communities. There are many local branches of the group.
- Working for economic justice – The group Church Action on Poverty works to tackle the causes of poverty. They also campaign for the wellbeing of refugees and asylum seekers in the UK today.
- The Church working for racial equality – The Church of England's Committee for Minority and Ethnic Anglican Concerns (CMEC) works to encourage the participation of ethnic minority groups in the Church. The Catholic Association for Racial Justice works to celebrate the equality and dignity of all God's people in a variety of ways.

For discussion

'Community cohesion is the responsibility of the government, not Christians.' Do you agree?

Summary

- Jesus helped and supported the social outcasts of his time and worked to promote a tolerant and compassionate society.
- The Catholic Church has worked and spoken in favour of a tolerant and fair society.
- Many Christians believe that a multi-ethnic society would help to prevent prejudice and violence.

4.5 The Ten Commandments

Learning outcomes

By the end of this lesson you should:

- know the Ten Commandments and understand what they teach
- understand why the Ten Commandments are important for Christians
- be able to evaluate the relevance of the Ten Commandments in the modern world.

Sacred texts

God gives the Ten Commandments to Moses
Exodus 20:2–17

The Ten Commandments teach love of God and neighbour
Mark 12:28–32

What are the Ten Commandments?

The Ten Commandments are perhaps the most famous set of rules ever written. They were given by God to Moses just after he had led the Jews from slavery in Egypt. The commandments can be divided into two groups:

- Three of the rules tell us how we should behave towards God himself.
- The other seven tell us how we should behave towards each other.

RESPECT FOR GOD

WORSHIP GOD ALONE

DO NOT USE GOD'S NAME IN VAIN

KEEP THE SABBATH DAY HOLY

RESPECT FOR OTHERS

HONOUR YOUR PARENTS

DO NOT MURDER

DO NOT COMMIT ADULTERY

DO NOT STEAL

DO NOT TELL LIES ABOUT YOUR NEIGHBOUR

DO NOT COVET YOUR NEIGHBOUR'S PROPERTY

DO NOT COVET YOUR NEIGHBOUR'S WIFE

Activities

1 Create a spider diagram of the Ten Commandments. See how many of them you can remember without having to copy them from the list.

Two laws

The Ten Commandments are the most fundamental of God's rules – the ones upon which all the other rules are based. Jesus, and many Jewish teachers before him, said they can be summarised as just two laws:

- We should love God because he created us.
- We should love all the other people that God has created.

Christians today always try to follow the Ten Commandments.

Loving God

The first three commandments are important to Christians because they stress the importance of their relationship with God, their father and creator.

- The commandment that only God should be worshipped tells Christians that God must come first in their lives, before money or possessions.
- Christians should only use God's name in a serious way. They speak of God in worship. If they are in court they may be asked to swear in God's name that they are telling the truth.
- For the Jews the Sabbath is Saturday but, following the resurrection, Christians changed it to Sunday, which they call the Lord's Day. It is a day for going to church to celebrate the Eucharist and for reflecting on their relationship with God. Where possible they try not to work on a Sunday, though that can be difficult in the modern world.

Loving others

Seven of the commandments tell Christians how they should treat other people.

- Christians should honour their parents. That can mean being grateful for all they have given, and taking care of them when they grow old.
- Christians shouldn't harm others but treat human life as sacred, to be cherished and respected.
- Stealing is also unacceptable, as is destroying someone else's relationship by committing adultery. In the same way Christians should always try to tell the truth.
- Christians also believe that it is possible to have sinful thoughts, by being jealous of what other people own, and by having lustful thoughts about someone else's husband or wife.

How do the Ten Commandments tell us how we should to treat the aged and infirm?

For discussion

Should shops and places of work be closed on Sundays? Discuss your reasons.

Why Christians follow the Ten Commandments in their lives today

- God gave the Ten Commandments, and that makes them more important than any man-made rules.
- Keeping the Ten Commandments shows respect for God and for his creation.
- The laws in the United Kingdom, and in many other countries, are based on the Ten Commandments.
- The Ten Commandments reflect many problems faced by Christians today. They teach about rejecting violence, about being faithful in marriage and not being jealous of other people's possessions. Some Christians also believe they condemn abortion and euthanasia.

Activities

2 Are there any laws in your country that contradict the Ten Commandments? Have a discussion in groups or with your teacher about this. If some laws do oppose the Commandments does that mean that Christians can sometimes be allowed to break the law?

3 Write Ten Commandments for today's world and explain briefly why you have chosen them. Is there one which you think would be the most important?

Summary

- The Ten Commandments tell us to honour God and to respect our family and our neighbours.
- Christians believe that if everyone obeyed the Ten Commandments the world would be a safer and more loving place.
- The Ten Commandments are the basis for many of the laws which are enforced throughout the world.
- Some people feel the Ten Commandments need to be updated and do not reflect the most important problems of the modern world.

4.6 The Sermon on the Mount and the Law of Moses

100

Learning outcomes

By the end of this lesson you should:

- know what Jesus taught about the Law of Moses
- understand how Jesus reinterpreted the Old Testament law
- understand what Jesus teaches about divorce
- be able to evaluate how difficult it is to live according to the teaching of Jesus.

edexcel ::: key terms

The Law of Moses – The laws God gave to Moses in the Old Testament.

The Sermon on the Mount – Jesus' description of Christian living.

The Sermon on the Mount

On one occasion during his public teaching Jesus preached a very important sermon which became known as **the Sermon on the Mount**. It can be found in Chapters 5–7 of St Matthew's Gospel. In this sermon, Jesus gave very clear teaching about the way he expected Christians to live. He said that he was not changing the Ten Commandments, or any of the other rules handed down by Moses, but the time was right to make them stricter.

Sacred texts

Jesus reinterprets the Law of Moses
Matthew 5:17–42

Jesus taught his disciples much stricter rules.

You have heard it said… (Law)	But I say to you… (Jesus' interpretation)
Do not kill	Don't even be angry with your brother
Do not commit adultery	Don't even look at another person lustfully
Divorce can sometimes be permitted	Divorce is strictly forbidden
You can demand eye for an eye	If someone wants your coat also give him your shirt
Love your neighbour, hate your enemy	Also love your enemies and pray for them

The new interpretation of the law

In the Sermon on the Mount Jesus is showing the difference between what people actually do and what they feel in their hearts.

- Most people may not actually kill anyone, but many do feel hatred in their heart.
- Although some people may not commit adultery they may be filled with lust for people other than their own husbands and wives.
- **The Law of Moses** allowed people to have revenge to equal the hurt that has been done to them ('an eye for an eye'), but Jesus wants his followers to forgive anyone who hurts them and not want revenge.
- In the same way he doesn't want them to love only those who are good to them. He wants them to do something much more difficult – to love everyone, even people who are unkind to them or people they consider to be their enemies.

Jesus believed that if people had bad thoughts in their hearts, such as hatred, or lust, or the desire for revenge, then those people were still sinning even if they hadn't acted on them.

Divorce

In the old Law of Moses, men could divorce their wives under certain circumstances. The law could be interpreted in a number of ways. Some Jewish teachers said you could divorce your wife if she wasn't a good housekeeper or cook. Others said it had to be a more serious reason, such as adultery. There is much more dispute about whether women were allowed to divorce their husbands.

In St Matthew's Gospel Jesus makes it very clear by declaring that men and women cannot be divorced once they have been married in the eyes of God. This is a very demanding law which the Catholic Church follows strictly, not permitting any divorced person to re-marry in a Catholic church. Some Christians do allow certain people who are divorced to re-marry in church, but only if the divorce was for a very serious reason.

Summary

- Jesus said he came not to destroy the Law of Moses but to complete it.
- The new laws set by Jesus are more demanding than the Law of Moses.
- Christians must not just pay attention to what they do, but they must also try to think and feel good things.
- In St Matthew's Gospel Jesus outlaws divorce, but apart from the Catholic Church, most other Christian Churches still permit divorce in serious circumstances.

4.7 The Sermon on the Mount and displaying religion

Learning outcomes

By the end of this lesson you should:

- know what Jesus says about displaying religion
- understand why this teaching is so important to Christians
- be able to evaluate the danger of being a hypocrite.

edexcel ⋮⋮⋮ key terms

Displaying religion – Making a show of your religion, e.g. by praying in the street.

Hypocrite – A person who acts in a way that contradicts what they say.

Displaying religion

If we believe in something we should be proud to let everyone know about it. Jesus wants his followers to pass on the good news they have received from God. He wants them to try to persuade others to live Christian lives. What he doesn't want is for people to show off about it.

Is it better to pray in private, or in public?

- Jesus says we should pray, but quietly, in private

DISPLAYING RELIGION

- We should give to charity, but privately
- We should fast during the penitential seasons, but we should not tell everyone we are doing it

Hypocrisy

The Sermon on the Mount is full of practical advice about how to live a good life which Christians try to follow. For example, Jesus tells us we should never be hypocrites. That means we should never say or do something which gives the impression we believe in one thing, and then do exactly the opposite. If ever we get a reputation for being a **hypocrite** we lose other people's trust.

Sacred texts

Avoid the hypocrisy of the Pharisees
Matthew 23

Do not make a show of your religion
Matthew 6:1–18

Jesus prays in private
Mark 1:35 and 14:34–40

Activities

1 Can you think of an occasion when you have been a hypocrite? Would you be prepared to share the story with others in class? Alternatively you could write a short story about someone who behaved like a hypocrite.

That means that we are doing all these things to please God, and not to get praise from others. There is the danger of hypocrisy here. It can look as though we are very religious, but in fact we just want others to think we are.

Jesus' teaching comes with a warning. If we show off about how good we are, the praise we receive from others is all the reward we will get. There will not be a second reward from God when we go to Heaven.

Why is this teaching about displaying religion important to Christians?

- In his teaching Jesus tells his followers something important about prayer. He says that it should be something personal. He also gave them the 'Our Father' as a model of how to pray.
- Christians are not to think themselves as better than anyone else. All people will be judged by how they behave rather than who they are.
- Jesus is not saying that Christians should be ashamed of their beliefs. He wants his followers to preach the Gospel and try to convert people. But Christians have to avoid being hypocrites because that may cause others to reject the teaching of Jesus.
- This teaching is about the personal side of religion. Jesus wants his followers to develop a close relationship with God, and this is best done privately, without showing off.
- Jesus does not forbid public worship, which is when the whole community comes together to show their respect for God. Jesus himself used to go to the synagogue on the Sabbath.

Activities

3 Explain in your own words how Christians should pray, fast and give to charity and why they should do it this way.

ResultsPlus
Build Better Answers

Should Christians only pray in private?
Give **two** reasons for your point of view. (4 marks)

■ **Basic, 1-mark answer**
One brief reason with no development, such as 'Christians should only pray in private because Jesus said so in the Sermon on the Mount.'

● **Good, 2-3-mark answer**
Develop the reason by mentioning that Jesus said that those who prayed on the street were acting like hypocrites. Add another reason, such as that Christians should imitate Jesus and he went off by himself when he wanted to pray.

▲ **Excellent, 4-mark answer**
Develop this second reason by giving an example, such as when Jesus was in the garden of Gethsemane before his arrest, and left the disciples to pray by himself.

Activities

2 Why do you think hypocrisy is such a serious fault? Try to explain why in your own words.

For discussion

Fewer people go to church these days. Do you think that religion has become a more private matter? Does it matter if people don't go to church?

Summary

- Jesus wants his followers to avoid becoming hypocrites.
- Jesus taught that his followers should practise their religion privately.
- Those who show off about religion will not receive any extra reward from God.
- Jesus wants his followers to preach the Gospel and to worship God as a community.

4.8 The Sermon on the Mount and money

104

'Money makes the world go round'

We spend a large part of our lives trying to make money and then spending it. A lot of crime is committed by people who want to steal other people's money. For some people trying to get rich becomes the one important aim of their life. But we all need to have at least enough money to buy food and pay for somewhere to live. Some people also give a lot of their money away to people who need it more.

Activities

1 Is money a good thing or a bad thing? Create two spider diagrams, one listing all the good things that money can help someone do and the other all the ways in which money is dangerous. Which list is longer?

God and money

Jesus was very concerned about people's attitude to money and it is one of the most important subjects in the Sermon on the Mount. Jesus put the matter very simply:

- He said you cannot serve both God and money at the same time, because you will end up loving one and hating the other. He said that some people worship money rather than God.
- We are only on the Earth for a short while, and because we cannot take anything with us when we die, Jesus said we should spend less time worrying about the comfort of our life on Earth. Instead we should try to make sure that we store up treasure in Heaven. That means we need to concentrate on living a good life so we will go to Heaven.

Should Christians be poor like Jesus or is it enough to share their wealth?

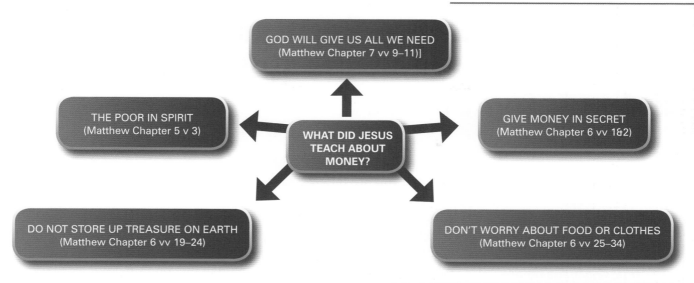

- The pursuit of wealth will mean that people forget the teachings of Jesus, and may even forget about God altogether. This would result in a world which was less loving and less peaceful because everyone would just be concerned for themselves.

These teachings help Christians to understand the value of money today. All Christians would agree that loving God and living a Christian life is more important than money and material possessions. However, Christians disagree about how these teachings should be followed.

How Christians should follow these teachings

Some Christians say that Jesus lived simply and that he wanted his followers to do the same. They think that being a Christian and being rich is a contradiction because being rich when others are poor cannot be either loving or fair. These Christians would therefore try to live a simple life themselves.

Other Christians think that what is important is 'poverty of spirit' – that means that we should not be selfish with what we have. We should be generous in sharing our wealth with others who are in need. We should also support the work of Christian charities such as the Catholic charity the SVP (see pages. 108–111). But Christians do not need actually to be poor to live a Christian life. These Christians would point out that money can be used for good works.

Activities

2 Copy out the spidergram. Look up the various sections of Matthew's Gospel and write in the boxes in your own words what you think Jesus is saying.

3 Prepare for a debate on Christians and wealth. Write a short speech either for or against the motion that 'A rich Christian is really no Christian at all.'

For discussion

Many Christian Churches seem very wealthy and own some very valuable land and buildings. Should they sell everything they own and give it to the poor? Why or why not?

Summary

- Jesus taught that wealth can make people forget about God and make them selfish.
- Christians should give to others, but not make a show of it.
- Christians should be more concerned about 'riches in Heaven'.
- Some Christians believe that to be wealthy when others are poor is a sin.
- Other Christians believe a Christian does not have to be poor to live a Christian life.

4.9 What does the Sermon on the Mount teach about the Golden Rule and judging others?

Learning outcomes

By the end of this lesson you should:

- know what Jesus teaches about how we should treat and judge others
- understand why the Golden Rule is important for Christians
- understand why it is wrong for Christians to judge others
- be able to evaluate the difference between judging actions and judging people.

Sacred texts

The Golden Rule in the Old Testament
Leviticus 19:18

Jesus teaches the Golden Rule
Matthew 7:1-12

The parable of the Sheep and the Goats
Matthew 25:31–46

Do not Judge
Matthew 7:1–5

Let the one without sin cast the first stone
John 8:7

One rule for all situations?

Imagine you are facing a difficult decision about how to behave. Perhaps someone is being bullied at school, and you have to decide what you should do about it. If you get involved you may get hurt yourself. If you tell a teacher you may be accused of being a sneak. If you don't do anything, someone may be hurt or distressed. There are so many things to think about you may just end up doing nothing.

Wouldn't it be helpful if there was just one rule that told you what you should do in a situation like this? For most of the world's religions, there is. It is called the Golden Rule. It simply says that we should treat others how we would want to be treated ourselves. So what should you do about the person you see being bullied? According to this rule, you should do what you would want them to do if they saw you being bullied.

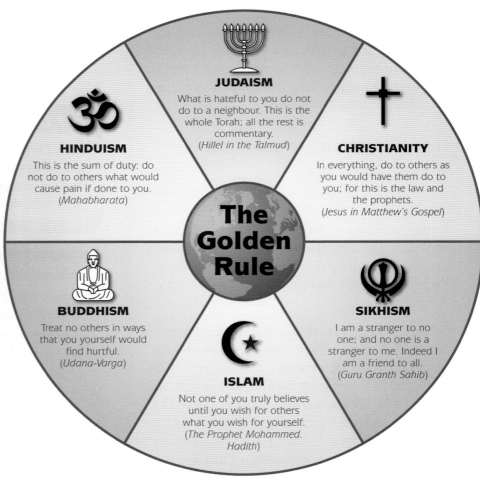

How do these world religions say we should treat each other?

Activities

1 Copy the Golden Rule diagram into your books. Which faith do you think sets out the rule most clearly?

2 Discuss some of the school rules. Do they encourage you to treat others as you would want to be treated?

Activities

3 Write a short story about someone who made a difficult moral choice by acting selfishly, in their own interests. Then show how things would have turned out differently if they had used the Golden Rule.

Why should Christians follow the Golden Rule

The Golden Rule wasn't invented by Jesus. As you can see from the diagram, it was an important rule for religions such as Hinduism and the Jewish faith, before the time of Christianity. But Jesus made it clear that he wanted his followers to abide by it. In other words it is the most important rule that Christians should follow.

- Jesus said the rule summed up the whole of the Jewish law and the teaching of the Prophets.
- In the parable of The Sheep and the Goats Jesus says that by following The Golden Rule Christians will get into Heaven.
- Jesus lived by the Golden Rule himself. He forgave people, he healed them, he taught them, and he consoled them. Christians should try to follow Jesus' example.
- The Golden Rule is a simple guide to making decisions in all situations – Christians should treat others as they would want to be treated themselves.

Why should Christians not judge others?

The Golden Rule also applies to judging others. In the Sermon on the Mount Jesus says we should be slow to judge others. He taught that those who judge others must expect to be judged themselves.

- Only those who have not sinned can judge others. In the story of the woman caught in adultery, Jesus shows that not many people are totally sinless.

- Jesus said it is important to put our effort into behaving well ourselves, rather than finding fault with others.
- Often judging others leads to gossip and sometimes to creation of false stories about people. In the Ten Commandments we are taught not to take away a person's good name (see page 98).
- Christians believe that it is acceptable to judge people's actions, but only God can say whether a person is good or bad. We can never fully know the reasons why people do what they do.

For discussion

If Jesus doesn't want us to judge others, does that mean that we cannot pass judgement on criminals? Should we always just try to understand and forgive them?

Summary

- The Golden Rule says we should treat others as we would want them to treat us.
- Jesus said the Golden Rule sums up the whole of the Law and the Prophets.
- Jesus taught the importance of the Golden Rule to his disciples and he lived by it himself.
- No one should be quick to judge others. Because no one is perfect, we should pay more attention to our own sins.
- Those who are quick to judge others can expect to receive a harsh judgement themselves.

4.10 Relieving suffering and poverty in the UK

Learning outcomes

By the end of this lesson you should:

- know the extent of poverty and suffering in the UK
- understand why there is poverty even in rich countries
- understand the work that the SVP does to relieve poverty and hunger
- evaluate the work of the SVP.

Activities

1 What examples of poverty and suffering have you seen in your local community? Discuss this in groups, and then share what you have discovered with the rest of the class.

Make a short list of the main examples of poverty and suffering that you have discussed.

Is there poverty in the UK?

Although the United Kingdom is one of the richest countries in the world, it has been estimated that one in five people in the UK do not have enough money to live on. They can't afford essential clothing, or fuel to heat their homes. There are four million children in the UK who live in homes with low incomes, and some of them go to bed hungry every night.

The reasons why some people live in poverty are quite complicated but there are some basic reasons such as unemployment, family break-up and illness.

The work of the SVP

The Saint Vincent de Paul Society (the SVP) is a Catholic organisation founded in Paris in the first half of the 19th century to help relieve poverty. It is named after a saint of the 17th century who dedicated his life to the care of the poor. Today all over the world, many Catholics volunteer to help people by working with the society. It has been active in England and Wales since 1844. There are branches of the SVP in many parishes and schools. Although they also work in developing countries, most of their work is done within their local community. For example, they collect second-hand furniture to distribute to those who can't afford to buy their own. More examples are shown in the spider diagram.

Why are there still people who sleep on the streets in the UK?

Here are some examples of the work they do:

Home visits
Volunteers visit people in their own homes. They provide company for the lonely and do shopping and other jobs for those who are housebound. They also help families to organise their finances. The SVP has 10,000 volunteers in England Wales and makes over half a million visit every year.

Soup runs
Soup runs provide a hot drink and food for homeless people and also offer them companionship.

Residential care
The SVP runs hostels for homeless people, and for helping those with mental health problems.

SVP

Holidays
The SVP organises holidays for children from poor and broken homes.

Support centres
The SVP provides support centres where people can go to get advice about dealing with debt and other financial problems. They also offer training in literacy and numeracy.

The SVP tries to help people find long-term solutions to their problems and works to fight the causes of poverty as well as the results of it. Therefore, although the SVP do provide money and material assistance when it is needed they also provide advice, training and support to try to help families and individuals raise themselves out of poverty.

The SVP produces material on their work that they will send to schools. You could contact the SVP and ask them to send some information to your school.

For more information about the history and work of the SVP go to www.heinemann.co.uk/hotlinks (express code 4257P) and click on the appropriate link.

Activities

2   Look again at the main examples of poverty you discussed earlier. What do you think are the principal causes of this kind of poverty and suffering in your local area?

   What could your school do to support the work of the SVP?

3   Prepare a short report for your class on the work of the SVP. The report could be a general one or it could focus on a particular aspect of their work, such as SVP1833 which is for volunteers aged 18–30.

Summary

- There is poverty, hunger and suffering even in wealthy countries like the United Kingdom.
- The SVP is a Catholic organisation set up to focus the efforts of Catholics in the United Kingdom to relieve this suffering.
- As well as working to relieve suffering, the SVP tries to raise awareness of the causes of poverty.

4.11 Why the SVP works for the poor

Learning outcomes

By the end of this lesson you should:

- understand what the Bible and the Catholic Church teach about social justice
- understand the reasons why the SVP works for the poor and those who suffer
- be able to evaluate the importance of the Church's commitment to the poor.

Sacred texts

Social Justice proclaimed by Isaiah
Isaiah 58:6–7

God demands both love and fairness
Micah 6:8

Jesus teaches the need for compassion
Luke 6:36–38

The Beatitudes
Matthew 5:3–12

Activities

1 Thought shower! What examples from the life of Jesus suggest that he thought it was important to care for others? Do this in groups and then see which group has produced the longest list.

'This is what the Lords asks of you, to act justly and to love tenderly…'

Following the example of Jesus

There are many organisations working to relieve suffering. Many people think we should help those who are suffering simply because they are our fellow human beings. But the SVP is a Catholic charity and the inspiration for its work comes from the Bible and from the teachings of the Catholic Church. Doing as Jesus did is particularly important.

Social justice and the Bible

The prophets in the Old Testament, and Jesus himself in the New Testament, made it clear that it is God's will that people care for the poor and suffering.

- In the Old Testament, Isaiah says that sharing our food, sheltering the homeless and protecting the oppressed is God's will.
- The prophet Micah says that acting justly is one of only three things that God demands of us.
- Jesus spent most of his life among people who were sick and poor and had a special care for outcasts. In the Sermon on the Mount, Jesus says that those who hunger and thirst for justice are especially blessed.

Social justice and the Church

The work of the SVP is also a response to over 100 years of Catholic teaching on the subject of social justice. More than a dozen important documents have been written by the Church instructing Catholics to work for a just society. Here is a summary of some of their key points:

To find out more about 'Populorum progressio' go to www.heinemann.co.uk/hotlinks (express code 4257P) and click on the appropriate link.

JUST LAWS

The Catechism of the Catholic Church teaches that every person has the God-given right to food, clothing, health, work, education and to be able to raise and care for a family. The SVP provides people with these things in the short term and helps people provide for themselves in the long term.

Catholics believe that every human being is their brother or sister.

THE COMMON GOOD

Every individual should be able to achieve their full potential, both in their human life and in their relationship with God. Catholics must not be interested simply in ensuring a good life for themselves. They must also work for the common good, a society in which everyone can flourish. Laws and policies that do not work for the common good are considered sinful and must be changed. Therefore, the SVP raises awareness and lobbies governments to try to change and improve legislation.

SOLIDARITY

Catholics must recognise that every other human being is their brother and sister. St Paul said that the Church is like a body, in fact it is the Body of Christ. If one part of the body suffers, then everyone shares that suffering. Solidarity should be the immediate response of every Catholic when they hear that someone else is suffering. The SVP works as a 'body' and helps everyone who needs it, regardless of gender, age, race or religion.

SERVICE

Finally, it isn't just a matter of feeling the pain of others. Catholics must follow in the footsteps of Jesus: they must go out among those who suffer and care for them. The SVP is a practical organisation which helps people face to face – it does not just give money.

Activities

2 Read the Beatitudes. These can be found at the start of Chapter 5 of St Matthew's Gospel. In what way does the work of the SVP try to respond to what Jesus taught in the Beatitudes?

3 See what you can find out about Pope Paul VI's letter about social justice called 'Populorum progressio' (which means 'the development of peoples'). What were the key points that Pope Paul VI made?

Summary

- The SVP is a Catholic charity which draws its inspiration from the Bible and the teaching of the Catholic Church.

- Both the Old and the New Testaments make it clear that working for social justice is an important duty for all Christians.

- For over 100 years the Catholic Church has taught the importance of working to make the world a fairer place for everyone.

KnowZone
Living the Christian life

Quick quiz

1 What is meant by 'charity'?

2 What is the 'Law of Moses'?

3 Name three things that Jesus said about 'displaying religion'.

4 Why did Jesus say Christians shouldn't judge others?

5 What kinds of support does the SVP give to the poor in the UK?

6 Why did Jesus think you cannot serve both God and money?

7 What is meant by a multi-ethnic society?

8 What is a permanent deacon?

9 Give two reasons why the Golden Rule is important for Christians.

10 Outline two occasions when Jesus helped someone who had been cast out of Jewish society.

Plenary activity

1 Design a poster or a Powerpoint® presentation for the SVP. You should show the different kinds of work the SVP does, and why they do this work. You could include some texts from Jesus' teaching, for example, or include some illustrations of Jesus helping others.

Student tips

I thought that because the Ten Commandments are so famous I already knew them off by heart, but when I started to revise I could only remember six or seven of them. As questions about the Ten Commandments often come up in the exam, I made sure I knew them all!

Student tips

I was told by my teacher that if a question asks about an organisation that helps to relieve poverty in the UK I cannot talk about the work of CAFOD. CAFOD does most of its work in developing countries. The most famous Catholic organisation that works to relieve poverty in the UK is the Society of St Vincent de Paul (the SVP).

Student tips

There are a number of parables that can be used to develop an answer about the Golden Rule. For example, the parable of The Good Samaritan says that everyone is our neighbour, and in the parable of The Sheep and the Goats Jesus says that if we do not help our neighbour then we cannot go to Heaven.

Find out more

The Catechism of the Catholic Church gives a good summary of how Catholics should live a Christian life. It has been compiled with the approval of the Pope and bishops. It has an index that is very easy to use.

There are a number of Christian and Catholic Encyclopaedias which may be available in your school library.

The SVP and many other Christian Charities have their own websites. They also produce materials for schools which you or your teacher could ask them to send .

'Progressio' is a Catholic organisation that works for social cohesion. It also has its own website.

The Vatican has its own website which is available in a number of languages. On this site you will be able to find a number of the Church's documents which talk about social cohesion and the relief of suffering. These include 'Populorum progressio' by Pope Paul VI and 'Sollicitudo Rei Socialis' by Pope John Paul II.

Have a look at the Documents of the Second Vatican Council. These are the official documents about Catholic teaching that were written in the 1960s. They were written following a great gathering in Rome of all the Bishops for what is called an Ecumenical Council. In the index you could look for references to 'holy orders' or 'vocation'. 'Gaudium et Spes' makes particular reference to the Catholic approach to social issues. Remember that the language will sometimes be quite difficult to understand.

Self-evaluation checklist

Read through the following list and evaluate how well you know and understand each of the topics.
How well have you understood the topics in this section? In the first column of the table below use the following code to rate your understanding:

Green – I understand this fully

Orange – I am confident I can answer most questions on this

Red – I need to do a lot more work on this topic.

In the second and third columns you need to think about:

● Whether you have an opinion on this topic and could give reasons for that opinion if asked

● Whether you can give the opinion of someone who disagrees with you and give reasons for this alternative opinion.

Content covered	My understanding is red/orange/green	Can I give my opinion?	Can I give an alternative opinion?
● What it means for Christians to have a 'vocation'.			
● How Christians show vocation in all aspects of their lives. What is meant by 'holy orders'.			
● Why some Christians show vocation by taking holy orders.			
● What is meant by 'social and community cohesion' and why some Christians are involved in working to achieve this.			
● How some Christians work for social and community cohesion.			
● How and why Christians use the Ten Commandments as a guide for living.			
● How Jesus re-interpreted the Law of Moses.			
● How and why Christians use Jesus' teaching about the Law of Moses to guide their lives.			
● What the Sermon on the Mount says about displaying religion and how and why Christians use this teaching to guide their lives.			
● What the Sermon on the Mount says about money and how and why Christians use this teaching to guide their lives.			
● What the Sermon on the Mount says about Judgement and the Golden Rule and how and why Christians use this teaching to guide their lives.			
● What work the SVP does to relieve poverty and suffering in the UK.			
● Why the SVP does this work.			

Introduction

In the exam you will be given a choice of two questions on this section. Each question will include four tasks (a-d) which test your knowledge, understanding and evaluation of the material covered; a 2-mark (a) question which will ask you to define a term; a 4-mark (b) question which will ask your opinion on a point of view; a 6 mark (d) question which will ask for your opinion on a point of view and ask you to consider an alternative point of view; an 8-mark (c) question which will ask you to explain a particular belief or idea.

You need to give a short accurate definition – just a single sentence. This is a key term so the definition would score full marks.

Don't just say what Jesus said about money, but try to explain what he meant. For example, Jesus said we shouldn't store up treasure for ourselves on earth. But why did he say that? He feared that people would forget that the most important treasure is eternal life in Heaven.

Now you have to give the opposite point of view, again using material you have learned during your studies. You don't have to say what you think about these alternative points of view, but you do need to give reasons why people might hold them.

Mini exam paper

(a) What is the Sermon on the Mount? (2 marks)

(b) Should priests be allowed to marry? (4 marks)

Give two reasons for your point of view.

(c) Explain how Jesus taught about money in the Sermon on the Mount. (8 marks)

(d) All Catholics should support the work of the SVP.

In your answer you should refer to Roman Catholic Christianity.

(i) Do you agree? Give reasons for your opinion. (3 marks)

(ii) Give reasons why some people may disagree with you. (3 marks)

You can give your own point of view, but be sure to give TWO reasons. If you don't have a point of view of your own, you can use reasons you have learned in class.

Make sure you read the question carefully. Note that it talks about ALL Catholics. You must ensure that your answer responds to that question, not 'should SOME Catholics support the SVP?'

You only need to give one point of view at this stage but you must give reasons why you hold this point of view.

ResultsPlus
Watch out!

Catholics sometimes talk about 'having a vocation' to mean being called to the priesthood or religious life. Of course some people believe they are called to become priests, monks or nuns. But in this examination the term 'vocation' refers more widely to a 'call from God to lead the Christian life'. This could also be a call to become a good parent, or a teacher, for example.

There may be a question about what Jesus taught about 'displaying religion'. This sometimes causes confusion. Jesus did ask his followers to live good lives, and to preach the Gospel to others. But in the exam 'displaying religion' refers to showing off, which Jesus condemns.

Support activity

1   A large part of this section of the course is about what Jesus taught in the Sermon on the Mount. This can be found in Chapters 5–7 of St Matthew's Gospel. It would be useful to know the sermon thoroughly.

Read the Sermon on the Mount and write down a list of all the things that Jesus says about the Law of Moses, displaying religion, money, Judgement and the Golden Rule.

Re-write what Jesus said on each of these topics in your own words.

ResultsPlus
Maximise your marks

(d)   'All Catholics should support the work of the SVP.'

(i)   Do you agree? Give reasons for your opinion. (3 marks)

(ii)   Give reasons why some people may disagree with you. (3 marks)

Student answer	Examiner comments	Improved student answer
I think all Catholics should support the work of SVP because they should follow the example of Jesus and he was always trying to help people. Others may disagree because they don't have enough money to spend on others.	This answer offers what can be described as a 'simple for and against'. It offers one correct but simple reason in support of the suggestion that all Catholics should support the SVP and one simple reason against. This would only reach Level 1 for both parts i and ii.	I think all Catholics should support the work of SVP because they should follow the example of Jesus and he was always trying to help people, such as when he did miracles that cured people. Jesus also taught us that we should treat others as we would like to be treated. This is called the 'Golden Rule' and supporting the SVP would be one way of doing this. Others may disagree because they don't have enough money to spend on others. Also, Catholics may choose to help people in other ways such as supporting other charities, praying for people or helping others directly.

Welcome to examzone

Revising for your exams can be a daunting prospect. In this part of the book we'll take you through the best way of revising for your exams, step by step, to ensure you get the best results possible.

Zone In!

Have you ever become so absorbed in a task that suddenly it feels entirely natural and easy to perform? This is a feeling familiar to many athletes and performers. They work hard to recreate it in competition in order to do their very best. It's a feeling of being 'in the zone', and if you can achieve that same feeling in an examination, the chances are you'll perform brilliantly.

The good news is that you can get 'in the zone' by taking some simple steps in advance of the exam. Here are our top tips.

UNDERSTAND IT

Make sure you understand the exam process and what revision you need to do. This will give you confidence and also help you to get things into proportion. These pages are a good place to find some starting pointers for performing well in exams.

FRIENDS AND FAMILY

Make sure that your friends and family know when you want to revise. Even share your revision plan with them. Learn to control your times with them, so you don't get distracted. This means you can have better quality time with them when you aren't revising, because you aren't worrying about what you ought to be doing.

DEAL WITH DISTRACTIONS

Think about the issues in your life that may interfere with revision. Write them all down. Then think about how you can deal with each so they don't affect your revision.

COMPARTMENTALISE

You might not be able to deal with all the issues that can distract you. For example, you may be worried about a friend who is ill, or just be afraid of the exam. In this case, there is still a useful technique you can use. Put all of these worries into an imagined box in your mind at the start of your revision (or in the exam) and mentally lock it. Only open it again at the end of your revision session (or exam).

DIET AND EXERCISE

Make sure you eat sensibly and exercise as well! If your body is not in the right state, how can your mind be? A substantial breakfast will set you up for the day, and a light evening meal will keep your energy levels high.

BUILD CONFIDENCE

Use your revision time not only to revise content, but also to build your confidence in readiness for tackling the examination. For example, try tackling a short sequence of easy tasks in record time.

Planning Zone

The key to success in exams and revision often lies in good planning. Knowing **what** you need to do and **when** you need to do it is your best path to a stress-free experience. Here are some top tips in creating a great personal revision plan.

First of all, *know your strengths and weaknesses.*

Go through each topic making a list of how well you think you know the topic. Use your mock examination results and/or any other test results that are available as a check on your self-assessment. This will help you to plan your personal revision effectively, putting extra time into your weaker areas.

Next, *create your plan!*

Remember to make time for considering how topics interrelate.

For example, in PE you will be expected to know not just about the various muscles, but how these relate to various body types.

The specification quite clearly states when you are expected to be able to link one topic to another so plan this into your revision sessions.

You will be tested on this in the exam and you can gain valuable marks by showing your ability to do this.

Finally, *follow the plan!*

You can use the revision sections in the following pages to kick-start your revision.

MAY

SUNDAY	MONDAY	TUES
	30	1
7	8	
13		
20	21	22
27	28	29

Be realistic about how much time you can devote to your revision, but also make sure you put in enough time. Give yourself regular breaks or different activities to give your life some variance. Revision need not be a prison sentence!

Find out your exam dates. Go to the Edexcel website **www.edexcel.com** to find all final exam dates, and check with your teacher.

~iew Secti~
~complete t~
~ractice ex~
~question~

Chunk your revision in each subject down into smaller sections. This will make it more manageable and less daunting.

Draw up a list of all the dates from the start of your revision right through to your exams.

Review Sectio~
complete three
practice exam
~tions

Review Sectio~
Try the Keywor~
Quiz again

Make sure you allow time for assessing your progress against your initial self-assessment. Measuring progress will allow you to see and be encouraged by your improvement. These little victories will build your confidence.

EXAM DAY!

In this section you will need to show the examiner that you:

- know the meaning of the different beliefs Christians have about God, and what they believe their faith tells them about how they should behave (AO1)

- understand why these beliefs and values are important for Catholics (AO2)

- can explain your own views about these beliefs and values and express why and how they differ from other possible views (AO2).

Here are some examples:

- You are expected to know that Christians believe in the Trinity. Although they believe there is only one God, they also believe that God has revealed himself as God the Father, God the Son and God the Holy Spirit. There are lots of similar facts that you will need to have learned. Here are just a few examples:

  - Christians believe God created the world.

  - They believe that Jesus was crucified and then rose from the dead.

  - They believe that the most important commandment is that people should love God and love each other.

- Belief in the Trinity is important for Catholics because, for example, it means that Jesus is more than just a teacher, he is also God. This is the most important Christian belief. There are non-Christians who believe that Jesus was a great teacher, even a prophet, but they do not believe he is God. They believe that his teachings are important – but Christians believe they must always try to live according to those teachings.

- Jesus taught that we should love everyone, even our enemies. Perhaps you disagree with this, and think it is too difficult to love people who hate you, or are trying to harm you. But it is important to show that you understand that other people may disagree with you, and to be able to explain why. The issue here is that you can be critical of your views and those of others, and can recognise the variety of beliefs that can be held.

Revision

Look back at the KnowZone pages at the end of this section (pages 28–31). Read through the Checklist and try to identify your stronger and weaker areas, so that you can focus on those things you are less confident about. You may like to try the Quick Quiz again or the Plenary activity at the end of the section, or the Support activity opposite.

Some people find it helpful to write out what they want to learn on to large sheets of paper and put them up on the walls around their room. You could make a list of what Christians believe about God, for example. If you write in large letters you will notice them whenever you walk into the room.

When learning about God, we often feel we know quite a lot about God the Father (for example, that he created the world, that he is the father of Jesus, that Jesus says we should call God 'Our Father') and God the Son (for example, that he was born to the Virgin Mary, that he taught and worked miracles, that he was crucified and rose from the dead). But how much can you remember about God the Holy Spirit? It can be more difficult to remember the teaching about the Holy Spirit, so it might be helpful to look at that spread again (on pages 14–15) and to make notes about the most important things that Christians believe on that topic.

When you feel you are ready for some exam practice, read through the KnowZone on pages 30–31. Then you could attempt the questions opposite.

Meet the exam paper

This diagram shows the front cover of the exam paper. These instructions, information and advice will always appear on the front of the paper. It is worth reading it carefully now. Check you understand it. Now is a good opportunity to ask your teacher about anything you are not sure of here.

Print your surname here, and your other names afterwards. This is an additional safeguard to ensure that the exam board awards the marks to the right candidate.

Here you fill in the school's exam number.

Ensure that you understand exactly how long the examination will last, and plan your time accordingly.

Note that the quality of your written communication will also be marked. Take particular care to present your thoughts and work at the highest standard you can, for maximum marks.

Here you fill in your personal exam number. Take care when writing it down because the number is important to the exam board when writing your score.

In this box, the examiner will write the total marks you have achieved in the exam paper.

Make sure that you understand exactly which questions from which sections you should attempt.

Don't feel that you have to fill the answer space provided. Everybody's handwriting varies, so a long answer from you may take up as much space as a short answer from someone else.

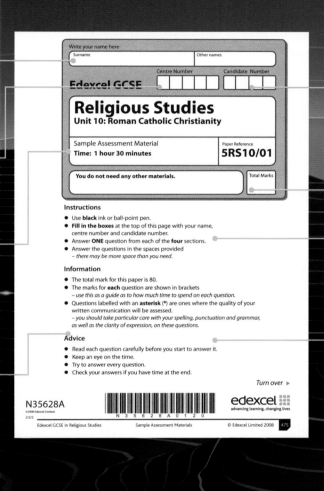

Practical tips on the exam paper

- You must use a black pen. Your paper is scanned into a computer for marking. If you write in any other colour, you risk your work not being seen clearly.

- You must choose your question carefully – cross out the one you are not going to do – to avoid changing a question half-way through answering it. This is a very common mistake and costs candidates lots of marks!

- Mark with an x at the top of the page which question you have chosen.

- Do not write outside the guidelines – your answer may get cut off by the scanning process.

- Do not use extra sheets and attach them unless it is absolutely necessary. If you need more space – for example, for a (b) question – continue into the (c) space and when you change question write your own (c). Do the same for (c) into (d). If you then run out, put an arrow and write at the end of the exam booklet.

Zone Out

This section provides answers to the most common questions students have about what happens after they complete their exams. For more information, visit the ExamZone website: Go to www.heinemann.co.uk/hotlinks (express code 4257P) and click on the appropriate link.

About your grades

Whether you've done better than, worse than, or just as you expected, your grades are the final measure of your performance on your course and in the exams. On this page we explain some of the information that appears on your results slip and tell you what to do if you think something is wrong. We answer the most popular questions about grades and look at some of the options facing you.

When will my results be published?

Results for summer examinations are issued on the **middle** two Thursdays in August, with GCE first and GCSE second. November exam results are issued in January, January exam results are issued in March and March exam results issued in April.

Can I get my results online?

Visit the resultsplus direct website: Go to www.heinemann.co.uk/hotlinks (express code 4257P) and click on the appropriate link, where you will find detailed student results information including the 'Edexcel Gradeometer' which demonstrates how close you were to the nearest grade boundary.

I haven't done as well as I expected. What can I do now?

First of all, talk to your subject teacher. After all the teaching that you have had, tests and internal examinations, he/she is the person who best knows what grade you are capable of achieving. Take your results slip to your subject teacher, and go through the information on it in detail. If you both think there is something wrong with the result, the school or college can apply to see your completed examination paper and then, if necessary, ask for a re-mark immediately. The original mark can be confirmed or lowered, as well as raised, as a result of a re-mark.

How do my grades compare with those of everybody else who sat this exam?

You can compare your results with those of others in the UK who have completed the same examination using the information on the Edexcel website: Go to www.heinemann.co.uk/hotlinks (express code 4257P) and click on the appropriate link.

I achieved a higher mark for the same unit last time. Can I use that result?

Yes. The higher score is the one that goes towards your overall grade. Even if you sat a unit more than twice, the best result will be used automatically when the overall grade is calculated. You do not need to ask the exam board to take into account a previous result. This will be done automatically so you can be assured that all your best unit results have gone into calculating your overall grade.

What happens if I was ill over the period of my examinations?

If you become ill before or during the examination period you are eligible for special consideration. This also applies if you have been affected by an accident, bereavement or serious disturbance during an examination.

If my school has requested special consideration for me, is this shown on my Statement of Results?

If your school has requested special consideration for you, it is not shown on your results slip, but it will be shown on a subject mark report that is sent to your school or college. If you want to know whether special consideration was requested for you, you should ask your Examinations Officer.

Can I have a re-mark of my examination paper?

Yes, this is possible, but remember that only your school or college can apply for a re-mark, not you or your parents/carers. First of all, you should consider carefully whether or not to ask your school or college to make a request for a re-mark. It is worth knowing that very few re-marks result in a change to a grade – not because Edexcel is embarrassed that a change of marks has been made, but simply because a re-mark request has shown that the original marking was accurate. Check the closing date for re-marking requests with your Examinations Officer.

When I asked for a re-mark of my paper, my subject grade went down. What can I do?

There is no guarantee that your grades will go up if your papers are re-marked. They can also go down or stay the same. After a re-mark, the only way to improve your grade is to take the examination again. Your school or college Examinations Officer can tell you when you can do that.

How many times can I re-sit a unit?

You may resit a modular GCSE Science or Mathematics module test once, prior to taking your terminal examination and before obtaining your final overall grade. The highest score obtained on either the first attempt or the re-sit counts towards your final grade. If you enter a module in GCSE Mathematics at a different tier, this does not count as a re-sit. If you are on the full modular Religious Studies GCSE course, and sat the first unit last year, you may re-sit module 1 when you sit module 2 to maximise your full course grade.

For much more information, visit the ExamZone website. Go to www.heinemann. co.uk/hotlinks (express code 4257P) and click on the appropriate link.

Glossary

This is an extended glossary containing definitions that will help you in your studies. Edexcel key terms are not included as all of these are defined in the lessons themselves.

abortion – The deliberate termination of a pregnancy, resulting in the death of the foetus.

anointing – Also known as 'unction', the application of oil to people or things, symbolising the presence of God within them.

apostles – The most important, original followers of Jesus. The word means 'messenger' or 'ambassador'.

ascension – When Jesus, after the **resurrection**, left his **apostles** and was carried up to heaven.

baptism – A **sacrament** in which water is blessed and then poured over the head of a person, usually an infant, to represent the washing away of **sin** and the beginning of a new life with God.

Bible – The sacred text of Christianity.

big bang – The theory that an enormous explosion started the universe around 15 billion years ago.

Body of Christ – As well as the physical body of Jesus, this also refers to the Roman Catholic Church as a whole and to the presence of Jesus' body in the Eucharist.

canonisation – The process by which a dead person is declared a saint.

causation argument – An argument for the existence of God which states that nothing happens by chance and everything has a cause, which is God.

communion of saints – Spiritual union of all Catholics, those alive, in **Purgatory** and in Heaven.

Confirmation – Sacrament in which baptismal vows are renewed and receiving the Holy Spirit is received.

contraception – Deliberately preventing or reducing the likelihood of pregnancy or childbirth.

deacon – First of the three Orders of ordination in the Roman Catholic Church: The other major orders are those of priest and bishop.

design argument – The belief that the universe is too complicated to have come about by chance, and must have a designer, God.

disciples – The twelve most important **apostles**.

Epiphany – A festival celebrated on the 6th January, commemorating the visit of the **Magi** to Jesus.

euthanasia – Deliberately ending the life of a sick person.

evolution – The gradual development of species over millions of years.

font – Article of church furniture used to contain water used for **baptism.**

Golden Rule – Rule shared by most of the world's religions, states that we should treat others as we would want to be treated ourselves.

Holy Spirit – The third person of the Trinity, equal with God the Father and God the Son. The Holy Spirit was the last piece of Trinitarian theology to be developed, and Christians more about God the Father and Jesus, God the Son, than about the Holy Spirit, not because they believe the Holy Spirit to be less important but because works the Holy Spirit works in ways that are less obvious. It is sometimes said to be like water, sometimes like fire and sometimes like the air (in the wind or in breath).

Last Supper – Final meal Jesus shared with his **disciples**.

Lent – Period of preparation and prayer for 40 days before Holy Week.

Magi – The three Wise Men who visited Jesus at the **epiphany**.

Mass – **sacrament** involving bread and wine, commemorating the Last Supper. Also known as Eucharist

Pentecost – When the **Holy Spirit** came down upon the **apostles**, after the **ascension** of Jesus.

Pontius Pilate – Roman governor who ordered the crucifixion of Jesus.

prayer – Act of addressing God.

priest – Second of the three Orders of ordination in the Roman Catholic Church: The other major orders are those of deacon and bishop.

Purgatory – Temporary place of purification to which people with unforgiven sins are believed to go before Heaven.

reconciliation – **sacrament** in which people are freed from sins committed after receiving Baptism.

reformation – Movement in the 15th and 16th centuries, when many believed that leaders of the Church had gone astray and broke away to form new Churches.

resurrection – The return to bodily life of Jesus after his crucifixion and death.

Sabbath – Day for going to Church to celebrate the **Mass** and for praying to God. Where possible Catholics try not to work on a Sunday, though that can be difficult in the modern world. For the Jews the Sabbath is Saturday but, following the **resurrection**, Christians changed it to Sunday, which they call the Lord's Day.

sin – An action which is against God's rules. Catholics believe that if we die without our sins being forgiven, we may go to **Purgatory** or even to Hell rather than to Heaven.

Ten Commandments – Set of rules given by God to Moses. Three commandments tell us how we should behave towards God , the other seven tell us how we should behave towards each other.

transfiguration – Event witnessed by some of the **Apostles** in which Jesus became radiant, spoke with Moses and Elijah, and was called 'Son' by God.

Viaticum – Latin word which signifies the journey from life through death to eternal life.

Index

In the following index, Edexcel key terms are given in bold and the first page number, also in **bold**, will lead you to the definition. For further definitions of unfamiliar words, see also the Glossary on page 122.

RE Dept